BLOOM'S

HOW TO WRITE ABOUT

Joseph Conrad

ROBERT P. MCPARLAND

Introduction by Harold Bloom

BLOOM'S
LITERARY CRITICISM
An imprint of Infobase Publishing

Bloom's How to Write about Joseph Conrad

Copyright © 2011 by Infobase Publishing
Introduction © 2011 by Harold Bloom

Bloom's Literary Criticism
An imprint of Infobase Publishing
132 West 31st Street
New York NY 10001

Library of Congress Cataloging-in-Publication Data
McParland, Robert.
    Bloom's how to write about Joseph Conrad / Robert P. McParland ; introduction by Harold Bloom.
        p. cm. — (Bloom's how to write about literature)
    Includes bibliographical references and index.
    ISBN 978-1-60413-714-9 (hardcover)
    1. Conrad, Joseph, 1857–1924—Criticism and interpretation. 2. Criticism—Authorship.
I. Bloom, Harold. II. Title. III. Title: How to write about Joseph Conrad.
    PR6005.O4Z7668 2010
    823'912—dc22   2010017430

You can find Bloom's Literary Criticism on the World Wide Web at
http://www.chelseahouse.com

Text design by Annie O'Donnell
Cover design by Ben Peterson
Composition by Mary Susan Ryan-Flynn
Cover printed by Art Print, Taylor, PA
Book printed and bound by Maple Press, York, PA
Date printed: October 2010
Printed in the United States of America

10 9 8 7 6 5 4 3 2 1

CONTENTS

SERIES INTRODUCTION

Bloom's How to Write about Literature series is designed to inspire students to write fine essays on great writers and their works. Each volume in the series begins with an introduction by Harold Bloom, meditating on the challenges and rewards of writing about the volume's subject author. The first chapter then provides detailed instructions on how to write a good essay, including how to find a thesis; how to develop an outline; how to write a good introduction, body text, and conclusion; how to cite sources; and more. The second chapter provides a brief overview of the issues involved in writing about the subject author and then a number of suggestions for paper topics, with accompanying strategies for addressing each topic. Succeeding chapters cover the author's major works.

The paper topics suggested within this book are open-ended, and the brief strategies provided are designed to give students a push forward in the writing process rather than a road map to success. The aim of the book is to pose questions, not answer them. Many different kinds of papers could result from each topic. As always, the success of each paper will depend completely on the writer's skill and imagination.

HOW TO WRITE ABOUT JOSEPH CONRAD: INTRODUCTION

by Harold Bloom

CONRAD WAS a last romantic who desired to free himself from any transcendental idealism, yet fortunately never quite managed it in his creation of character. I want here to center on his masterwork, *Nostromo*, and two of its High Romantics, Decoud and Nostromo.

Decoud, though very sympathetic, is a study in a subtle form of nihilistic decadence, unable to believe either in the self or in any value outside the self. His suicide illustrates the great Conradian theme of immersing in the destructive element, the true test for Conrad's protagonists. Most of them are destroyed by that immersion; Nostromo survives but only for a time and then is destroyed by his own heroic myth.

Conrad's study of Nostromo is endlessly subtle, for so vainglorious is this would-be hero who can achieve a sense of reality only in regard to what others think about him. And yet is that not true also of Homer's Achilles in the *Iliad* and of Tolstoy's heroic Chechen Hadji Murad? If there is a difference, what is it? Is Nostromo's death meaningless, or does it have a tragic dimension?

Part of Conrad's challenge is that he is so enigmatic a moralist. We sense that there is judgment hovering in his atmosphere but he will not help us locate it. After being heavily influenced by the middle phase of Henry James—*The Spoils of Poynton, What Maisie Knew, The Awkward*

Age—Conrad swerved away from James in *Nostromo*. Can we believe in Conrad's detachment toward his most magnificent character, Nostromo?

Writing about Conrad you learn to answer questions with more questions. And yet he became the dominant influence on the generation of Hemingway, Scott Fitzgerald, and Faulkner by suggesting to them a mode of what might be called compromised tragedy. Profoundly skeptical of Nostromo's moral ruin, Conrad nevertheless yields to the sublimity of a natural leader, a man of the people, who perhaps triumphs in his own self-defeat. Audacity is a two-sided virtue in Conrad but particularly in Nostromo, an authentic man of action who never can believe in his own myth.

Compared to Nostromo, Fitzgerald's Gatsby, Hemingway's Robert Jordan, and even Faulkner's Sutpen lose much of their richness. Gatsby comes closest, because his absurd love for Daisy defies the woman's inadequacy. Nothing is more Conradian than to die, while still retaining your Platonic faith in your own dream of glory. Conrad remains perpetually relevant despite his own skepticism as to that glory.

HOW TO WRITE
A GOOD ESSAY

By Laurie A. Sterling and Robert P. McParland

WHILE THERE are many ways to write about literature, most assignments for high school and college English classes call for analytical papers. In these assignments, you are presenting your interpretation of a text to your reader. Your objective is to interpret the text's meaning in order to enhance your reader's understanding and enjoyment of the work. Without exception, strong papers about the meaning of a literary work are built upon a careful, close reading of the text or texts. Careful, analytical reading should always be the first step in your writing process. This volume provides models of such close, analytical reading, and these should help you develop your own skills as a reader and as a writer.

As the examples throughout this book demonstrate, attentive reading entails thinking about and evaluating the formal (textual) aspects of the author's works: theme, character, form, and language. In addition, when writing about a work, many readers choose to move beyond the text itself to consider the work's cultural context. In these instances, writers might explore the historical circumstances of the time period in which the work was written. Alternatively, they might examine the philosophies and ideas that a work addresses. Even in cases where writers explore a work's cultural context, though, papers must still address the more formal aspects of the work itself. A good interpretative essay that evaluates Charles Dickens's use of the philosophy of utilitarianism in his novel *Hard Times*, for example, cannot adequately address the author's treatment of the philosophy without firmly grounding this discussion in the book itself. In other words, any analytical paper about a text, even one that seeks to evaluate the work's cultural context, must also have a firm handle on the work's themes, characters, and language. You must look for and evaluate these aspects of a work, then, as you read a text and as you prepare to write about it.

WRITING ABOUT THEMES

Literary themes are more than just topics or subjects treated in a work; they are attitudes or points about these topics that often structure other elements in a work. Writing about theme therefore requires that you not just identify a topic that a literary work addresses but also discuss what the work says about that topic. For example, if you were writing about the culture of the American South in William Faulkner's famous story "A Rose for Emily," you would need to discuss what Faulkner says, argues, or implies about that culture and its passing.

When you prepare to write about thematic concerns in a work of literature, you will probably discover that, like most works of literature, your text touches upon other themes in addition to its central theme. These secondary themes also provide rich ground for paper topics. A thematic paper on "A Rose for Emily" might consider gender or race in the story. While neither of these could be said to be the central theme of the story, they are clearly related to the passing of the "old South" and could provide plenty of good material for papers.

As you prepare to write about themes in literature, you might find a number of strategies helpful. After you identify a theme or themes in the story, you should begin by evaluating how other elements of the story—such as character, point of view, imagery, and symbolism—help develop the theme. You might ask yourself what your own responses are to the author's treatment of the subject matter. Do not neglect the obvious, either: What expectations does the title set up? How does the title help develop thematic concerns? Clearly, the title "A Rose for Emily" says something about the narrator's attitude toward the title character, Emily Grierson, and all she represents.

WRITING ABOUT CHARACTER

Generally, characters are essential components of fiction and drama. (This is not always the case, though; Ray Bradbury's "August 2026: There Will Come Soft Rains" is technically a story without characters, at least any human characters.) Often, you can discuss character in poetry, as in T. S. Eliot's "The Love Song of J. Alfred Prufrock" or Robert Browning's "My Last Duchess." Many writers find that analyzing character is one of the most interesting and engaging ways to work with a piece of literature and to shape a paper. After all, characters generally are human, and we all know something about being human and living in the world. While it is always important to remember that these figures are not real people but creations of the writer's imagination, it can be fruitful to begin evaluating them as you might evaluate a real person. Often you can start with your own response to a character. Did you like or dislike the character? Did you sympathize with the character? Why or why not?

Keep in mind, though, that emotional responses like these are just starting places. To truly explore and evaluate literary characters, you need to return to the formal aspects of the text and evaluate how the author has drawn these characters. The twentieth-century writer E. M. Forster coined the terms *flat* characters and *round* characters. Flat characters are static, one-dimensional characters that frequently represent a particular concept or idea. In contrast, round characters are fully drawn and much more realistic characters that frequently change and develop over the course of a work. Are the characters you are studying flat or round? What elements of the characters lead you to this conclusion? Why might the author have drawn characters like this? How does their development affect the meaning of the work? Similarly, you should explore the techniques the author uses to develop characters. Do we hear a character's own words, or do we hear only other characters' assessments of him or her? Or, does the author use an omniscient or limited omniscient narrator to allow us access to the workings of the characters' minds? If so, how does that help develop the characterization? Often you can even evaluate the narrator as a character. How trustworthy are the opinions and assessments of the narrator? You should also think about characters' names. Do they mean anything? If you encounter a hero named Sophia or Sophie, you should probably think about her wisdom (or lack thereof), since *sophia* means "wisdom" in Greek. Similarly, since the name Sylvia is derived from the word *sylvan*, meaning "of the wood," you might want to evaluate that character's relationship with nature. Once again, you might look to the title of the work. Does Herman Melville's "Bartleby, the Scrivener" signal anything about Bartleby himself? Is Bartleby adequately defined by his job as scrivener? Is this part of Melville's point? Pursuing questions such as these can help you develop thorough papers about characters from psychological, sociological, or more formalistic perspectives.

WRITING ABOUT FORM AND GENRE

Genre, a word derived from French, means "type" or "class." Literary genres are distinctive classes or categories of literary composition. On the most general level, literary works can be divided into the genres of drama, poetry, fiction, and essays, yet within those genres there are classifications that are also referred to as genres. Tragedy and comedy, for example, are genres of drama. Epic, lyric, and pastoral are genres of poetry. *Form,* on the other hand, generally refers to the shape or structure of a work. There are many clearly defined forms of poetry that follow specific patterns of meter, rhyme, and stanza. Sonnets, for example, are poems that follow a fixed form of 14 lines. Sonnets generally follow one of two basic sonnet forms, each with its own distinct rhyme scheme. Haiku is another example of poetic form, traditionally consisting of three unrhymed lines of five, seven, and five syllables.

While you might think that writing about form or genre might leave little room for argument, many of these forms and genres are very fluid. Remember that literature is evolving and ever changing, and so are its forms. As you study poetry, you may find that poets, especially more modern poets, play with traditional poetic forms, bringing about new effects. Similarly, dramatic tragedy was once quite narrowly defined, but over the centuries playwrights have broadened and challenged traditional definitions, changing the shape of tragedy. When Arthur Miller wrote *Death of a Salesman,* many critics challenged the idea that tragic drama could encompass a common man like Willy Loman.

Evaluating how a work of literature fits into or challenges the boundaries of its form or genre can provide you with fruitful avenues of investigation. You might find it helpful to ask why the work does or does not fit into traditional categories. Why might Miller have thought it fitting to write a tragedy of the common man? Similarly, you might compare the content or theme of a work with its form. How well do they work together? Many of Emily Dickinson's poems, for instance, follow the meter of traditional hymns. While some of her poems seem to express traditional religious doctrines, many seem to challenge or strain against traditional conceptions of God and theology. What is the effect, then, of her use of traditional hymn meter?

WRITING ABOUT LANGUAGE, SYMBOLS, AND IMAGERY

No matter what the genre, writers use words as their most basic tool. Language is the most fundamental building block of literature. It is essential that you pay careful attention to the author's language and word choice as you read, reread, and analyze a text. Imagery is language that appeals to the senses. Most commonly, imagery appeals to our sense of vision, creating a mental picture, but authors also use language that appeals to our other senses. Images can be literal or figurative. Literal images use sensory language to describe an actual thing. In the broadest terms, figurative language uses one thing to speak about something else. For example, if I call my boss a snake, I am not saying that he is literally a reptile. Instead, I am using figurative language to communicate my opinions about him. Since we think of snakes as sneaky, slimy, and sinister, I am using the concrete image of a snake to communicate these abstract opinions and impressions.

The two most common figures of speech are similes and metaphors. Both are comparisons between two apparently dissimilar things. Similes are explicit comparisons using the words *like* or *as*; metaphors are implicit comparisons. To return to the previous example, if I say, "My boss, Bob, was waiting for me when I showed up to work five minutes late today—the snake!" I have constructed a metaphor. Writing about his experiences fighting in World War I, Wilfred Owen begins his poem "Dulce et decorum est" with a string of similes: "Bent double, like old beggars under sacks, / Knock-kneed, coughing like hags, we cursed through sludge." Owen's goal was to undercut clichéd notions that war and dying in battle were glorious. Certainly, comparing soldiers to coughing hags and to beggars underscores his point.

"Fog," a short poem by Carl Sandburg, provides a clear example of a metaphor. Sandburg's poem reads:

> The fog comes
> on little cat feet.
>
> It sits looking
> over harbor and city
> on silent haunches
> and then moves on.

Notice how effectively Sandburg conveys surprising impressions of the fog by comparing two seemingly disparate things—the fog and a cat.

Symbols, by contrast, are things that stand for, or represent, other things. Often they represent something intangible, such as concepts or ideas. In everyday life we use and understand symbols easily. Babies at christenings and brides at weddings wear white to represent purity. Think, too, of a dollar bill. The paper itself has no value in and of itself. Instead, that paper bill is a symbol of something else, the precious metal in a nation's coffers. Symbols in literature work similarly. Authors use symbols to evoke more than a simple, straightforward, literal meaning. Characters, objects, and places can all function as symbols. Famous literary examples of symbols include Moby Dick, the white whale of Herman Melville's novel, and the scarlet *A* of Nathaniel Hawthorne's *The Scarlet Letter.* As both of these symbols suggest, a literary symbol cannot be adequately defined or explained by any one meaning. Hester Prynne's Puritan community clearly intends her scarlet *A* as a symbol of her adultery, but as the novel progresses, even her own community reads the letter as representing not just *adultery,* but *able, angel,* and a host of other meanings.

Writing about imagery and symbols requires close attention to the author's language. To prepare a paper on symbolism or imagery in a work, identify and trace the images and symbols and then try to draw some conclusions about how they function. Ask yourself how any symbols or images help contribute to the themes or meanings of the work. What connotations do they carry? How do they affect your reception of the work? Do they shed light on characters or settings? A strong paper on imagery or symbolism will thoroughly consider the use of figures in the text and will try to reach some conclusions about how or why the author uses them.

WRITING ABOUT HISTORY AND CONTEXT

As noted above, it is possible to write an analytical paper that also considers the work's context. After all, the text was not created in a vacuum. The author lived and wrote in a specific time period and in a specific cultural context and, like all of us, was shaped by that environment. Learning more about the historical and cultural circumstances that surround the author and the work can help illuminate a text and provide you with productive material for a paper. Remember, though, that when you write analytical papers, you should use the context to illuminate the text. Do not lose sight of your goal—to interpret the meaning of the literary work. Use historical or philosophical research as a tool to develop your textual evaluation.

Thoughtful readers often consider how history and culture affected the author's choice and treatment of his or her subject matter. Investigations into the history and context of a work could examine the work's relation to specific historical events, such as the Salem witch trials in seventeenth-century Massachusetts or the restoration of Charles II to the English throne in 1660. Bear in mind that historical context is not limited to politics and world events. While knowing about the Vietnam War is certainly helpful in interpreting much of Tim O'Brien's fiction, and some knowledge of the French Revolution clearly illuminates the dynamics of Charles Dickens's *A Tale of Two Cities,* historical context also entails the fabric of daily life. Examining a text in light of gender roles, race relations, class boundaries, or working conditions can give rise to thoughtful and compelling papers. Exploring the conditions of the working class in nineteenth-century England, for example, can provide a particularly effective avenue for writing about Dickens's *Hard Times.*

You can begin thinking about these issues by asking broad questions at first. What do you know about the time period and about the author? What does the editorial apparatus in your text tell you? Similarly, when specific historical events or dynamics are particularly important to understanding a work but might be somewhat obscure to modern readers, textbooks usually provide notes to explain historical background. With this information, ask yourself how these historical facts and circumstances might have affected the author, the presentation of theme, and the presentation of character. How does knowing more about the work's specific historical context illuminate the work? To take a well-known example, understanding the complex attitudes toward slavery during the time Mark Twain wrote

Adventures of Huckleberry Finn should help you begin to examine issues of race in the text. Additionally, you might compare these attitudes to those of the time in which the novel was set. How might this comparison affect your interpretation of a work written after the abolition of slavery but set before the Civil War?

WRITING ABOUT PHILOSOPHY AND IDEAS

Philosophical concerns are closely related to both historical context and thematic issues. Like historical investigation, philosophical research can provide a useful tool as you analyze a text. For example, an investigation into the working class in Dickens's England might lead you to a topic on the philosophical doctrine of utilitarianism in *Hard Times*. Many other works explore philosophies and ideas quite explicitly. Mary Shelley's famous novel *Frankenstein,* for example, explores John Locke's tabula rasa theory of human knowledge as she portrays the intellectual and emotional development of Victor Frankenstein's creature. As this example indicates, philosophical issues are more abstract than investigations of theme or historical context. Some other examples of philosophical issues include human free will, the formation of human identity, the nature of sin, or questions of ethics.

Writing about philosophy and ideas might require some outside research, but usually the notes or other material in your text will provide you with basic information, and often footnotes and bibliographies suggest places you can go to read further about the subject. If you have identified a philosophical theme that runs through a text, you might ask yourself how the author develops this theme. Look at character development and the interactions of characters, for example. Similarly, you might examine whether the narrative voice in a work of fiction addresses the philosophical concerns of the text.

WRITING COMPARISON AND CONTRAST ESSAYS

Finally, you might find that comparing and contrasting the works or techniques of an author provides a useful tool for literary analysis. A comparison and contrast essay might compare two characters or themes in a single work, or it might compare the author's treatment of a theme in two works. It might also contrast methods of character development or analyze an author's differing treatment of a philosophical concern in two works. Writing comparison and contrast essays, though, requires some special consideration. While they generally provide you with plenty of material to use, they also come with a built-in trap: the laundry list. These papers often become mere lists of connections between the works. As this chapter will discuss, a strong thesis must make an assertion that you want to prove or validate. A strong comparison/contrast thesis, then, needs to comment on the significance of the similarities and differences you observe. It is not enough merely to assert that the works contain similarities and differences. You might, for example, assert why the similarities and differences are important and explain how they illuminate the works' treatment of theme. Remember, too, that a thesis should not be a statement of the obvious. A comparison/contrast paper that focuses only on very obvious similarities or differences does little to illuminate the connections between the works. Often, an effective method of shaping a strong thesis and argument is to begin your paper by noting the similarities between the works but then to develop a thesis that asserts how these apparently similar elements are different. If, for example, you observe that Emily Dickinson wrote a number of poems about spiders, you might analyze how she uses spider imagery differently in two poems. Similarly, many scholars have noted that Hawthorne created many "mad scientist" characters, men who are so devoted to their science or their art that they lose perspective on all else. A good thesis comparing two of these characters—Aylmer of "The Birthmark" and Dr. Rappaccini of "Rappaccini's Daughter," for example—might initially identify both characters as examples of Hawthorne's mad scientist type but then argue that their motivations for scientific experimentation differ. If you strive to analyze the similarities or differences, discuss significances, and move beyond the obvious, your paper should move beyond the laundry list trap.

PREPARING TO WRITE

Armed with a clear sense of your task—illuminating the text—and with an understanding of theme, character, language, history, and philosophy, you are ready to approach the writing process. Remember that good writing is grounded in good reading and that close reading takes time, attention, and more than one reading of your text. Read for comprehension first. As you go back and review the work, mark the text to chart the details of the work as well as your reactions. Highlight important passages, repeated words, and image patterns. "Converse" with the text through marginal notes. Mark turns in the plot, ask questions, and make observations about characters, themes, and language. If you are reading from a book that does not belong to you, keep a record of your reactions in a journal or notebook. If you have read a work of literature carefully, paying attention to both the text and the context of the work, you have a leg up on the writing process. Admittedly, at this point, your ideas are probably very broad and undefined, but you have taken an important first step toward writing a strong paper.

Your next step is to focus, to take a broad, perhaps fuzzy, topic and define it more clearly. Even a topic provided by your instructor will need to be focused appropriately. Remember that good writers make the topic their own. There are a number of strategies—often called "invention"—that you can use to develop your own focus. In one such strategy, called *freewriting*, you spend 10 minutes or so just writing about your topic without referring back to the text or your notes. Write whatever comes to mind; the important thing is that you just keep writing. Often this process allows you to develop fresh ideas or approaches to your subject matter. You could also try *brainstorming*: Write down your topic and then list all the related points or ideas you can think of. Include questions, comments, words, important passages or events, and anything else that comes to mind. Let one idea lead to another. In the related technique of *clustering*, or *mapping*, write your topic on a sheet of paper and write related ideas around it. Then list related subpoints under each of these main ideas. Many people then draw arrows to show connections between points. This technique helps you narrow your topic and can also help you organize your ideas. Similarly, asking journalistic questions—Who? What? Where? When? Why? and How?—can lead to ideas for topic development.

Thesis Statements

Once you have developed a focused topic, you can begin to think about your thesis statement, the main point or purpose of your paper. It is imperative that you craft a strong thesis, otherwise, your paper will likely be little more than random, disorganized observations about the text. Think of your thesis statement as a kind of road map for your paper. It tells your reader where you are going and how you are going to get there.

To craft a good thesis, you must keep a number of things in mind. First, as the title of this subsection indicates, your paper's thesis should be a statement, an assertion about the text that you want to prove or validate. Beginning writers often formulate a question that they attempt to use as a thesis. For example, a writer exploring the theme of isolation and community in Conrad's *Lord Jim* might ask, `Why are Jim's decisions always closely related to the needs and realities of the communities of which he is a part?` While a question like this is a good strategy to use in the invention process to help narrow your topic and find your thesis, it cannot serve as the thesis statement because it does not tell your reader what you want to assert about isolation and community. You might shape this question into a thesis by instead proposing an answer to that question: `In Lord Jim, the character of Jim experiences the pull and influence of the lives of those around him. The story presents his isolation in his moral dilemmas. The novel demonstrates his need for a core of decision making and responsibility within the larger communities of which he is a part.` Notice that this thesis provides an initial plan or structure for the rest of the paper, and notice, too, that the thesis statement does not necessarily have to fit into one sentence. For example, after discussing Jim's plight on the *Patna* you could examine the ways in which community is presented as important in this novel and then theorize about what Conrad is saying about human relationships more generally; perhaps you could discuss how the common responsibility to preserve life in the light of this irresponsibility is a flaw not only in Jim but in the society in which this story is set. That is, Conrad might be suggesting that Jim's moral mistake arises not only from his youthful romanticism but also from the wider society that encourages this.

Second, remember that a good thesis makes an assertion that you need to support. In other words, a good thesis does not state the obvious. If you tried to formulate a thesis about isolation and community by simply saying, `Isolation and community are aspects of Lord Jim,` you have done nothing but rephrase the obvious. Since Conrad's novel is centered on his protagonist Jim and his issues, there would be no point in spending three to five pages supporting that assertion. You might try to develop a thesis from that point by asking yourself some questions: `How does Marlow, the narrator of this part of the novel, perceive Jim's social responsibility? How is Jim's sense of heroism derived from Western culture` and specifically from his maritime community on board the *Patna*? After the fateful incident has occurred, how does Jim seek to belong and to regain his honor within the human community? When he has become a central figure of the Patusan community in Asia, how do his decisions relate to his new leadership role? Does the novel appear to indicate that responsibility is an inevitable part of belonging to a community of people? Such a line of questioning might lead you to a more viable thesis, like the one begun in the preceding paragraph.

As the comparison with the road map also suggests, your thesis should appear near the beginning of the paper. In relatively short papers (three to six pages) the thesis almost always appears in the first paragraph. Some writers fall into the trap of saving their thesis for the end, trying to provide a surprise or big moment of revelation, as if to say, "TA-DA! I have just proved that in *Lord Jim* the community of the Patusan islanders are more humane and responsible than the crew of the *Patna* and Jim has also learned to be more humane and responsible." Placing a thesis at the end of an essay can seriously mar the essay's effectiveness. If you fail to define your essay's point and purpose clearly at the beginning, your reader will find it difficult to assess the clarity of your argument and understand the points you are making. When your argument comes as a surprise at the end, you force your reader to reread your essay in order to assess its logic and effectiveness.

Finally, you should avoid using the first person ("I") as you present your thesis. Though it is not strictly wrong to write in the first person, it is difficult to do so gracefully. While writing in the first person, beginning writers often fall into the trap of writing self-reflexive prose (writing *about* their paper *in* their paper). Often this leads to the most dreaded of opening lines: "In this paper I am going to discuss . . ." Not only does this self-reflexive voice make for very awkward prose, but it frequently allows writers to boldly announce a topic while completely avoiding a thesis statement. An example might be a paper that begins as follows: *Lord Jim,* one of Joseph Conrad's most powerful stories, begins with a description of Jim, who, in the Far East, will be called Tuan Jim, or Lord Jim. In this paper I will discuss why. The author of this paper has done little more than announce a general topic for the paper: why

Jim is called "Tuan Jim." While there may be a potential thesis here, the writer fails to present an opinion about the significance of this. To improve this attempt at formulating a thesis, the writer would need to back up a couple of steps. First, the announced topic of the paper is too broad; it largely summarizes an event in the story, without saying anything about the ideas of the story. The writer should highlight what she considers the meaning of the story. What is the story about? The writer might conclude that the name given to Jim in Patusan, in the Far East, denotes qualities of his character, or that its use suggests something about the natives. A writer who chooses to explore Jim's name might craft a thesis that reads: `Lord Jim is a story that explores the isolation and human connection of a man who is compelled by events to learn the responsibility of moral decision making and how the trust placed in him, exemplified by the name bestowed on him—Lord Jim— heightens this sense of responsibility.`

Outlines

While developing a strong, thoughtful thesis early in your writing process should help focus your paper, outlining provides an essential tool for logically shaping that paper. A good outline helps you see and develop the relationship among the points in your argument and assures you that your paper flows logically and coherently. Outlining not only helps place your points in logical order but also helps you subordinate supporting points, weed out any irrelevant points, and decide if there are any necessary points that are missing from your argument. Most of us are familiar with formal outlines that use numerical and letter designations for each point. However, there are different types of outlines; you may find that an informal outline is a more useful tool for you. What is important, though, is that you spend the time to develop some sort of outline—formal or informal.

Remember that an outline is a tool to help you shape and write a strong paper. If you do not spend sufficient time planning your supporting points and shaping the arrangement of those points, you will most likely construct a vague, unfocused outline that provides little, if any, help with the writing of the paper. Consider the following example:

`Thesis: Lord Jim is a story that explores the impact of the consequences that result from the choices of one man,`

Jim, whose isolation from the human community leads him to poor choices and from whose later heroism in the Far East comes a name, "Lord Jim," which underscores in him a deepened sense of conscience and his responsibilities to the human community of the islanders.

I. Introduction and thesis: Jim's romantic isolation and bad choices

II. Jim and the *Patna*
    A. Isolation and romanticism.
    B. Failure of will and poor choices.

III. Jim and the Patusans
    A. Jim's actions in the Far East.
    B. Admiration for Tuan Jim.
    C. Challenges and Jim's role in decision making.

IV. Conclusion
    A. Jim faces a crisis in Patusan that challenges him to exercise his sense of responsibility for the villagers.

This outline has a number of flaws. First, the major topics labeled with the Roman numerals are not arranged in logical order. If the paper's aim is to show how Jim gradually develops a more responsible character, the writer should establish the particulars of this process toward growth by showing the flaws in Jim's romantic self-image. Similarly, the thesis makes no reference to the process of Jim's growth and development. It has been argued by some critics that Jim never really grows much or changes fundamentally in his romantic idealism. If the writer, in contrast with this view, sees a change in Jim during the course of this story, this change should be demonstrated. The writer could argue that loneliness or shame and the need to prove himself as honorable drive Jim farther east to a place where he adopts a kind of valor.

Another problem with this outline is the inclusion of a section A in the conclusion. An outline should not include an A without a B, a 1 without a 2, and so forth. The final problem with this outline is the over-all lack of detail. None of the sections provide much information about the contents of the argument, and it seems likely that the writer has not given sufficient thought to the content of the paper.

A better start to this outline might be the following:

    I. Introduction and thesis: Jim's overcoming of
       romantic isolation and bad choices

   II. Jim's decisions on the *Patna*
       A. Isolation, romanticism, and Jim's decision
          making.
          1. The essential aloneness of human
             beings.
          2. Jim's dreams of honor and glory and
             romantic idealism.
       B. Jim's failure of will and poor choices.
          1. Abandoning the *Patna*: a bad decision.
          2. Fear and the loss of honor and moral
             standing.

  III. Jim and the Patusans: Learning about community
       and responsibility
       A. Jim's struggle with his past decision.
       B. Jim's shame and his attempt to escape by
          going east.
       C. Jim's learning about community and
          responsibility among the Patusans.
          1. Admiration for Tuan Jim.
          2. Learning about leadership.
       D. Challenges in Patusan: Jim's decisions
          and mistakes.
          1. Protecting the people.
          2. Jim's mistakes in handling Gentleman
             Brown.

This new outline would prove much more helpful when it came time to write the paper.

An outline like this could be shaped into an even more useful tool if the writer fleshed out the argument by providing specific examples from the text to support each point. Once you have listed your main point and your supporting ideas, develop this raw material by listing related supporting ideas and material under each of those main headings. From there, arrange the material in subsections and order the material logically.

For example, you might begin with one of the theses cited above. `In Lord Jim, the protagonist, Jim, is driven by the need to come to terms with his mistakes and to fashion, with integrity, a more socially responsible character who is less deluded by romantic dreams and a romantic self-image.` As you develop your thesis, consider opposing viewpoints. Can he do this? Or is Jim still persuaded by romantic illusions? One could argue that the Gentleman Brown incident toward the end of the novel shows that Jim has not shed his romantic illusions and has been overly influenced by flattery and false honor among the Patusans. Some critics say that he is far too kind to this invader and should have responded more decisively. However, you could argue, with support from the text, some change has begun to occur in Jim. You could argue that Jim has not entirely failed and that he has become more genuinely heroic. You might add that Marlow, for all of his ambivalence about Jim's moral failings, also recognizes this. As noted above, a thesis already gives you the beginning of an organization. You might start by supporting the notion that community values play an important role in Jim's development. Perhaps he is not always the romantic egotist that some critics claim he is.

Joseph Conrad began writing *Lord Jim* in 1898 shortly after writing his short story "Youth." He then put his initial draft of *Lord Jim* aside and wrote his famous novel *Heart of Darkness.* Then he returned to writing *Lord Jim,* incorporating many innovative techniques. One of these is how the story is told. In "Youth" and in *Heart of Darkness,* as well as in *Lord Jim,* a middle-aged sailor named Marlow becomes a narrator who tells us the story. If the writer is working on an essay on *Heart of Darkness,* the same sense of organization and development can be brought to developing a thesis and an outline. For example, if the writer is considering the setting and landscape of *Heart of Darkness* and the human drive for adventure, one might ask questions about how the environment compels this spirit of adventure. You might begin your outline with four topic headings:

An informal outline might look like this:

    I. Focus on nature as being like a character and
       on the importance of setting.

   II. Discuss setting in the first section of the
       novel.

  III. Discuss Marlow as a storyteller and his view
       of man and nature.

   IV. Battle on the boat and the strength of the
       river.

You would set about writing a formal outline with a similar process, though in the final stages you would label the headings differently. A formal outline for a paper that observes that nature and setting play a large role in *Heart of Darkness* might look like this:

    I. Introduction
       A. Conrad focuses on nature as a character.
       B. Setting is important to the theme of the
          story.
       C. The element of water, like the river, is
          a symbol of dualism in nature.

   II. Discussion of first section of the novel.
       A. Immediately, the setting is Conrad's
          focus.
       B. The power of the sea and sky and other
          symbols is stressed.
       C. The list of ships is deceptive. It is the
          great Thames that has carried them all.

  III. Discuss Marlow.
       A. He is a storyteller.
          1. His style resembles the author's.

2. He is distinct in the world of "yarn spinning sailors."
B. Marlow's philosophy of man and nature.
1. One person's life and the span of humankind are moments in comparison to the ancient and enduring Earth.
2. Nature's power is like water: slow and soft, but more powerful than fire.

IV. Example of the Roman soldiers parallel Marlow's own journey.

V. Battle on the boat.
A. River is remarkably stronger than a man.

VI. Conclusion
A. Conrad is in awe and fear of nature but still in favor of exploration and adventure.
B. There is a sense in which the struggle is inescapable and the game must be played.

As in the previous sample outline, the thesis provides the seeds of a structure, and the writer was careful to arrange the supporting points in a logical manner, showing the relationships among the ideas in the paper. There are many ideas here that will support this writer's creation of a strong paper. However, this outline needs some revision. Sections IV and V are incomplete and require more detail. The direction that the writer will take in Section IV needs to be indicated. In section V, there should be no A without a B. This more detailed outline will help the writer as he works to write these sections. Yet, there is another problem here. In section three, the writer confuses Marlow, the narrator, with Conrad, the author. Conrad has created Marlow's style of narration. The writer of this paper has to be careful not to directly associate the narrator with the author who created this narrator. Many critics have pointed out that some of Conrad's characters emerge from Conrad's own experiences. However, it would take a great deal of effort to demonstrate that Marlow's style of narration resembles that of Conrad, the author. More interesting here is the idea that Marlow is distinct in the world of "yarn spinning sailors." This phrase itself is interesting because one might think of a ball of yarn with its threads unfolding. That kind of unfolding of his story is what Marlow accomplishes. This writer is astute in bringing a discussion of Marlow's narration into his paper. The way that Marlow tells this tale is itself an ample subject for a whole paper. This viewpoint narration is a very important aspect of Conrad's novel. However, it might be best for the writer to find a way to focus on Marlow directly in connection with his overall theme of the power of nature and the importance of setting. This is taken up in section B. It should also be considered, in some way, in section A.

An inquiry into Marlow's philosophy of man and nature (part III, section B) is a very interesting subject. In this part of the paper, the writer can discuss the interactions between the individual and the natural world and its power. In his outline, the writer has captured a sense of the limitations of the person against the scale of nature and the span of history. Conrad's attention to the inexorable force of nature is something that can also be found in the theory of Charles Darwin, in which he pointed to the process of natural selection. This was part of the intellectual context in which Conrad wrote. The writer might explore that here. If so, the writer ought to integrate that well into his essay. This writer chooses to consider how the first pages of the novel describe the Roman legions that once inhabited Britain. He sees a comparison between their historic encounter with Britain and Marlow's own modern journey. Here in part IV, it would be helpful if the writer could take this into some further detail, as he has done with the plan for part III of the paper. The writer will devote a section of his paper, in Section V, to the battle on the boat. This is an important incident in Conrad's story. The outline indicates that the writer will show how the river is stronger than a man. However, this raises a question: What does Conrad mean by showing this strength of the river over man? The writer needs to address this question and it would be a good idea to develop this within his outline.

Finally, the conclusion that Conrad himself is in awe and fear of nature is a conjecture based on the story he has written. It might be clearer to say that Marlow, his character, suggests this awe and fear through the story he tells. The writer will show that the struggle is inescapable. He also intends to assert that the game of exploration, adventure, and expedition "must be played." These ideas would make for a strong thesis that would unify the entire essay. They might be introduced early on the paper, supported with evidence, and returned to here at the end of the paper, in the conclusion.

Body Paragraphs

Once your outline is complete, you can begin drafting your paper. Paragraphs, units of related sentences, are the building blocks of a good paper, and as you draft you should keep in mind both the function and the qualities of good paragraphs. Paragraphs help you chart and control the shape and content of your essay, and they help the reader see your organization and your logic. You should begin a new paragraph whenever you move from one major point to another. In longer, more complex essays you might use a group of related paragraphs to support major points. Remember that in addition to being adequately developed, a good paragraph is both unified and coherent.

Unified Paragraphs:

Each paragraph must be centered around one idea or point, and a unified paragraph carefully focuses on and develops this central idea without including extraneous ideas or tangents. For beginning writers, the best way to ensure that you are constructing unified paragraphs is to include a topic sentence in each paragraph. This topic sentence should convey the main point of the paragraph, and every sentence in the paragraph should relate to that topic sentence. Any sentence that strays from the central topic does not belong in the paragraph and needs to be revised or deleted. Consider the following paragraph about how Marlow in *Heart of Darkness* considers the idea of adventure and the environment of the novel. Notice how the paragraph veers away from the main point that in Conrad's novel the setting is treated much like a character.

> Joseph Conrad does something rare in that he treats the setting, the environment in which the characters exist and in which the action takes place, as a virtual character in itself. The deeds and the very lives of the characters in this story are tenuous in that they are suspended in the awesome and immutable power of nature. Nature is something eternal, whereas men and

women are transitory. Once upon a time, there were
Romans in ancient Britain. They discovered a new world.
When Marlow discusses them, surely he is speaking not
just of the Romans in his imagination but the misplaced
outposts of the Congo in his memory. Human beings
have a short burst of impact, and their strength is
apparent. So the subtle and slow moving power of nature
is noticeably greater than the sudden and short-lived
power of human beings.

Although the paragraph begins solidly, and the second sentence provides
the central idea of the paragraph, the author soon goes on a tangent. If
the purpose of the paragraph is to demonstrate that setting is almost
like a character and that humans are transitory and dwarfed by their
environment, the sentences about the Romans are tangential here. They
may find a place later in the paper, but they should be deleted from this
paragraph.

Coherent Paragraphs:

In addition to shaping unified paragraphs, you must also craft coherent paragraphs, paragraphs that develop their points logically with sentences that flow smoothly into one another. Coherence depends on the
order of your sentences, but it is not strictly the order of the sentences
that is important to paragraph coherence. You also need to craft your
prose to help the reader see the relationship among the sentences.

   Consider the following paragraph about nature and setting in *Heart
of Darkness.* Notice how the writer uses the same ideas as the paragraph
above yet fails to help the reader see the relationships among the points.

The setting and environment in which these characters
exist is like a character itself. The deeds and the
very lives of the characters in this story are tenuous
in that they are suspended in the awesome and immutable
power of nature. Everybody's life is like a flicker.
Life is fleeting, like a wave breaking and receding.
Life is full of changes. It is incredible that nature
is so powerful. That power is everywhere represented by
the image of water. Water is soft and yielding; someone

can splash it or scoop it or do anything to it. All
of nature is like that. It can be like a storm. It can
boil or freeze. It takes beatings without resistance.
But Conrad wants to show that nature can and does bite
back and has great power, even if this power is hidden.

This paragraph demonstrates that unity alone does not guarantee paragraph effectiveness. The argument is hard to follow because the author
fails both to show connections between the sentences and to indicate
how they work to support the overall point.

A number of techniques are available to aid paragraph coherence.
Careful use of transitional words and phrases is essential. You can use
transitional flags to introduce an example or an illustration (*for example, for instance*), to amplify a point or add another phase of the same
idea (*additionally, furthermore, next, similarly, finally, the*), to indicate
a conclusion or result (*therefore, as a result, thus, in other words*), to signal a contrast or a qualification (*on the other hand, nevertheless, despite
this, on the contrary, still, however, conversely*), to signal a comparison
(*likewise, in comparison, similarly*), and to indicate a movement in time
(*afterward, earlier, eventually, finally, later, subsequently, until*).

In addition to transitional flags, careful use of pronouns aids coherence and flow. To see how helpful transitional aids are, compare the
paragraph below to the preceding paragraph about nature and setting in
Heart of Darkness. Notice how the author works with the same ideas and
quotations but shapes them into a much more coherent paragraph whose
point is clearer and easier to follow.

Marlow mentions men and their lives being a flicker.
He comments, for example, on the fleeting quality of
human life, and, in the same sentence, offers a plea on
behalf of his race that it may enjoy as much time as the
Earth itself. One can note both morbidity and valiance
in his tone when he speaks this way, with prayers for
blessings that he knows cannot be realized. He mourns
the inescapable, fast approaching end, yet he faces
it with a strong heart and a passionate love for his
precious few years, as well as for his species, however
abominable some of its members may be. Marlow reveals

```
by his examples of fire and lightning his sentiments
about the way to go about living a short life. Marlow
lives life aggressively. He recognizes this all-powerful
force and presence of nature and feels that humankind
must lash back at it. Men are like bolts of lightning and
flashes of fire for Marlow; they are briefly occurring,
voracious, wild, and consuming entities.
```

Similarly, the following paragraph from a paper on the significance of setting in *Heart of Darkness* demonstrates both unity and coherence. In it, the author argues that Conrad draws the story's setting to prepare us to see how it inspires adventure. He concludes that without a river and an ocean, there would be no adventure:

```
The first narrator, who is a man on a ship with the
main hero, Marlow, begins to describe the water and
the surrounding town and the ship. He makes reference
to the similarities and the differences between the
work of nature and the work of man. Man's work is
made to seem inferior to nature's work, and this is a
corroboration of the great power and superiority that
nature possesses. Next, Conrad has his narrator go on a
short rant, listing the numerous ships and valiant men
that have traveled down the Thames and onto the sea.
The list is deceptive in that it seems to praise the
men and their sturdy ships, which it does, but a point
that jumps out on inspection is that, though many great
men have traveled down the river, the river has always
been, long before them and long after, one enduring and
eternal thing. There would be nothing to say of those
adventurers if there had not been a river to carry them
or a sea to carry them to.
```

Introductions

Introductions present particular challenges for writers. Generally, your introduction should do two things: capture your reader's attention and explain the main point of your essay. In other words, while your introduction should contain your thesis, it needs to do a bit more work than that. You are likely to find that starting that first paragraph is one of the most difficult parts of the paper. It is hard to face that blank page or screen, and as a result, many beginning writers, in desperation to start somewhere, start with overly broad, general statements. While it is often a good strategy to start with more general subject matter and narrow your focus, do not begin with broad sweeping statements such as "Everyone likes to be creative and feel understood." Such sentences are nothing but empty filler. They should begin to fill the blank page, but they do nothing to advance your argument. Instead, you should try to gain your readers' interest. Some writers like to begin with a pertinent quotation or with a relevant question. Or, you might begin with an introduction of the topic you will discuss. If you are writing about Conrad's presentation of landscape in *Heart of Darkness,* for instance, you might begin by talking about how nature and an environment are understood to affect people psychologically. Another common trap to avoid is depending on your title to introduce the author and the text you are writing about. Always include the works' author and title in your opening paragraph.

Compare the effectiveness of the following introductions:

1. Joseph Conrad's novel is filled with interesting characters and settings. There are Marlow and Kurtz, and there are the Congo and men that have come from ships into the jungle. Characters are described and we see what they look like and what they are doing and saying. Yet, in this story, Conrad does something interesting and rare. He treats the setting and the environment in which the characters exist and in which the action takes place as a virtual character in itself. Conrad shows us the characters in context. The deeds and the very lives of the characters in this story are tenuous in that they are suspended in the awesome and immutable power of nature.

2. A common element in fictional literature is the dominating focus on the characters in a story: who they are, what they look like, what they are doing and saying. Joseph Conrad describes

his characters in *Heart of Darkness*, but he does something rare: He treats the setting, the environment in which the characters exist and in which the action takes place, as a virtual character in itself. He wants us to see his characters in context. The deeds and the very lives of the characters in Joseph Conrad's *Heart of Darkness* are tenuous in that they are suspended in the awesome and immutable power of nature.

The first introduction begins with a vague, overly broad sentence; cites unclear, undeveloped examples; and then moves abruptly to the thesis. Notice, too, how a reader deprived of the paper's title does not know the title of the story that the paper will analyze. The second introduction works with the same material and thesis but provides more detail and is consequently much more interesting. It begins by discussing a novelist's understandings of character, gives specific examples about what novelists do, and then shows how Conrad uniquely focuses on the importance of the setting. The paragraph ends with the thesis, which includes both the author and the title of the work to be discussed.

The following paragraph provides another example of an opening strategy. It begins by introducing the author and the text it will analyze, and then it moves on, briefly introducing relevant details of the story in order to set up its thesis.

Joseph Conrad's short novel *Heart of Darkness* shows that nature has great power, even if it is hidden. He treats the setting, the environment in which his characters exist and in which the action takes place, as a virtual character itself. The sea and its water, as well as the Congo and its vast jungles, exemplify the power that nature possesses. Marlow, the story's principle narrator, recalls a journey of discovery, in which he has learned firsthand about these environments. He has recognized that the subtle and slow moving power of nature is noticeably greater than the sudden and short-lived power of human beings. The deeds and the very

```
lives of the characters in this story are tenuous in
that they are suspended in the awesome and immutable
power of nature.
```

Conclusions

Conclusions present another series of challenges for writers. No doubt you have heard the adage about writing papers: "Tell us what you are going to say, say it, and then tell us what you have said." While this formula does not necessarily result in weak papers, it does not often result in good ones, either. It will almost certainly result in boring papers (especially boring conclusions). If you have done a good job establishing your points in the body of the paper, the reader already knows and understands your argument. There is no need to merely reiterate. Do not just summarize your main points in your conclusion. Such a boring and mechanical conclusion does nothing to advance your argument or interest your reader. Consider the following conclusion to the paper about nature and adventure in *Heart of Darkness:*

```
These examples show the point I am making. That is, one
can see that Conrad focuses on nature as a character
and that setting is important to the theme of this
story. Humanity is stuck in a material world and is
suffocated by nature. The sea is vast, the jungle is
harsh, and the river is stronger than a man. There
is a sense in which the struggle is inescapable and
the game must be played.
```

Besides starting with a mechanical transitional device, this conclusion does little more than summarize the main points of the outline (and it does not even touch on all of them). It is incomplete and uninteresting (and a little too depressing).

Instead, your conclusion should add something to your paper. A good tactic is to build on the points you have been arguing. Asking "why?" often helps you draw further conclusions. For example, in the paper on *Heart of Darkness* you might speculate or explain why the idealistic Kurtz, who sets out for Africa with grand hopes, turns into a ruthless leader who is worshipped like a god. Scholars often discuss this story as an adventure or conquest that raises questions about the goals and objectives of Western civilization, and your conclusion could present your analysis of ambition, adventurousness, and civilized progress. Another method for successfully concluding a paper is to speculate on other directions in which to take your topic by tying it into larger issues. You might do this by envisioning your paper as just one section of a larger paper. Having established your points in this paper, how would you build on this argument? Where would you go next? In the following conclusion to the paper on *Heart of Darkness*, the author reiterates some of the main points of the paper but does so in order to amplify the discussion of the story's central message and to connect it to other texts by Joseph Conrad:

> Through these few examples, one can see how Conrad, as channeled through the character Marlow, holds a view that nature is cold and cruel. Not only this, but it is superior to mankind in all ways. It is the sum of the obstinacy of the world in resistance to the progress and aspirations of humankind. This theme stretches from Conrad's early novels like *Almayer's Folly* and *Outcast of the Islands*, through *Nostromo*, where nature often appears cruel or resistant to human ambitions, to his later works, *Chance*, *The Rescue*, and *The Rover*, in which the sea plays a large role. *Heart of Darkness*, like these other tales, is a testimony to Conrad's awe and reverence for the wild. Apart from his descriptions of nature's opposition to human progress, Conrad frequently raises the question of whether or not progress is an absolute good. He acknowledges that there may be a reason for the world's deadly defenses. Perhaps humankind is too ambitious for its own good or for the good of the world.

Citations and Formatting
Using Primary Sources:
As the examples included in this chapter indicate, strong papers on literary texts incorporate quotations from the text in order to support

their points. It is not enough for you to assert your interpretation without providing support or evidence from the text. Without well-chosen quotations to support your argument you are, in effect, saying to the reader, "Take my word for it." It is important to use quotations thoughtfully and selectively. Remember that the paper presents *your* argument, so choose quotations to support *your* assertions. Do not let the author's voice overwhelm your own. With that caution in mind, there are some guidelines you should follow to ensure that you use quotations clearly and effectively.

Integrate Quotations:

Quotations should always be integrated into your own prose. Do not just drop them into your paper without introduction or comment. Otherwise, it is unlikely that your reader will see their function. You can integrate textual support clearly and easily with identifying tags, short phrases that identify the speaker. For example:

> The narrator describes Jim's appearance as "spotlessly neat, apparalled [spell] in manner as one immaculate white" and that he "displayed a kind of dogged self-assertion which had nothing aggressive in it."

While this tag appears before a quotation, you can also use tags after or in the middle of the quoted text, as the following example demonstrates:

> In *Heart of Darkness*, Marlow suggests that the explorers had lost their bearings. "We were cut off from the comprehension of our surroundings; we glided past like phantoms . . ." he says, adding that they were wondering at everything "like sane men would be before an enthusiastic outbreak in a madhouse."

You can also use a colon to formally introduce a quotation:

> Jim's strengths and weaknesses are clear:

When you quote brief sections of poems (three lines or fewer), use slash marks to indicate the line breaks in the poem:

```
As the poem ends, Dickinson speaks of the power of the
imagination: "The revery alone will do, / If bees are
few."
```

Longer quotations (more than four lines of prose or three lines of poetry) should be set off from the rest of your paper in a block quotation. Double-space before you begin the passage, indent it 10 spaces from your left-hand margin, and double-space the passage itself. Because the indentation signals the inclusion of a quotation, do not use quotation marks around the cited passage. Use a colon to introduce the passage:

```
After Marlow is introduced, he becomes the narrator,
telling his story to the men on deck. He begins by
looking back in time to when the ancient Romans landed
in the place that would one day become Britain:

I was thinking of very old times, when the Romans
first came here, nineteen hundred years ago—the other
day. . . Light came out of this river ever since—you
say Knights? Yes, but it is like a running blaze on a
plane, like a flash of lightning in the clouds. We live
in the flicker—may it last as long as the old earth
keeps rolling!
```

It is also important to interpret quotations after you introduce them and explain how they help advance your point. You cannot assume that your reader will interpret the quotations the same way that you do.

Quote Accurately:
Always quote accurately. Anything within quotation marks must be the author's exact wording. There are, however, some rules to follow if you need to modify the quotation to fit into your prose.

1. Use brackets to indicate any material that might have been added to the author's exact wording. For example, if you need to add any words to the quotation or alter it grammatically to allow it to fit into your prose, indicate your changes in brackets:

As Marlow anticipates getting to his destination, Kurtz's station, he realizes that the journey will take longer than he has expected. On the evening of the second day, Marlow says that they were considering their distance and "judged [themselves to be] about eight miles from Kurtz's station." Marlow says, "I wanted to push on; but the manager looked grave, and told me the navigation up there was so dangerous that it would be advisable, the sun being very low already, to wait where we were till the next morning.

2. Conversely, if you choose to omit any words from the quotation, use ellipses (three spaced periods) to indicate missing words or phrases:

Towards the evening of the second day we judged ourselves about eight miles from Kurtz's station. I wanted to push on; but the manager looked grave, and told me the navigation up there was so dangerous that it would be advisable . . . to wait where we were till the next morning. Moreover, he pointed out that if the warning to approach cautiously were to be followed, we must approach in daylight—not at dusk, or in the dark. That was sensible enough (109).

3. If you delete a sentence or more, use the ellipses after a period:

Towards the evening of the second day we judged ourselves about eight miles from Kurtz's station. I wanted to push on; but the manager looked grave, and told me the navigation up there was so dangerous that it would be advisable, the sun being very low already, to wait where we were till the next morning. . . . That was sensible enough (109).

4. If you omit a line or more of poetry, or more than one paragraph of prose, use a single line of spaced periods to indicate the
   omission:

   ```
   To make a prairie it takes a clover and one bee,
   . . . . . . . . . . . . . . . . . . . . . . .
   And revery.
   The revery alone will do,
   If bees are few.
   ```

Punctuate Properly:

Punctuation of quotations often causes more trouble than it should.
Once again, you just need to keep these simple rules in mind.

1. Periods and commas should be placed inside quotation marks,
   even if they are not part of the original quotation.

   ```
   "No longer is Conrad accused of unfaithfulness
   to his Polish heritage," wrote Adam Gillon in his
   review of "Conrad's Reception in Poland" (217).
   ```

   The only exception to this rule is when the quotation is
   followed by a parenthetical reference. In this case, the period
   or comma goes after the citation (more on these later in this
   chapter):

   ```
   In Joseph Conrad and the Fiction of Autobiography
   (Harvard, 1966), Edward Said looked at Joseph
   Conrad's "immense struggle with himself" (4).
   Some have speculated that Conrad was remaking
   his life, over and over. In his characters human
   connections are broken. His characters are often
   vulnerable.
   ```

2. Other marks of punctuation—colons, semicolons, question
   marks, and exclamation points—go outside the quotation
   marks unless they are part of the original quotation:

> In the Sherry Commemorative volume, Nadjer points
> out emphatically that Conrad was a dedicated
> writer; he was a "writer passionately concerned
> with the problems of moral responsibility"! (79).

Documenting Primary Sources:

Unless you are instructed otherwise, you should provide sufficient information for your readers to locate material you quote. Generally, literature papers follow the rules set forth by the Modern Language Association (MLA). These can be found in the *MLA Handbook for Writers of Research Papers* (sixth edition). You should be able to find this book in the reference section of your library. Additionally, its rules for citing both primary and secondary sources are widely available from reputable online sources. One of these is the Online Writing Lab (OWL) at Purdue University. OWL's guide to MLA style is available at http://owl.english.purdue.edu/owl/resource/557/01/. The Modern Language Association also offers answers to frequently asked questions about MLA style on this helpful Web page: http://www.mla.org/style_faq. Generally, when you are citing from literary works in papers, you should keep a few guidelines in mind.

Parenthetical Citations:

MLA asks for parenthetical citations in your text after quotations. When you are working with prose (short stories, novels, or essays), include page numbers in the parentheses:

> In the view of Barbara Kocowna, "Conrad heard Polish
> voices in his soul; he dreamt of Poland and—being
> emotionally a conservative—remained always a Pole even
> while everything in his daily life was alien to him"
> (196).

This quotation is from Barbara Kocowna, "The Problem of Language" in *Joseph Conrad: A Commemoration,* ed. Norman Sherry. London: Macmillan, 1976. pp. 194–205. Reference to her article would be placed on your works cited page at the end of your paper.

When you are quoting poetry, include line numbers:

Dickinson's speaker tells of the arrival of a fly: "There interposed a Fly– / With Blue– uncertain stumbling Buzz– / Between the light– and Me–" (12-14).

Works Cited Page:

These parenthetical citations are linked to a separate works cited page at the end of the paper. The works cited page lists works alphabetically by the author's last name. An entry for the above reference to Conrad's *The Heart of Darkness* would read:

Conrad, Joseph. *The Heart of Darkness.* Ed. Ross C. Martin. Boston and New York: Bedford Books, St. Martin's Press, 1996.

The *MLA Handbook* includes a full listing of sample entries, as do many of the online explanations of MLA style.

Documenting Secondary Sources:

To ensure that your paper is built entirely on your own ideas and analysis, instructors often ask that you write interpretive papers without any outside research. If, on the other hand, your paper requires research, you must document any secondary sources you use. You need to document direct quotations, summaries or paraphrases of others' ideas, and factual information that is not common knowledge. Follow the guidelines above for quoting primary sources when you use direct quotations from secondary sources. Keep in mind that MLA style also includes specific guidelines for citing electronic sources. OWL's Web site provides a good summary: http://owl.english.purdue.edu/owl/resources/557/09/.

Parenthetical Citations:

As with the documentation of primary sources, described above, MLA guidelines require in-text parenthetical references to your secondary sources. Unlike the research papers you might write for a history class, literary research papers following MLA style do not use footnotes as a means of documenting sources. Instead, after a quotation, you should cite the author's last name and the page number.

> "Heart of Darkness does not claim to be a dependable traveler's guide, but it does depict the threatening atmosphere of isolation quite convincingly" (Najder 134).

If you include the name of the author in your prose, then you would include only the page number in your citation. For example:

> According to Zdzislaw Najder, "In place of romance and adventure he found ruthless competition for trade and power, and an organization bent on making quick, huge profits" (136).

If you are including more than one work by the same author, the parenthetical citation should include a shortened yet identifiable version of the title in order to indicate which of the author's works you cite. For example:

> (Najder, Chronicle 140)

Similarly, and just as important, if you summarize or paraphrase the particular ideas of your source, you must provide documentation:

> Najder points out that instead of finding romance and adventure in the colonial territories, Joseph Conrad witnessed a lot of competition and struggling for power and trade (136).

Works Cited Page:

Like the primary sources discussed above, the parenthetical references to secondary sources are keyed to a separate works cited page at the end of your paper. Here is an example of a works cited page that uses the examples cited above. Note that when two or more works by the same author are listed, you should use three hyphens followed by a period in the subsequent entries. You can find a complete list of sample entries in the MLA *Handbook* or from a reputable online summary of MLA style.

WORKS CITED

Berthoud, Jacques. *Joseph Conrad: The Major Phase.* Cambridge: Cambridge University Press, 1978.

Fleishman, Avrom. *Conrad's Politics: Community and Anarchy in the Fiction of Joseph Conrad.* Baltimore, MD: Johns Hopkins University Press, 1967.

Hewitt, Douglas. *Conrad: A Reassessment.* Cambridge: Bowes and Bowes, 1952.

Jordan, Elaine. *Joseph Conrad.* Macmillan New Casebooks. New York: Macmillan, 1996.

Leavis, F. R. *The Great Tradition: George Eliot, Henry James, Joseph Conrad.* London: Chatto and Windus, 1948.

Meyers, Jeffrey. *Joseph Conrad.* New York: Charles Scribner's Sons, 1991.

Najder, Zdzislaw. *Joseph Conrad: A Chronicle.* New Brunswick, NJ: Rutgers University Press, 1983.

Plagiarism

Failure to document carefully and thoroughly can leave you open to charges of stealing the ideas of others, which is known as plagiarism, and this is a very serious matter. Remember that it is important to include quotation marks when you use language from your source, even if you use just one or two words. For example, if you wrote Conrad at first believed in the high-minded propaganda about bringing the benevolent light of civilization to the dark continent you would be guilty of plagiarism, since you used Jeffrey Meyers's distinct language without acknowledging him as the source. Instead you should write According to Jeffrey Meyers, "Conrad at first believed in the high-minded propaganda about bringing the benevolent light of civilization to the dark continent" (96). In this case, you have properly credited Meyers.

Similarly, neither summarizing the ideas of an author nor changing or omitting just a few words means that you can omit a citation. Jeffrey Meyers's biography of Joseph Conrad contains the following passages about the novel *Heart of Darkness.*

Heart of Darkness is the first significant work in English literature to deny the idea of progress, which has been a dominant idea in European thought for the past four hundred years, and to question the very foundations of Western civilization (191).

Below are two examples of plagiarized passages:

1. English literature had to wait until Heart of Darkness before an author seriously challenged the idea of progress in European thinking. Few authors until Conrad had questioned Western civilization's notion.

2. The idea of progress, which has been dominant in Europe for 400 years, is denied in Heart of Darkness. This was the first major novel to question the very foundations of Western civilization.

While the first paragraph does not use Meyers's exact language, it does list the same ideas he proposes as the critical themes informing the stories without citing his work. Since this interpretation is Meyers's distinct idea, this constitutes plagiarism. The second passage has shortened his passage, changing some wording, and included a citation, but some of the phrasing is Meyers's. The first paragraph could be fixed with a parenthetical citation. Because some of the wording in the second remains the same, though, it would require the use of quotation marks, in addition to a parenthetical citation. The passage below represents an honestly and adequately documented use of the original passage:

According to Jeffrey Meyers, a major element of Conrad's Heart of Darkness was its challenge to the Western idea of progress. In Conrad's view, colonialism was not necessarily progressive. Meyers says that Conrad was suggesting that humane values were needed to right this situation (191).

This passage acknowledges that the interpretation is derived from Meyers while appropriately using quotations to indicate his precise language.

While it is not necessary to document well-known facts, often referred to as "common knowledge," any ideas or language that you take from someone else must be properly documented. Common knowledge generally includes the birth and death dates of authors or other well-documented facts of their lives. An often-cited guideline is that if you can find the information in three sources, it is common knowledge. Despite this guideline, it is, admittedly, often difficult to know if the facts you uncover are common knowledge or not. When in doubt, document your source.

Sample Essay

Ryan Nardi
Dr. McParland
ENG 123
March 22, 2011

THE POTENCY OF NATURE IN *HEART OF DARKNESS*

In his short novel *Heart of Darkness*, Joseph Conrad employs a peculiar tactic through which he achieves several effects. A common element in much fictional literature is a dominating focus on the characters: who they are, what they look like, what they are doing and saying. Although Conrad certainly treats his characters as well as should be expected and answers all of those questions about them, he does something rare in that he treats the setting, the environment in which the characters exist and in which the action takes place, as a virtual character in itself—arguably the most important character. Whereas adventure stories tend to treat the adventurer, the hero, as a miracle in himself, an individual in the purest sense, Conrad leads the reader's attention to something that had been overlooked, or undertreated, in the past. Neither men nor their adventures could be at all without the rivers and oceans, the jungles and savannahs, the very concreteness of the world. Nothing exists out of context. Indeed, the individual cannot even be distinguished without a platform and background on which to stand and stand out. Conrad has realized this, presumably, and has taken up the task in "Heart of Darkness" to introduce his readership to the world. The deeds and the very lives of the characters in this story are tenuous in that they are suspended in the awesome and immutable power of nature. This kind of storytelling is innovative and insightful and merits closer inspection.

Some good examples of Conrad's method of conveying this idea, the magnitude and importance of nature, come almost immediately, within the first few pages. The narrator, who is imbedded in the opening scene, as opposed to being some hovering, all-seeing third person, in describing the view from the deck of the waiting ship, says, ". . . the sea and sky were welded together without a joint." This seemingly innocuous statement is easy to pass by without giving a second thought during the course of a leisurely reading, but, on a close and deliberate inspection, one can see a hint at the developing theme. The sea and sky are certainly not welded together literally, they do not even touch, they only appear to touch—and Conrad was doubtlessly aware of this fact. This must, then, be a metaphor. The sea and sky are metaphorically welded. In order to understand the purpose of this metaphor, it is important to understand the purpose of metaphors in general. A metaphor takes two disparate ideas or objects and draws a connection between them in order to illustrate a third idea. In this case, Conrad is treating the sea and sky, natural bodies, and welding, a human invention. So, what is the third idea? Conrad says, through the narrator, that "the sea and sky were welded together *without a joint*." And it is in that last part of the phrase that the potency of the metaphor lies. When a man welds two pieces of metal together, there is not only a seam between the two pieces but the seam is jagged and rough, and often there are separate points, pockmarks, when spot welding is employed. It seems that Conrad, a sailing man, was familiar with the look of welded metal that he had seen on ships and drew the distinction between the shoddiness of the seams in objects welded by men and the smoothness of the seam between sky and sea welded by nature. This points, however subtly, to the superiority of nature in relation to mankind.

Conrad has his narrator go on a short rant, listing the numerous ships and valiant men who have traveled down the Thames and onto the sea. The list is deceptive in that it seems to praise the men and their sturdy ships, which it does, but the point that jumps out during this kind of close reading is that, though many great men have traveled down the river, the river has always been, long before them and long after, one enduring and eternal thing, and there would be nothing to say of those men if there had not been a river to carry them or a sea to carry them to.

As Marlow, the hero of the story, is introduced, and as the reader gets to know him better, this theme becomes even more apparent. The narrator describes Marlow as being different from the other men. Specifically, his "yarns," or his stories, are different from those of most other sailors. No doubt Marlow, as most protagonists are for their authors in at least some capacity, is an avatar for Conrad himself, a reflection of his personality and a channel for his personal thoughts. The narrator comments on Marlow's storytelling style, saying, ". . . to him the meaning of an episode was not inside like a kernel but outside, enveloping the tale which brought it out only as a glow brings out a haze . . ." It appears that Conrad is calling attention to this concentration on setting, as well as patting himself on the back for his own unorthodox approach to the adventure story.

Marlow remarks, in his short commentary that follows the narrator's comment on his peculiarity, not only on the grandness of nature spatially but also temporally. Nature is something eternal whereas men are something transitory. He says, "We live in the flicker—may it last as long as the old earth keeps rolling!" He goes on to compare an individual's life but to "a running blaze on a plain, like a flash of lightning in the clouds." Marlow's plea for the long lasting of this "flicker" is not one for which he could honestly hope, not with the deep knowledge he has about the vast difference in weight and endurance between the Earth and its lowly inhabitants. One can note both morbidity and valiance in his tone when he says those words; he mourns the inescapable, fast approaching end, yet he faces it with a strong heart and a passionate love for his precious few years, as well as for his species, however abominable some its members may be.

Marlow reveals, through his analogies to fire and lightning, his sentiments about the human spirit and the way to go about living one's short life. Marlow lives life aggressively. He recognizes this all-powerful force and presence of nature and feels that humankind must lash back at it. Men are like bolts of lightning and flashes of fire for Marlow; they are briefly occurring, voracious, wild, and consuming entities. When Marlow harkens back to the Romans, he imagines them exploring the Thames almost two millennia in the past. He conjures up images, "Sand-banks, marshes, forests, savages,— precious little to eat, nothing but Thames water to drink." The wilderness, for Marlow/Conrad, is something separate from the explorer. That is not to say that all humans are alien to nature—he mentions "savages" in the list of nature's defenses—but those who seek to conquer it are treated like viruses, foreign bodies. According to Marlow, nature wants to destroy the explorer, to starve him and consume him before he has the chance to consume it, like the fiery thing he is.

He foreshadows the tale of his latest adventure, the main story of the book, as well, that must be brewing in his head at this point, when he speaks about the Romans discovering Britain. When he says, "Here and there a military camp lost in a wilderness, like a needle in a bundle of hay . . . death skulking in the air, in the water, in the bush," he is surely speaking of not just the Romans in his imagination but the misplaced outposts in the Congo in his memory, from which he has recently returned—and where the reader is soon to go back with him. He goes on in a hauntingly passionate tone that further confirms he is not thinking of some fictional band of soldiers from ancient history: "Land in some swamp, march through the woods, and in some inland post feel the savagery, the utter savagery, had closed in around him." For Marlow, nature is not only formidable and defensive but aggressive and violent; it swallows those who would dare challenge its power.

Later in the story, in the second chapter, Marlow relates a skirmish between the people on board his steamboat and the natives lurking in the forest along the bank of the river. During the fight, an African man working with Marlow is shot and killed. About the treatment of his corpse, Marlow says this, "Oh! he was heavy, heavy; heavier than any man on earth, I should imagine. Then without much more ado I tipped him overboard. The current snatched him as though he had been a wisp of grass, and I saw the body roll over twice before I lost sight of it forever." In this brief piece of the story one can see the theme repeated. This slain man was massive by human standards, "heavier than any man on earth," Marlow says. Yet the river carries him away like so much vegetation. Here is seen the incomparability of the strength of a man, even the biggest of men, and the strength of nature. The river swallows him like it would a frog or a stone. It does not even notice him. And the constant occurrence of phrases such as this throughout the story makes it clear that it is Marlow's/Conrad's intention that the reader draw such a conclusion about the brutal potency of the wilderness.

Through these few examples, of the many from which there are to choose, one can see how Conrad, as channeled through the character Marlow, holds an anthropomorphic view of nature. It is utterly opposed to human beings and human progress, yet it feels and acts in human ways. It is the sum of the obstinacy of the world in resistance to progress and the aspirations of humankind. *Heart of Darkness* is a testimony to Conrad's awe, fear, and reverence for the wild. Apart from his descriptions of nature's opposition to human progress, Conrad frequently raises the question of whether or not progress is an absolute good. He acknowledges that there may be a reason for the world's deadly defenses. Perhaps humankind is too ambitious for its own good or for the good of the world. But there remains, even in such sobriety, a fascination with the uncharted, the dangerous, the wilderness.

HOW TO WRITE ABOUT
JOSEPH CONRAD

JOSEF TEODOR Konrad Korzeniowski, the writer we know as Joseph Conrad, was born in December 1857 in Poland, in a section of the Ukraine, at a time when the country was occupied by Russia. His father was a Polish patriot, and his family was sent into exile in northern Russia when the young Conrad was only four years old. As a young man, he sailed to sea to the Far East, to the Congo in Africa, and to South America. His adult life was spent as a writer in England. He was the son of a patriot exile, an orphan at the age of 11, an emigrant in England in his twenties. That is the broad outline of the life of Joseph Conrad, one of the great writers of the late nineteenth century and of the early part of the twentieth century. Conrad chose to write in English and brought his international experience to bear on the making of the modern novel. Conrad knew the high seas, life in Malaysia and Borneo, the stories of gun runners and African traders, life in the English countryside, and the grimier setting of London: its docks, its streets, its working class, and its literary life of agents and editors, publishers and authors. Conrad wrote diligently, developing innovations in point of view and uses of irony that have influenced many authors who followed him. He took a long, hard look at the world around him and told tales in which individuals faced moral decisions. At times, his stories highlighted his characters' aloneness and the claims of the human community on them. The writer on Conrad can find ways to explore the concepts of individual and society that are central to his work.

Joseph Conrad is notable for his highly original narrative technique. His fictional methods vary and his subjects change from story to story, but there is a moral core to his work. He often breaks with linear progression in his narratives to underscore the fragmentary nature of experience and how individuals look at the world differently from one another. Conrad makes use of "nonrealist" techniques. His most characteristic techniques are the time shift, multiple narrators, and symbolic description. There is throughout his work a deep concern about the psychological and philosophical implications of experience. Conrad's work also reveals a profound epistemological and metaphysical skepticism. Because of his unique style, Conrad is often challenging for readers. His fiction is also a challenge for anyone who would write on his work.

In writing on Joseph Conrad, one should attempt to develop a careful and well-ordered essay. While your essay will be orderly, that essay could be about the moments of disorder in Conrad's stories. For in Conrad's work, we see that life is not always logical, orderly and neat. The ironic method is prevalent in many of Conrad's stories. There is a difference between the way that things appear to the characters in the story and how they appear to the reader.

In looking for general patterns in Conrad's work, you may find that Conrad's stories are filled with concrete images, things that we see, things that urge us to keep looking for deeper meaning. Conrad wrote, "My task is, before all, to make you see." A writer might consider the ways that Conrad makes us see the world through his fiction. To what does he guide our eyes? Conrad's work is often about perspective. His characters and narrators "see" the world in many different ways. He is an author seeking meaning. Conrad prefigures modern existentialist fiction. He is concerned with the individual in society, matters of conscience and angst, the basis of moral commitment. Commitment to the human community is deeply tested in the early works. Integrity is required of the individual, who paradoxically is intended for relation with society. Conrad approaches this with intellectual skepticism about what the individual can know about the world. He must face the darkness within, as well as the darkness outside.

As you read Conrad's fiction, you may notice that Conrad is a philosophical novelist whose position is frequently that of a skeptic. Conrad probes the individual consciousness in relation to the outside world.

Between 1896 and 1900, he chiefly pursued the issue of the self and the world in which that self lives. He probed human subjectivity: whether how the world is and how one sees it is compatible. He examined illusion and disillusion, communal life and isolation. There is a distinctive moral outlook throughout the tales: An individual's choices and actions determine his character and his fate. Conrad's stories argue for human solidarity—for personal engagement in the life of the human community. This ensures stability of the self and a kind of moral character. There is a fundamental conflict between the needs of the individual and that of the society. An individual's egoism is self-enclosing. In the case of Kurtz in *Heart of Darkness* this is disastrous. One must, rather, make personal and social commitments. There is "solidarity" with humanity, a faithfulness to others that must be fulfilled. Conrad seeks honor and to uphold duty. Without this, the individual is adrift. Conrad is skeptical about the human mind. The intellect alone cannot give meaning to reality. Fidelity is central and is humanity's moral core.

Conrad makes use of autobiographical elements in his stories. Yet, he transforms these, as one would take raw material and turn it into something. Conrad drew on his personal suffering to create beauty and bring forth "a wealth of ideas," says his leading Polish critic, Zdzislaw Najder (495). Conrad wrote indirectly about his experiences. He never wrote directly about his inner life. Some biographers note his periods of illness, his struggles with malaria, rheumatism and gout, or his "nervous instability." Ian Watt asks how such a figure as they depict could have penned 20 volumes of fiction and have "the moral strength and sanity that remain unrivalled in the literature of our century" (25). Even so, Conrad worked hard at his craft. His goal was to write for a wide enough public to become financially secure. With his eyes to the market, he engaged in writing a romance, *Almayer's Folly,* his first novel, which included exotic adventure. Calling on his experiences, he wrote fiction that paralleled the popular stories of Kipling and Stevenson that were set in the Far East.

Yet, Joseph Conrad was also a writer of the sea. You will notice that he romanticizes the sea. He makes frequent use of adventure and romance material. A writer who deals with melodramatic tests of violence and conflict as Conrad did has to find a method of working thoughtfully with this. The exotic and the adventurous are brought home for his readers. Conrad wishes to distinguish himself in this regard from writers like

H. Rider Haggard. For Conrad, Haggard writes "a good story for young people." However, he is "essentially a writer of action." Conrad seeks to do something more in his fiction: He tries to explore human motivation.

A writer may reflect on Conrad's descriptive power. From his first novel to his last, Conrad was descriptive. He had a sharp memory for landscapes. This power of seeing suggests the ability to determine what the landscape discloses. By looking at what is visible, the individual can develop a sense of its meaning. He provides careful attention to topography, to character and activities, what the reader sees and feels in this location.

Conrad is also a master of technique, who wrote in English. However, he came to this language later in life and he had to work steadily at it. His writing bears traces of Polish and French grammar and rhetorical style. His careful attention to the craft of writing emerges, in part, from the French influences of Gustave Flaubert and Guy de Maupassant. Conrad carried the legacy of spoken and written Polish throughout his life. He was likewise fluent in French and spoke it idiomatically. Referring to his choice to write in English, Conrad claimed, "it was I who was adopted by the genius of the language." He said that he "had the right to be believed when I say that if I had not written in English I would not have written at all" (*Personal Reminiscences* v–vi).

Conrad portrays human emotion with restraint. Skepticism and irony are characteristic of his writing. Conrad's youth was "gloomy" and unsettled. He spent long years as a seaman. Later, he lived in England, among many who did not readily accept or understand him. This may be a reason why Conrad writes about the tragic in human existence. He is concerned about the failings of human nature, faithfulness to people and to causes, matters of moral responsibility. There is an understated compassion for the fate of humanity. An émigré from Poland to England, Conrad pondered alienation and human solidarity. He found himself living in an alien land, apart from familiar structures of culture and family. Conrad wrote from the feeling that he was an outsider. Yet, as he notes in his preface to *The Nigger of the "Narcissus,"* he implicitly believed in human fellowship and wrote in "conviction of our fellow-men's existence."

Readers who become familiar with a writer's works often read a biography to add perspectives to their understanding, as Conrad's biographer Najder points out. You might want to do this also. Najder adds that, in his view, understanding the author's life "is only marginally important for understanding and appreciating his work" (vii). Yet, he recognizes, as should we, that we do gain something when we learn about a writer's influences and the ways in which he may have transformed personal experience into literary texts.

TOPICS AND STRATEGIES

This section will give you ideas about how you might approach writing an essay about Conrad. You will have to select a certain work or works to focus on, since you will not be able to write about all of Conrad's works in one essay. The sample topics will give you suggestions about which texts you might use in connection with a particular topic. As you plan your essay, think about how you will structure your essay. How long will it be? What are the main points you would like to cover? Which of Conrad's works do you want to consider as you plan your paper? Can you write on this work that you have selected in a meaningful way in the time and space you have allotted for this essay? If you plan to make use of more than one Conrad story, why? Your reader might be assisted if you can provide a rationale for grouping the texts you do in your essay. Perhaps you have chosen stories that focus on a specific theme or that include the same character, such as Marlow. You might let your reader know that you have chosen to explore how Conrad made use of Marlow as a narrator. How is Marlow a mouthpiece for Conrad's concerns? You may have selected pieces that span Conrad's writing life in order to demonstrate developments in his thinking. For example, some critics have charged that there was a "decline" in Conrad's work in his later novels after 1915. What if you want to contest this claim? You would probably make comparisons between some of his earlier novels with his later ones. If you are sure of your reasons for choosing certain texts for your comparison and your essay makes those reasons clear to readers, then you can be confident that your selection will not appear random and that your argument will be strong.

Joseph Conrad was an innovator, one of the originators of modernism in England. The techniques he developed in voice, characterization, and narrative point of view were quite influential for later writers. However, they present some challenges to the writer of a research paper or an essay on Conrad's literary methods or on the social or philosophical implications of his stories. We will look at some of these issues that are involved in writing about Conrad's fiction. Then we will consider a number of possible paper topics and some strategies for working on each of these topics.

Themes

Many of Conrad's works engage similar themes. You might study, for example, artistic expression, the nature of romantic love, the effects of war on the individual, or the human being's relationship with nature in almost any of Conrad's literary works. The sample topics below offer you suggestions as to which works you might focus on for a given topic, but the lists they provide are by no means exclusive. Feel free to include another work or substitute a work you find particularly interesting in place of one suggested in the topic. Once you have selected the works you want to study, you will want to reread each of them carefully, paying special attention to any passages that pertain to your topic, analyzing these passages and keeping careful notes. Attentive reading includes noting your impressions and asking questions as you read. Exploring these questions could lead to an essay. When you engage in careful questioning, this begins to reveal patterns, issues, or themes. Such close reading can begin as you identify the central themes and ideas that recur in the novel you have chosen to work on. Then comes the interesting part: You will begin crafting an essay. You will want to compare the notes you have taken about each of the works you have selected and synthesize your findings. This may help you to discover new and insightful ideas about the story.

Sample Topics:

1. **Isolation:** How does Conrad portray human isolation in his work?

   Several of Conrad's characters are solitary, and this raises the issue of human isolation. When you write you are probably alone, but you may be thinking of other people as you write. Are we connected with one another in our human relationships or essentially isolated? In several Conrad stories, an individual is beset by a situation that strips him of his anchors in the world: Friendship, society, moral supports, and love are taken away. You might explore how the character responds to the situation he or she faces.

In story after story, Conrad shows that the individual lives within a context. We see the interaction between a man or a woman and this sense of order or the lack of it. When does an individual character deviate from the norm? How is one's conduct limited by society? What happens when order breaks down? Look for occasions when the wilderness separates men and women from the civilized and ordered world. Locate moments when a character faces chance, chaos, irrationality and has to survive. Conrad's characterizations often show that the individual is limited. To be fully human is to be fully conscious of this limitation. In *Heart of Darkness*, for example, the boat immobilized, submerged, and stuck in the mud may suggest the resistance of the world. Yet, this story suggests an imperative of action, a requirement that the characters act and not remain passive. Do you see any of Conrad's characters acting to overcome isolation? Or are they isolated by their actions?

2. **Chance:** What do Conrad's stories have to say about chance?

In Conrad's early novels, characters are put to the test. In *Lord Jim,* we encounter the chance occurrence that the *Patna* has struck something and is beginning to sink. This unexpected disaster requires a response from those on board. It tests Jim's humanity and his moral decision making with respect to the human community. You might explore how this is a test of his courage and of his integrity. Sadly, Jim fails. As you write, you may consider how this brings a moral awareness. Chance also looms large in Conrad's later novels. In later works, like *Under Western Eyes* or *Victory,* there is an apparently chance meeting of characters that makes a great difference in their lives. How do Conrad's characters respond to chance occurrences? What might Conrad be saying about the place of chance in our lives?

Look for patterns of chance happenings across Conrad's works. In *Lord Jim,* chance is what calls Jim to the test of his humanity in a fundamental way. Chance like this tests his physical courage and his moral character. In "The Secret Sharer," it seems only by chance occurrence that Leggatt, the captain's alter-self or double, appears. Yet, the captain has something profoundly personal to work out because of this. In *Under Western Eyes,* Razumov's life is changed by the chance occurrence of an assassin hiding in his room. *Chance* (1913), *Victory* (1915), *The Shadow Line* (1917), and *The Rescue* (1920) all have elements of chance in them. What do you think about this element of chance in life and in Conrad's stories?

3. **Romance:** What romantic adventures or journeys do you see in Conrad's novels?

When Conrad started writing, adventure novels were popular. Conrad often presents romantic adventures ironically. This can be seen in *Almayer's Folly, Heart of Darkness,* and "Youth." In these stories, characters have dreams and goals that often do not work out according to their expectations. You can look at stories like these for romantic dreamers and adventurers, characters on a quest who make mistakes along the way. How does Conrad get significance and seriousness out of these conventions of the escapist boy's novel of adventure? You might also explore the relationships between women and men in some of Conrad's stories, like *Victory.* Where do you see types of romance and adventure present in Conrad's novels? In which character's actions do you see romantic hopes turning into disaster?

Characters

When you write about Conrad, consider character development and how he employs and pursues it in his work. As you read his novels and stories, observe how the characters act. Do his characters change? Do they reveal themselves as the story progresses? Your paper can focus on questions of character development or the author's method of characterization. It is helpful to investigate how we come to know the characters. In Conrad's work, this is particularly tricky at times because of the shifting of viewpoint narrators. So read closely. Characters in Conrad's work often use language and mannerisms of speech peculiar or uniquely matched to them. The way in which a character speaks or inhabits a space can offer clues to his or her inner workings and motivations.

Conrad made an effort to make us *see* his characters. He presents us with complex characters whose behavior can be considered psychologically, socially, or ethically. These characters are, at times, seen through the eyes of a viewpoint narrator and thus we get that narrator's interpretation. In this we see Conrad's investigations of the self, particularly in relation to community. In many stories we see the isolation of characters and the need for solidarity with others. Writing on characters in Conrad is a valuable approach that one can take because Conrad's characters are often so complex and well drawn. Conrad wrote that he sought to give readers of his fiction a chance to pause "for a look, for a sigh, for a smile . . ." If a moment can be caught in fiction, as Conrad hoped, how do his characters' dreams, struggles, or challenges appear to us at any given point? How might you use well-chosen details to write descriptively about this?

Sample Topics:

1. **Conrad's social worlds:** What is the fictional social context in which the characters of Conrad's stories live?

   It is helpful for a writer to reflect on Conrad's idea of society. How do the social worlds in his novels impact the lives of his characters? What is expected of them? Where do they commit themselves and when do they withdraw? When they retreat from society, what are the consequences? The writer should pay careful attention to the mix of characters that make up Conrad's fictional society in each of his stories. Conrad, as a novelist, is a historian of society, much like Balzac, Tolstoy, James, or Austen, Thackeray, Eliot, and Dickens. When characters in *Nostromo* or in *Heart of Darkness* are self-deceiving, how do they affect the public good? When you are writing about the fictional society of the novel of your choice, consider how characters affect one another, the ways that characters speak, and the habits of this society.

   Many of Conrad's novels and stories inquire into isolation and community. How do these works portray the sailor or the entrepreneur or the adventurer? Is the character a hero, a villain, or an ordinary human who has been put in an extraordinary situation? You might choose to focus on *Heart of Darkness, Lord Jim, Victory*, or "The Secret Sharer" to examine the isolation of characters and how this affects them. How do they deal with the experiences they have participated in? What do these characters have in common? What generalizations can you make about Conrad's portrayal of these characters?

2. **Ambiguity:** What uncertain and mysterious qualities and complexity can be seen in Conrad's characters?

When writing on Conrad's characters, one has to work through their ambiguity, or the complexity of their traits, motivations, and behavior. For example, Jim, the central character of Conrad's novel *Lord Jim*, appears to us through the interpretation and story of Marlow. Jim is a middle-class British youth who has grown up reading boys' adventure stories. He dreams of a heroic life and decides to go to sea to fulfill these dreams. The storybook romance of Jim's dreams clashes with realities that do not unfold like those in a romantic adventure story. How does this affect Jim and what, if anything, does he learn?

Any approach to Jim is likely to be heavily affected by Marlow's perceptions of him. Marlow is our narrator for much of the story. He tries to fit together the fragments of what he has witnessed and what he has heard of Jim's life into a coherent narrative. Yet, Marlow has his own sense of the maritime code and morality. He enters into a variety of contradictory positions about Jim. When writing on *Lord Jim*, the writer has to move through Marlow's narrative, which presents Jim as something of an enigma. Conrad's story is no simple adventure story following a causal sequence. Jim moves through a series of crises. He struggles with apparent failure, with how to belong, and how to be a person of virtue or character. The writer working on this novel can make a good deal of this complexity.

3. **Ships and crews:** How are ships and their crews symbols of humanity and the journey of life?

Often Conrad's setting is on a ship or in a place that a ship has sailed to. If you read closely and ask questions about what you have read, you will find symbols throughout Conrad's writing. Symbols may represent large issues that are present in the story. In several stories, the ship is both a setting and a symbol. For example, ask yourself, how is the world represented on this ship, among this assemblage of people in a crew?

In "The Secret Sharer," *The Nigger of the "Narcissus,"* "The End of the Tether," and *The Shadow Line,* the action takes place on board ships. Lord Jim's first fateful decision as a young man takes place on a ship that is apparently sinking. You might explore how this is symbolic. On each ship a segment of humanity is isolated from the rest of the world, while forced to live as a working community. Settings are often significant in Conrad's fiction. You might think about other settings in Conrad's fiction and how these environments affect the characters. In the Congo of *Heart of Darkness* and the province coast of Sulaco in *Nostromo,* people are confined to a region where they must work out their destiny. The natural seascape and landscape inevitably have an impact on the characters. By exploring these environments, you can develop ideas about how nature, setting, and characters interact and how settings may act as symbols that suggest meaning.

4. **Modern tragic heroes:** How are many of Conrad's characters like tragic figures from ancient drama?

Conrad's characters stand out from society, much like the heroes of Greek tragedy. They act in isolated worlds, dealing with their inner problems. Jim struggles with the strain of the mistakes in his past. He becomes central to the fate of the inhabitants of Patusan. The captain in "The Secret Sharer" knows he must command the ship, even while his awareness of his "other self," Leggatt, weighs on his mind and his moods may make him less able to lead his crew. Conrad gives us tragic heroes who struggle to work out their relationship with society. Unlike the Greek heroes, they are not highborn and there is little glory that they move toward. They have moral issues to contend with; call them inner issues, if you will. You might give some attention to how these inner problems of the characters are mirrored in the external landscape or in the events of the story you are writing on.

History and Context

Another approach to Conrad's work is through context and history. Conrad sets his story in specific locations and times. Several of Conrad's stories deal with events that emerge from the European colonial enterprise in different regions of the world. You might consider doing some research on the issues of colonialism. A Conrad story may be discussed in its historical or political context. Several writers have approached Conrad's novels in this way. Through research, your paper could explore the reasons why characters act as they do in this context.

Write in your own voice and your own style. It certainly is sometimes difficult for students to read Conrad. His language is innovative, and his style of storytelling is not always straightforward. The modernity of Conrad's work appeals to many readers today. However, reading Conrad can be challenging. As a member of the avant garde seeking literary innovation, he participated in the origins of British modernism. In expressing problems of his own times, he echoes the problems of our own time. If you spend some time doing some research, you will learn about ideas that were important in the society in which Conrad was writing. That will help you to determine the spirit of the times and what Conrad's view was on many aspects of his world.

Sample Topics:

1. **Colonialism:** What do Conrad's works have to say about the psychological and economic aspects of colonialism?

You might want to begin your work with some background reading on colonialism and the late nineteenth century. You might try *Conrad and the Nineteenth Century* by Ian Watt to get a grasp of Conrad within his historical and cultural context. As for primary texts, *Heart of Darkness* and *Nostromo* each deal with imperialism, but in different ways. They would make particularly good choices for the study of colonialism. As you investigate these novels, look for the social and economic impact made by the colonizers on the society of the region. You might also look at how this affects the colonizers themselves. How does the colonial experience seem to have affected Almayer in *Almayer's Folly* or Marlow and Kurtz in *Heart of Darkness?* Do any of them seem to be struggling with or caught up in aspects of this enterprise? Based on the information you are provided in the text, how are these characters affected?

2. **Politics:** What does Conrad's work say about the politics of colonialists, adventurers, anarchists, and revolutionaries?

You might wish to begin with some background reading on European history and Conrad's native Poland, in which Russia had a critical and powerful position. You might also remember that Conrad's parents were sent into exile by the Russians and that complications resulting from this likely led to their deaths. Consequently, Conrad is quite critical of the political practice of Russia, and this critical stance appears in *Under Western Eyes, The Secret Agent,* and other works. The city of London is the scene of anarchist plotting in *The Secret Agent.* In this story, several Russian figures lurk in the background. There are more Russian characters in *Under Western Eyes.* How are they portrayed? You might read on the movement of anarchism just before the turn of the twentieth century and afterward. Eloise Knapp Hay provides some interesting perspectives in her book *The Political Novels of Joseph Conrad* (1963). What politically motivated actions do you see in Conrad's stories, like *Under Western Eyes* or *The Secret Agent?*

Philosophy and Ideas

Conrad can be explored for his political and philosophical beliefs. We find in Joseph Conrad's work themes of isolation and community, meditations on death, concerns with guilt and shame, reflections on language, admonitions to see clearly and avoid illusions, understandings of human interaction with nature, and assertions of individuality, the power of love, and the value of hard work. As you read through his novels, you will see that Conrad offers his readers characters and situations that compel us to think about moral decision making, human sympathy and pity, the value of restraint and moderation, and the importance of honor. In Conrad's life and works, there is an emphasis on ethics, inquiries into colonialism, opposition to anarchism, and reflections on romance, marriage and family, science, and the emerging modern world.

In writing about a Conrad novel, you might examine a few of the philosophical ideas that arise. With Conrad, you will have to spend some time reflecting on issues of identity, isolation, community, subjectivity and individuality, knowledge and skepticism. He was a writer who was concerned with ethics and responsibility and with knowledge and subjectivity. To inquire into ideas or problems such as these, you can look at the questions that the characters themselves ask. One might also work to identify themes that move through the novel.

Sample Topics:

1. **Meaning:** What is Conrad's struggle to affirm meaning in the world of his stories? How is this related to his larger worldview?

   Conrad's work is open to many different readings. Some critics have pointed to a kind of nihilism in Conrad's fiction, even while others point to human affirmation. You might try to decide whether Conrad's story points to something meaningful. Some critics see Conrad's works as implying a universe that is indifferent. They see in Conrad's works the struggle to find meaning and affirm identity in an apparently absurd world. Others suggest that his characters do find meaning in love, in commitment, or in a code of conduct. The politics of Conrad's novels have also drawn the attention of critics who recognize that moral interests are at the center of many of his most important works. Today's debate over colonialism, or postcolonial criticism, has turned toward Conrad because Conrad challenged romantic ideas about colonialism. However, some critics have suggested that Conrad himself was implicated in this. Given the complexity of issues of colonialism, race, gender, and class, there are many possible topics for writers to consider when writing about Conrad's stories.

2. **Alienation:** What kind of comment is Conrad making about alienation?

For Conrad, alienation is a universal condition that people have to face. He recognizes that sometimes people feel lonely or disconnected. In several stories, you may see that his solution is that one must make a commitment. A person has to morally and personally *affirm* something. A man gains honor by this personal commitment in concrete acts and deeds. In *Lord Jim*, we hear "Woe to stragglers!" (223) and "we exist only in so far as we hang together." Biographers of Conrad have suggested that this sense of aloneness may have emerged from his early loss of his parents, his life at sea as a young man, or his distance from Poland and life in England. As you look at a story of the sea like *Lord Jim* or *The Nigger of the "Narcissus,"* or an adventure like *Heart of Darkness* or *Nostromo*, does Conrad suggest a way out of alienation or a set of ethical principles to deal with the environment?

3. **Community:** How is the individual character in a Conrad story or novel related to the larger community?

Joseph Conrad had an extensive sea career as a sailor. One might imagine how lonely it must be at times to sail for many days and look out on the vast ocean. You may imagine also how important the other sailors become to the person who is living at sea. How is the sea central to Conrad's meditations? In his essay "The Silence of the Sea," Conrad wrote, "time passes and the sea alone remains unchanged." A man, however, is changed by his experience. "No man who has lived for many years with and by the sea, and even in certain measure for the sea, could be willfully false to that character-moulding element and continue to live on in the hope of saving his soul" (84). (*Daily Mail*, September 18, 1909; cited in *Congo Diary*, ed. Zdzislaw Najder, New York: Doubleday, 1978.) Can you determine, from comparing and contrasting Conrad's characters, what Conrad would consider an appropriate sense of connection between the members of a community? Or does Conrad's work suggest that such a thing as community is not possible, and each sailor or adventurer must constantly struggle with his conscience and adjust to the world?

4. **Duty:** Identify and evaluate the models of duty that are presented in Conrad's work.

Why is duty important to Joseph Conrad? The author wrote in a cablegram in 1920: "For Poles the sense of duty and the imperishable feeling of nationality preserved in the hearts and defended by the hands of their immediate ancestors in open struggle against the three powers and in indomitable defiance of crushing opposition for more than three hundred years is sufficient inducement to assist in reconstructing the independent dignity and usefulness of the reborn republic." Does this sentiment lie behind much of his work?

In Conrad, we often see life as a tenacious struggle, a heroic effort for moral balance and dignity. Conrad probes the meaning of duty, seeing in life a fundamental struggle with the elements in nature and in mankind. Conrad was keenly aware of moral complexities in the human condition. This was a novelist assured that he should control his distance from his material. He would encourage his readers to look carefully and to "see" the world. In this, he often fashioned narrators, sometimes within his stories, who tell us, the readers, the stories. Conrad dislocates time, casting aside chronology in favor of the halting and fragmented way in which stories are sometimes told. By this method, Conrad places a challenge on our judgments and our sense of sympathy for his characters. We are brought into imaginative worlds that compel us to reflect more deeply on our own. Do you find that you are sympathetic toward any of Conrad's characters? Record all the details you can about the characters in the works you have chosen to study. Probe the effort this character is making to balance duty and dignity.

Form and Genre

When you are asked to consider form and genre, you want to ask your-self how a literary work is put together and what kind of story it is. In Conrad's work, one frequent aspect of form is narrative point of view. In reading the novel or short story, you will want to examine how the story is told, who tells it, and why. While initially these factors seem to be outside of the story proper, they are in fact an integral part of the narrative. Keep in mind that the author and the narrator are separate entities. You have Conrad, the author, who is writing the story, and you have the narrators, characters that Conrad creates to tell the story. If you remember to think of these narrators as storytellers created by the author, you will often gain interesting insights into the work's themes and meanings.

Considering the form and genre of Conrad's novels offers another way of thinking about literary works. It is often clear whether a literary work is a tragedy, a comedy, or a romance. However, with some of Con-rad's novels, this leads us directly into interpretation. For example, *Lord Jim* may be read as tragedy. However, it might also be read as a critique of romance. If one considers Jim a mock heroic character, then one's reading moves into the region of dark comedy. A paper could question not only the genre of *Lord Jim* but how different emphases on tragedy, romance, or comedy in reading the novel affects how it is read.

Sample Topics:

1. **Narration:** Examine the narration and its effects on our inter-pretation of selected texts.

   Studying the viewpoints and tone of narration in Conrad's sto-ries can be interesting. When you read a Conrad story, you will want to think about whether or not the narrator is a character in the story or is an outside observer. Conrad sometimes gives us both within the same story. Ask what kinds of information your narrator is aware of and what biases he or she might have. What is this narrator's motivation for telling the particular story he or she is telling? How might this motivation affect the way the narrator presents the story and, consequently, the way a reader interprets it? You can study narration in any of

Conrad's works, but Marlow is one especially interesting case, and he appears in *Lord Jim,* "Youth," and *Heart of Darkness.*

2. **Biographical connections:** How does Conrad focus on the isolation of the individual from the community? Does this concern have anything to do with Conrad's own life?

When writing on Conrad, it is useful for the writer to think about how the values, beliefs, and structures of the social and political community impinge on his characters. Biographers have often commented on Conrad's own isolation. Some critics, from Gustav Morf to V.S. Pritchett, believe that Conrad personally felt some guilt for leaving Poland in a kind of self-exile to England. Conrad's father was a Polish hero and martyr. Yet, Conrad sought a life at sea and a writing career in England. Many of his characters carry a sense of remorse about their distance from the human community. A writer considering this could probe the biographies of Conrad for ways that his biography and psychology might be conveyed in his fiction. A writer has to be careful, however, about too closely identifying this author with his characters or his narrators. Some are based on people that Conrad experienced, yet are reworked through imagination. Others are purely imaginative creations. What the writer on Conrad might look for is how Conrad took the stuff of personal experience and reimagined it.

As you look through the stories, you can see that many of Conrad's works might be interpreted as retellings of his own experiences. Critics have also pointed out connections between Conrad and Marlow. You might explore these. Read about Conrad's family, his career at sea and in the Far East, and his writing career. There are many biographies, from Frederick Karl's *Joseph Conrad: The Three Lives, A Biography* to Jeffrey Meyers's *Joseph Conrad: A Biography.* Read on Conrad's life and compare what you have learned about his life and his sources to the fictional representations he creates in his characters. Is there some connection that you see? Investigate this connection and explore how it might help you to better understand Conrad and the literary work he has created.

3. Exploring genre: Is the work you have selected a tragedy or a romance?

You may ask, is *Lord Jim* a tragedy or a romance? Jim's idealistic dreams and his striving might tug at your sympathy. Is Jim a romantic hero, like Goethe's Werther, who is not able to adjust to society? Is he a mock heroic character like Don Quixote, whose foibles lead us to question chivalry? Ought he to be viewed as Dante engaged in a moral journey? Or is Jim a kind of tragic Hamlet? If Jim has absorbed popular cultural forms and the colonial adventure stories he has read have led to a distorted perception of life, is this saying anything about the culture? Do you think that Conrad might be contesting British culture or questioning Western civilization? Conrad provides documents of adventure at sea. Considering the epic of Homer, *The Odyssey,* as an archetypal tale of voyage, a writer may explore the quality of myth that Conrad's sea stories carry. *The Secret Agent,* in the form of a thriller, explores the psychology of revolution and the issue of despotism. Is this a detective novel or something else?

4. Different points of view: How does Conrad make use of point of view?

One of Conrad's important technical innovations was his use of different points of view to convey a story. This shifting of narrators and time sequences makes reading some of his novels difficult for readers. Someone writing about Conrad has to take into account his use of frame narrators and first-person narrators, who only know some aspects of the story they tell. These narratives may also include the use of irony, which can make reading challenging. In addition, Conrad's *Lord Jim* and *Nostromo* are told out of sequence, rather than in the chronological pattern usually expected by readers. To write about these matters requires careful attention and the ability to discern themes.

Conrad was a persistent experimenter. In his preface to *The Nigger of the "Narcissus,"* Conrad said that no single point of view could adequately provide the detachment a work of art requires. Skeptical of a single point of view's grasp of reality, Conrad presents several actions and points of view in connection with one another. He builds an overlapping of characters. Marlow interprets events. He refracts the material. In *Lord Jim* and *Heart of Darkness* we meet a Marlow who interprets events that have already occurred. Marlow looks in retrospect, perhaps in an effort to give meaning to the past.

5. **Time:** How does Conrad make use of time shifts in his fiction?

Among Conrad's concerns is the breaking up of time sequences. His stories require us to look at time in new ways— as does the fiction of Virginia Woolf, William Faulkner, or James Joyce. Conrad's early novels, *Almayer's Folly* and *Outcast of the Islands,* are fairly straightforward. *The Nigger of the "Narcissus"* is also conventional in its use of time and chronology. However, the early stories start to show experimentation. In *Lord Jim,* we are given some interiority of the character's mind. Larger experiments with time come in *Nostromo, Chance,* and *Victory.* Conrad's later uses of time have much in common with montage in film, Frederick Karl has pointed out (69). This biographer also notes that Conrad worked out "time shift techniques." These, he says, involved: 1. A careful selection of details to give an idea of the passage of time. 2. The indirect and interrupted method of handling interviews and dialogues to give a sense of complexity to the past and present meeting. 3. A sense of paralleling and opposing situations that provide time conflicts and tensions. 4. Getting a character in and then working backward and forward over his past. 5. The use of a "gathered up" summary that permits the novelist to sweep from past to present and break into the chronological narrative. 6. The use of time to provide the general effect that life has on mankind (70–71). Where do you see these techniques at work in Conrad's fiction?

In his early work, Conrad used flashback. *Almayer's Folly* has a single simple plot, in contrast with Victorian multiple-plot novels. It uses one flashback. In contrast, *Nostromo* dwells in different time sequences. You will see that Conrad moves back and forth in time, thus filling out the scene. A direct narrative is shifted and replaced by a fragmentary one. For example, Jim's psychology is borne out by scenes with other characters, such as the brief scene with Brierly, with the French naval officer, and with Stein, as Karl has pointed out (48). Conrad seems to ask: Is life a series of chances and rumors? How does Marlow suggest this? Marlow is the narrator who controls the sequence of events. "Through Marlow we enter into the creative process itself, into the collaboration between "many tellers and many listeners," writes Frederick Karl (51). [*A Reader's Guide to Joseph Conrad.* Frederick Karl. New York: Farrar, Straus and Giroux, 1969.]

Symbols, Imagery, and Language

One way to reflect on Conrad's use of symbols and imagery is to look at his details. How do they suggest something larger? Symbolism is of particular importance in much of Conrad's fiction. Your essay can probe the meaning of these symbols.

A significant or major symbol can serve as the anchor or the center of a novel. As you read, look for images, objects, or settings that seem to have particular resonance. Perhaps an image is repeated, or it gradually becomes clear to you that it represents something more. An object, an action, or a word that calls forth associations may be a symbol.

Sample Topics:

1. **Recurring symbols:** What symbols do you see repeating in Conrad's stories?

   Conrad uses symbols often within his fiction. Ships, "darkness," and the sea all carry symbolic resonance. Conrad's use of symbol within scenic presentation is noted by Frederick Karl, who points out that in *The Secret Agent* "A cab ride through the London streets to the charity home . . . the grimness and meanness of a London scene" reflects "the inhumanity of innocent people to each other" (19b) (*Secret Agent*). Many readers recognize that Conrad's use of symbolism contributes to his writing of stories. An insightful move you can make in your writing about Conrad's works is to analyze and evaluate Conrad's use of a symbol in one or more of his works. For example, often Conrad's setting is on a ship or in a place that a ship has sailed to. In "The Secret Sharer," *The Nigger of the "Narcissus,"* "The End of the Tether," and *The Shadow Line,* the action takes place on board ships. Lord Jim's first fateful decision as a young man takes place on a ship that is apparently sinking. What is the relationship among sailors, ships, and the sea?

2. **Many languages:** How does Conrad's facility with many languages appear in his stories?

Anyone writing about Joseph Conrad will notice Conrad's interesting uses of language. Conrad was from a Polish background and his writing, while in English, had some Polish mannerisms. He was also fluent in French. Conrad's first novel, *Almayer's Folly,* begins with words in Malay. In *Lord Jim,* a French lieutenant tells Marlow his story in French. Marlow then retells it in English. Conrad's collaboration with Ford Maddox Ford, *Romance,* includes some Spanish. In his last work, *Suspense,* there are Italian phrases. Conrad, growing up in Poland amid some Russian- and Yiddish-speaking people, knew bits of these languages as well. This added linguistic dexterity and richness to his uses of the English language. Despite this verbal flexibility, Conrad was also aware that written expression may be difficult for any writer. Speaking also has its challenges. Experience may be something different from how one talks about it. The English teacher who is the narrator of *Under Western Eyes* recognizes this when he says, "Words, as is well known, are the great foes of reality" (3). Where do you see Conrad carefully using language to help us to see his fictional world and his characters? What does he think about language and how we name or describe things and talk about the world?

Compare and Contrast Essays

The important thing to keep in mind when you are writing a comparison and contrast essay is that your essay should be analytical and thoughtful. It should do more than point out similarities and differences among several literary works. It is your job to explain to your readers the significance of these similarities and differences. With descriptive detail and analysis, you can turn your observations into an interesting interpretation or argument. You can organize a comparison or contrast by a block method. In this method, you write to define one term of your comparison—a person, place, or object that you intend to contrast with another. Then you write on the other one, defining it carefully in your next paragraph or paragraphs. Once your readers understand your definitions of these terms, you can begin a point-by-point method. For example, if you are contrasting the differences or the similarities between Marlow and Kurtz, you might make a list of these differences. Then you would write about each of these characters by looking at their traits, their actions, or what the other characters say about them. You might devote a paragraph or two to describing Marlow and then a paragraph or two to describing Kurtz. At this point, you would transform your list of similarities or differences into a clear paragraph in which you could indicate the specific features that each character has that make them similar or different from each other.

Sample Topics:

1. **Contrast elements across Conrad's works:** Compare and contrast an aspect of Conrad's work, such as a type of character or a certain theme, across several of his works.

   Joseph Conrad was an inventor of fictional techniques. He was an explorer. He is able to offer us multiple viewpoints. From novel to novel he is innovative. As you read Conrad, you may notice that several stories that Conrad wrote recall other stories he wrote. He concerns himself with issues of community, moral responsibility, and the plight of the individual. The kinds of inefficiency we see in *Heart of Darkness* may be repeated in other ways in "The Secret Sharer." The quest and the journey and an unavoidable moral reality pervade his work. The climate of nightmares that gathers in works like *Heart of Darkness* and "The Secret Sharer" may be seen in Jim's dilemma in *Lord Jim*. Conrad's symbols are anchored in concrete images, direct and distinct action. Conrad appeals to our imaginations and the difficult moral situation. He sets up stories of test and betrayal. You may want to start by choosing two or more texts that seem to you to have some significant connection.

2. **Different characters and their values:** How do the narrators and characters of Conrad's story express contrasting values?

Writers need to use words. Marlow is an oral narrator, using words to tell us stories. Marlow is often on a journey; he is a wanderer. The way that he looks at the world is distinctive. His stories often emerge within frame narratives, as in *Heart of Darkness.* This story begins with an anonymous narrator who introduces Marlow to us and then is one of the people listening to Marlow. The narratives that Marlow unfolds are thus like stories within a story. What values does Marlow express, and how is his perspective different from that of other characters? Which characters in the story you are working on express values? How do these values and perspectives differ?

In the course of his work, Conrad's goal appears to have been to define universal values and to insist on commitment and craft. He experimented with thematic recurrence, shifts in narrative sequence, frame narrators, and parallel situations. He reworked the material of the novel and its form. His ethic was to give things his love and care. For 29 years, from 1895 to 1924, he wrote 31 volumes of novels, short stories, essays and plays and more than 3,000 letters. Why should a writer give care and attention to his or her writing? In your view, which characters exercise love and care and which don't? What values was Conrad trying to express through his writing?

Bibliography
Primary Sources

Conrad, Joseph. *The Complete Works of Joseph Conrad.* 26 vols. Garden City, NY: Doubleday, Page and Company, 1926.

———. *The Cambridge Edition of the Works of Joseph Conrad.* Cambridge, 1990.

———. *The Collected Edition of the Works of Joseph Conrad.* 22 vols. London: J. M. Dent and Sons, 1946–55.

————. *The Collected Letters of Joseph Conrad.* Ed. Frederick R. Karl, Laurence Davies, J. H. Stape and Owen Knowles. 7 vols. Cambridge: Cambridge University Press, 1983.

Jean-Aubry, G. *Joseph Conrad: Life and Letters,* 2 vols. Garden City, NY: Doubleday, Page and Company, 1927.

Secondary Sources

Achebe, Chinua. "An Image of Africa." *Massachusetts Review* 18.4 (Winter 1977): 782–94.

Baines, Jocelyn. *Joseph Conrad: A Critical Biography.* London: Weidenfield and Nicholson, 1959. Rpt. Westport: Greenwood Press, 1960.

Berman, Jeffrey. *Joseph Conrad: Writing as Rescue.* Boston: Astra Books, Twayne, 1977.

Berthoud, Jacques. *Joseph Conrad: The Major Phase.* Cambridge: Cambridge University Press, 1978.

Carrabine, Keith. *Joseph Conrad: Critical Assessments.* 4 vols. Mountfield, East Essex, England: Helm Information, 1992.

Daleski, H. M. *Joseph Conrad: The Way of Dispossession.* Boston: Twayne, 1982.

Fleishman, Avrom. *Conrad's Politics: Community and Anarchy in the Fiction of Joseph Conrad.* Baltimore, MD: Johns Hopkins University Press, 1967.

Ford, Ford Maddox. *Joseph Conrad: A Personal Remembrance.* New York: Ecco Press, 1924, London: Duckworth and Company, 1924.

Gillon, Adam. *Joseph Conrad.* Boston: Twayne, 1982.

————. *Conrad and Shakespeare and Other Essays.* New York: Astra Books, 1976.

Green, Robert. *Ford Madox Ford, Prose and Politics.* Cambridge: Cambridge University Press, 1981.

Guerard, Albert J. *Conrad the Novelist.* Cambridge, MA: Harvard University Press, 1958.

Gurko, Leo. *Joseph Conrad: Giant in Exile.* New York: Macmillan, 1962.

Hay, Eloise Knapp. *The Political Novels of Joseph Conrad.* Chicago: University of Chicago Press, 1963.

Hendrickson, Bruce. *Nomadic Voices: Conrad and the Subject of Narrative.* Urbana: University of Illinois Press, 1992.

Hewitt, Douglas. *Conrad: A Reassessment.* Cambridge: Bowes and Bowes, 1952.

Jean-Aubry, Gerard. *The Sea Dreamer: A Definitive Biography of Joseph Conrad.* Garden City, NY: Doubleday, 1957.

Jones, Susan. *Conrad and Women.* Oxford: Clarendon Press, 1999.

Karl, Frederick R. *A Reader's Guide to Joseph Conrad.* New York: Farrar, Straus, and Giroux, 1969.

———. Joseph Conrad: *The Three Lives, A Biography.* New York: Farrar, Straus, and Giroux, 1979.

Knowles, Owen and Gene M. Moore. *Oxford Reader's Companion to Conrad.* Oxford: Oxford University Press, 2000.

Leavis, F. R. *The Great Tradition: George Eliot, Henry James, Joseph Conrad.* New York: George W. Stewart, 1948.

Meyer, Bernard C. *Joseph Conrad: A Psychoanalytic Biography.* Princeton, NJ: Princeton University Press, 1967.

Meyers, Jeffrey. *Joseph Conrad: A Biography.* New York: Charles Scribner's Sons, 1991.

Miller, J. Hillis. *Poets of Reality: Six Twentieth-Century Writers.* Cambridge, MA: Harvard University Press, 1965.

Moore, Gene M. ed. *Conrad on Film.* Cambridge: Cambridge University Press, 1997.

Moser, Thomas C. *Joseph Conrad: Achievement and Decline.* Cambridge, MA: Harvard University Press, 1957.

Mudrick, Marvin. *Conrad: A Collection of Critical Essays. Twentieth Century Views.* Englewood Cliffs, NJ: Prentice Hall, 1966.

Najder, Zdzislaw. *Joseph Conrad: A Chronicle.* Trans. Helena Carroll-Najder. Cambridge: Cambridge University Press, 1983.

———. *Conrad in Perspective: Essays on Art and Fidelity.* Cambridge: Cambridge University Press, 1997.

Palmer, John A. *Joseph Conrad's Fiction: A Study in Literary Growth.* Ithaca, NY: Cornell University Press, 1968.

Peters, John G. *Conrad and Impressionism.* Cambridge: Cambridge University Press, 2001.

———. *The Cambridge Introduction to Joseph Conrad.* Cambridge: Cambridge University Press, 2006.

Sherry, Norman. *Conrad's Eastern World.* Cambridge: Cambridge University Press, 1966.

———. *Conrad's Western World.* Cambridge: Cambridge University Press, 1971.

Stape, J. H. ed. *The Cambridge Companion to Joseph Conrad.* Cambridge: Cambridge University Press, 1996.

Swisher, Clarice. ed. *Readings on Joseph Conrad.* San Diego: Greenhaven Press, 1998.

Tennant, Roger. *Joseph Conrad: A Biography.* New York: Atheneum, 1981.

Thorburn, David. *Conrad's Romanticism.* New Haven and London: Yale University Press, 1974.

Warren, Robert Penn. "Introduction," *Nostromo* by Joseph Conrad. New York: The Modern Library, 1951.

Watt, Ian. *Conrad in the Nineteenth Century.* Berkeley: University of California Press, 1979.

Zabel, Morton Dauwen. "Introduction," *The Portable Conrad.* New York: Viking Press, 1947.

HEART OF DARKNESS

READING TO WRITE

R EADERS OF *Heart of Darkness* are often struck by the complexity of Conrad's style of storytelling. This includes the use of multiple points of view. These complexities make Conrad's novel an interesting one to write about. Whatever a writer chooses to discuss, he or she has to think through the complex nature of Conrad's use of point of view. This chapter will demonstrate how to read a few passages in *Heart of Darkness* in preparation for writing a paper. An attentive reader may move toward broader questions about the story. By asking questions, the writer may find the ideas that can become the center of his or her essay. They can lead the writer to examine issues, themes, and ideas that shed light on the possible ways the story can be read and understood. It may be helpful for you to annotate as you read. Jot down your ideas, impressions and questions. After you have read a portion of the story, see what sense you can make of this. What points might you develop for a paper?

Conrad's story begins in the voice of a frame narrator, who is one of the men on board the deck of a ship, the *Nellie*. This narrator introduces Marlow, who becomes the central narrator of the story. Marlow recalls the past in stops and starts, in a somewhat discontinuous way. He assembles the fragments of memory into a story. In the short story "Youth," Charlie Marlow, a sailor of experience, recalls his own youthful innocence, vitality, and sense of wonder about a life of adventure on the sea. *Heart of Darkness*, likewise, is a story told from memory. Marlow tells this story to a group of company men on board the *Nellie*, which is on the Thames, London's great central river. These modern listeners—an accountant, a lawyer, a director of companies—are soon set against the distant past of Roman Britain, as Marlow says, "And this also has been one of the dark places of the earth" (9). The "darkness" becomes identified with this remote time in history and with the vast wilderness of Africa. The story then launches into the Congo, which was Belgian territory under King Leopold. The writer might question why Conrad's story seems to exempt Britain from criticism in the colonial enterprise. In Marlow's view, the darkness of these regions will be enlightened by civilization. He sits on deck asserting this like a cross-legged Buddah, whose *bodhi* tree is the mizzenmast of the ship. He claims to have been naive or innocent when he first went to the Congo. A writer might explore how Marlow's narrative suggests the struggle of losing moral balance in the midst of a traumatic experience. Marlow has passed through experience into some knowledge of the darkness.

An important technique you can use to identify a topic, or to provide evidence for a claim you have already formulated, is close reading. When you closely read a passage, you read it many times, paying careful attention to the language. Ask yourself why Conrad selected and arranged the words of this paragraph in the way that he did. This can help you to focus on a theme. For example, the theme of journey and navigation is central in *Heart of Darkness*. What if the reader is paying careful attention to the journey Marlow takes through this wilderness and to Marlow's sense of anticipation as he approaches Kurtz? Could it be that Marlow is not only finding Kurtz elusive but is trapped in a wilderness that can no longer be defined morally? The reader of a Conrad story is much like the traveler who faces the wilderness and he has to find his way. It is important to read Conrad slowly and carefully.

> The earth for us is a place to live in, where we must put up with sights, with sounds, with smells too, by Jove!—breathe dead hippo, so to speak, and not be contaminated. And there, don't you see? Your strength comes in, the faith in your ability for the digging of unostentatious holes to bury the stuff in—your power of devotion, not to yourself, but to an obscure, back-breaking business. (50)

Let's examine this passage. In what sense is this place moral wilderness, as well as physical wilderness? This passage begins with a statement that the earth is a place for humanity to live in. Yet, the words "dead hippo" and "contaminated" immediately confront us. In the midst of this experiencing of putting up with unpleasant sounds and smells, there is an affirmation of strength. One digs down for this strength. You might ask what is being said here about determination and dedication to work. How does Marlow realize this "power of devotion" or strength? What is he devoted to beyond himself? In what ways does he believe in the usefulness and validity of this enterprise? This passage occurs before the meeting between Marlow and Kurtz in the third part of the story. The writer may consider whether Marlow already sees the "horror" in experience. If he does, what moral insight is possible from this? How does this narrator find the words to articulate this experience and this awareness?

A close reading of a passage can raise questions and ideas. As you read Conrad's story, look for passages that raise questions for you or ones that you think will lead you toward some answers. Focus on analyzing these passages to reach your own conclusions about them and to develop a claim on which you can build your essay.

TOPICS AND STRATEGIES

This section of the chapter will discuss possible topics for essays on *Heart of Darkness* and will offer some general approaches to these topics. This is a series of suggestions intended to inspire your own inquiry. You may find a topic that follows a useful place from which to start your essay. Use this material to prompt your thinking about the novel. After you jot down your ideas and analyze relevant passages in the novel, you should formulate your claim, the argument you want your essay to make. Then, you can go back to your notes and begin to provide the evidence for your claim, organizing and arranging your thoughts into a persuasive essay.

Themes

A novel's themes are those major ideas or issues that the story is considering. There are several key questions that Joseph Conrad reflects on in his works. Each work expresses a distinct perspective on the themes with which it deals. Your job as a writer is to discover and articulate this perspective in your essay. *Heart of Darkness* is filled with themes and ideas such as concerns about individual and society, colonialism, power, civilization, and moral action. Writers who approach this novel may begin by identifying a central theme of Conrad's novel and then think about how this theme is addressed by the story. In your view, what is being said about this theme? If you read closely and ask questions about what you have read, you will find something to say. Focus on close reading and what you think the story is saying about a particular issue. This will help you to develop a claim on which to build your essay. Always make sure to write to express the point that you have to make about the themes that you see in this novel. It is important to be aware of the main points that you want to make. You do not need to write about the entire novel; stick to your main idea. Avoid straying into unrelated tangents of thought. Bring your essay back to focus on your main points.

The writer might ask if *Heart of Darkness* is mostly about the problems of European colonialism. Is this story intended as some kind of a moral tale? Is Conrad's story saying something about the unconscious? Or is it a traveler's tale, some kind of an adventure story? The writer on Conrad's *Heart of Darkness* might argue for any of these interpretations. There is much in the story to support a psychological reading or a political one. Some critics have called this novel an indictment of imperialism. Others have asserted that Conrad is implicated in the colonialism he has described. The complexity of this story will challenge the writer to interpret the story in any of a variety of ways. Whatever your interpretive approach, it should be supported with evidence from the text.

The complexity in the novel's critical reception is characteristic of much of Conrad's work. Whatever lies in the setting or environment of "the heart of darkness" also lies within the viewer, the reader, or the traveler. Joseph Conrad once wrote that he sought to make us "see." One might add that he sought to make us see ourselves, as well as the world of his fiction—and to see in new ways. Your job as a writer is to help your own readers to see Conrad's story in new ways.

Sample Topics:

1. **Perspective:** We see this world through Marlow's perspective. This story is characterized by his angle of vision. The writer can gain insight into this novel by examining Marlow's attitude and his character. Does Marlow gain greater awareness, courage, and insight as he goes along? What is the point of Marlow's journey?

One might argue that Marlow's navigation is not going to add much to the existing record of this place. This area of the African continent has already been charted. Marlow's mission is not that of the anthropologist or the ethnographer. Rather, it is a commercial venture more than an exploratory one. It is a journey outward that is also an inward journey into the darkness of the self. The writer may examine Marlow's expeditions as a psychological-spiritual journey. Why is Marlow thinking of his journey as one like "travelling back to the earliest beginnings of the world"? (35) How is he trapped in a bewildering world? He moves beyond the bounds of Western civilization. What is possible here? How does Marlow see the world around him? What do we see through Marlow's angle of vision?

2. **Civilization:** What does the work say about civilization?

Writing on *Heart of Darkness* can be enhanced by asking critical questions. You can open with a general idea about the story. Then allow this thought to branch out into new ideas that are supported with specific evidence as the paper develops. Can people consciously lead a moral existence? Does this story say that people are flawed and are so caught up in social constraints that they fall apart when those constraints are lifted, or when they are exposed to life-threatening perils? Is this a story about civilized people becoming savages, while wearing the masks of propriety?

In gathering evidence to support your view, you ought to listen carefully to how Marlow tells his story. Marlow's story opens onto a world that is not restrained by civilization. The dark landscape evokes the tragic cost of civilization, in which the sharp contest of competitors leads to destruction. The colonial enterprise brought together commercial objectives and evangelistic goals to improve African life. "I had immense plans," Kurtz says (65). When writing on *Heart of Darkness*, the writer might ask whether Marlow approves of colonialism or opposes and rejects it. Does he feel devoted to British colonialism for its efficiency, while rejecting Belgian colonialism for a perceived lack of it? Is the goal of improving the non-Western world with education and technology and Christian religion adequate? In this novel, it is never clear whether Conrad indicts all colonial experience in Africa or only some of it.

3. **Darkness and death:** What kind of commentary is the novel making about darkness or about death?

Is "darkness" in this story and in its title to be equated with death or with something else? Is death "the horror," or is "the horror" something more than death? Marlow's narrative concludes shortly after Kurtz's death, following his exploration of Kurtz's character in conversation. How is the story that Marlow has just told an effort to make meaning from his experience? Is Kurtz's death meaningful or meaningless? Look for passages in the text in which Marlow comments on the "darkness." What do these signify? How does Marlow feel about death? Compare his perception of death or of "darkness" with the perspectives of other characters.

4. **Nature:** How does the natural world play a role in *Heart of Darkness?* What relationship exists between human beings and nature?

What impact does the setting have on the quest? Does the setting symbolize anything internal, as well as being an external place? This is a story that occurs on land more than on water. Is this significant? Consider passages in which human technology is described. Why are objects described in this way? How does technology fit into this novel's message about humans' relationship to nature and their enterprise in Africa?

Character

A careful consideration of a novel's characters can help you to interpret the novel's themes. As you write on *Heart of Darkness,* you can focus on the ways in which main characters in this story change and how they develop across the course of the novel. For example, Marlow's perspective on Kurtz changes throughout the narrative he provides for us. In your work at analysis, reread the text and mark the passages that you think suggest something about the character you have selected to write about. Give your attention to Marlow's narration to develop a sense of how he views the people he has encountered. Also, consider the dialogue between Marlow and other characters. A writer might look at Conrad's means of characterization. How do our interpretations of Marlow or Kurtz change as the novel proceeds? To write on character, the writer will take a close look at how readers come to know these characters. One might also look at how these characters come to know one another. Marlow's narration is a good place to start. In exploring the characters, a writer can examine the dialogue between them. Characters often have a particular way of speaking. The way that characters speak and how they interact with one another also provide clues about what each character is like.

Reflect on how the character you have selected changes through the course of the novel. Why has this character changed? You might focus on Kurtz, for example, and use your analysis to determine how Conrad views him. Is he a "remarkable man," as Marlow says, or a villain? It is possible to make a convincing argument about Conrad's attention to a particular idea through an analysis of his characters or his primary narrator, Marlow. For example, what is Marlow's attitude toward isolation, commitment, or the colonial enterprise?

Sample Topics:

1. **Solitariness:** Which of Conrad's characters are alone and what impact does this isolation have on this character's actions and how the story develops?

   Conrad's characters are often quite alone. In Marlow's narrative, he dwells on the isolation of individuals. He asserts, "We live, as we dream, alone." What does this sense of an essential loneliness have to do with Marlow's story? Does the personal nature of his adventure make it difficult for him to tell us about it? Each experience is a "fact dazzling, to be seen, like the foam on the depths of the sea, like a ripple on an unfathomable enigma [. . .]" (43). The writer may explore what Conrad is suggesting that separates people. As Kurtz dies, we read: "It was as though a veil had been rent. I saw on that ivory face the expression of somber pride, of ruthless power, of craven terror—of an intense and hopeless despair" (68). What veil has been torn and what has been revealed? What is the "darkness" that Kurtz, or Marlow, has faced? How do the characters Marlow and Kurtz express the aloneness of individuality? How are they affected by the society in which they participate?

2. **Marlow:** Explore the significance of Marlow and his journey.

Much critical emphasis has been placed on the psychology of Conrad's characters as they encounter "the dark continent." Some critics remind us that Marlow's moral dilemma lies at the center of *Heart of Darkness.* We see in Marlow's journey the nihilistic imagery of an indifferent natural world that appears set inexorably against humanity. Marlow's seaman's code is a stay against this decline and pessimism. The writer should observe how Marlow is a reflective person who stands within a set of values and expresses duty. In writing on Conrad, one may consider how the reader participates in the story through Marlow and his recollections. We see via the way that he has seen things, the way he tells us about them. One might analyze how Marlow enlisted in an adventure and participates in the exploitation of the land and of the Africans. He cannot keep his assumptions of moral superiority or about the civilizing mission of Europe. Marlow is forced to meet the darkness within his own being. He has the courage and faithfulness to endure without breaking. Yet, he appears overpowered by the darkness that is Mr. Kurtz.

As the writer follows Marlow's impressions and experiences, he or she can write about how Marlow tries to avoid the truth he is confronted with. How does Marlow attempt to maintain some sense of moral "rightness"? How does he struggle with the harsh truth of the imperialistic disruption and destruction he sees? In what ways does his narration show an effort to accommodate this? *Heart of Darkness* may move the writer to explore the ways in which Western civilization attempts to dominate others in the interest of civilizing values. The writer might question whether the novel suggests that there is something in the unconscious of the West that is tragic and self-destructive.

3. Kurtz: What does the writer think of Kurtz?

The writer should reflect on how Marlow's narrative has led to the meeting of Kurtz and to how Kurtz appears. The writer might pay special attention to the stirring encounter between Marlow and Kurtz in Kurtz's final scene:

> "He cried in a whisper at some image, at some vision—he cried out twice, a cry that was no more than a breath—
>
> "The horror! The horror!"
>
> I blew the candle out and left the cabin. The pilgrims were dining in the mess room, and I took my place opposite the manager, who lifted his eyes and gave me a questioning glance, which I successfully ignored. He leaned back, serene, with that peculiar smile of his sealing the unexpressed depth of his meanness. A continuous shower of small flies streamed on the lamp, on the cloth, on our hands and faces. Suddenly the manager's boy put his insolent face in the doorway, and said in a tone of scathing contempt—
>
> "Mistah Kurtz—he dead." (68–69)

How does Conrad make us feel present at this occasion? How is the ordinary juxtaposed with the extraordinary?

In what ways does Marlow appear to suppress the economic reasons why he and others have gone to colonial Africa? Marlow traces stories of the whereabouts of Mr. Kurtz, who is heralded by some as heroic. Kurtz has engaged in plunder and murder in the quest for ivory. He is revered as a god by a group of the Africans. Is Kurtz a hero or an antihero, a villain?

4. Doubling: Do any characters reflect or "double" as shadows of each other?

As in *Lord Jim* and "The Secret Sharer," Marlow encounters in *Heart of Darkness* his double in the form of the mad Kurtz. The writer might investigate the ways in which Marlow wonders about Kurtz and how he may be similar or different from him. The writer may reflect on how Marlow's unacknowledged inner self appears in Kurtz, deranged, demonic, and obsessed by "the horror." Marlow returns to England disturbed by this meeting. His ideal of "civilization" has been shattered. An essay can be developed concerning Marlow's ideals and how they have been challenged by his experience.

History and Context

Another important approach to Conrad's novel is to research and write about the historical and social conditions surrounding the story. In one's effort to understand the motivation of the characters and the setting and action of this story, it is helpful to understand the novel's historical and social context. Conrad's *Heart of Darkness* is set in a specific place and time: the Belgian Congo in the nineteenth century. The European colonial enterprise of the late nineteenth century is central to this novel. While the novel specifically indicts the practices of King Leopold of Belgium in the African Congo, the imperial practice of Britain is also implicated. A curious writer will explore this by looking at books such as *Empire* by Niall Ferguson (Basic Books, 2004); *The Rise and Fall of the British Empire* by Lawrence James (St. Martin's, 1997); and *The Decline and Fall of the British Empire* by Piers Brendon (Knopf, Doubleday, 2008). To discuss the novel in historical context, one might consider the Boer War in South Africa and make a comparative study of British colonialism in Africa, India, Australia, and the Far East. Papers can explore how Conrad's novel engages politics. One might look at Conrad's uses of terms or references to King Leopold and Belgium or to Britain and other European countries that held colonies in Africa in the latter part of the nineteenth century. One might successfully write a paper that compares European colonial enterprise with today's postcolonial situation.

Sample Topics:

1. **The psychology of imperialism:** What kind of commentary is the novel making about imperialism?

The writer on *Heart of Darkness* can examine the psychology of imperialism generally or of Marlow in particular. Imperialism presents a strong topic for the writer. It is one that calls for some historical research. From 1870 to 1914, more than a quarter of the globe was colonized by about a dozen countries, dividing the world into dominant "advanced" states and weaker "developing" nations. Imperialism led to spheres of influence, and imperialistic extension into these territories was accompanied by political, social, emotional, patriotic, and racial appeals. Colonial conquest by Westerners led to their encounter with the traditional cultures of indigenous people. Colonialism represented a broad range of influences from European institutions, discourses, and practices. The scramble for Africa has been called primarily economically driven. France occupied much of West Africa. The Belgians occupied central Africa, or the Congo, where *Heart of Darkness* is set. The British, Dutch, and Germans all had economic interests in Africa. Political elites of the developing world recognized that it was profitable for them to westernize, and images, ideas, and aspirations were shaped by education in Western ways.

2. **Western civilization:** What kind of commentary is the novel making about Western civilization in relation to the conquest of the African continent?

Themes in *Heart of Darkness* can be approached from more than one perspective. Marlow himself appears to not believe that Africa is being redeemed through Western civilization. Instead, "a rapacious and pitiless folly" occurs in which the so-called civilizers themselves appear devoid of any virtue or civilizing qualities. Yet, Marlow commits himself to the enterprise and appears to believe in it. The reader might explore this ambivalence in Marlow's attitude.

Conrad wrote *Heart of Darkness* eight years after his own experiences in the Congo. His six months in the Congo were a significant experience in his life and had an "enormous physical and moral impact," notes Najder in his introduction to *The Congo Diary* (1). The memories and illness clung to Conrad and he used the setting for *Heart of Darkness*. He has created Marlow's story, and the writer may ask what this experience has meant to Marlow. The writer may examine the ways in which Marlow appears impressionable. As he moves beyond the bounds of Western civilization, he seeks the wonder of a new world, yet he finds terror in it. How does he feel vulnerable? Is there potential for a different definition of "reality" here? Marlow wonders whether he should "talk openly with Kurtz." He concludes that "my speech or my silence, indeed any action of mine, would be mere futility. What did it matter what anyone knew or ignored?" Is this a statement of nihilism? Is there a sense that all human achievement is futile? Or that underneath it all is a deep darkness?

Philosophy and Ideas

Conrad is often regarded as a philosophical novelist. That is, he frequently explores questions of human identity, isolation, and community, and how different people each see the world from a unique point of view. An approach to formulating an argument about Conrad's novel is to inquire, like Conrad, into the philosophical ideas that move through this story. To discover these ideas, or philosophical problems, a writer may begin with the broad themes that the novel develops. What is implied here about how we come to get to know one another? As one follows Marlow, the very idea of human inquiry and exploration is present. What does this novel say about power and authority? When the boat is bogged down in the mud and the river is impassable, how does this reflect being stuck in one's action and attitudes? In what ways are these characters faced with existential issues or questions of meaning?

To write an essay on philosophical ideas, reread Conrad's story with this in mind. How do characters who are associated with your topic and passages express various philosophies? Analyze these characters and the passages you have identified, so that you can make a claim in your essay about this topic. If you wish to discuss ethics, for example, you might look closely at Marlow's attitudes toward the colonial enterprise and the people involved in it. You might evaluate the comments that are made by other characters in this story. Does Conrad enlist our sympathy for any of these characters? Why? Your analysis might lead you to a conclusion that Marlow has an ethical code, which is as necessary to abide by in the jungle as on the sea. However, Kurtz's goals have apparently led him elsewhere, to other actions and conclusions.

Sample Topics:

1. **Identity:** Does the novel suggest that our characters have already been shaped or that we are in the process of self-creation? How do these characters exercise free will?

Consider the scenes in which Marlow struggles with questions like these. You might also look at Kurtz's transformation. What do the stories of people who have encountered Kurtz, or who have heard about him, tell us about how his character has changed during the African experience? Think also about how this adventure affects Marlow. As his narrative proceeds, reflect on the choices that he is making. What is Marlow's sense of himself now, as he recalls his experience? What is his attitude toward his younger self and his encounters on this epic journey? If Marlow's storytelling is an effort to make meaningful sense of the past, how is it also an effort to cast or to construct identity? How are the characters determined by circumstances or by the environment?

2. **Ethics:** What kind of commentary does the novel make about ethics, or moral responsibility?

How do the characters decide what is ethical or acceptable in an environment so detached from normal, civilized society? Choose several characters and study the way in which they determine wrong from right. Marlow is presented by Conrad as an experienced sailor and a valued member of the English elite. It is clear that he is sociable enough to tell a story and that he embodies Victorian values. Marlow is, in this sense, representative of the preservation of these values. He is a man who has gone through a spiritual crisis. The writer, considering this, may look at how Britain itself was going through a crisis of moral awareness about its imperialist policies. Bertrand Russell has observed that Joseph Conrad "thought of civilized and morally tolerable human life as a dangerous walk on a thin crust of barely cooled lava which at any moment might break and let the unwary sink into fiery depths" (321).

[*The Autobiography of Bertrand Russell,* 1872–1914, vol. 1. Boston: Little Brown and Company, 1967, p. 321]

Feeling this wilderness, Marlow approaches Kurtz. He later says: "I couldn't have felt more of lonely desolation somehow, had I been robbed of a belief or had missed my destiny in life" (48). Could it be that he is trapped in a wilderness that can no longer be defined morally? Does the novel seem to suggest any character's choices or approach to life is the proper ethical approach? Does it suggest that any of these characters' ethics are wrong? Or does Conrad's story suggest that each individual must develop his or her own code according to his or her conscience?

3. **Racism:** What is the work expressing about race?

Nigerian novelist Chinua Achebe has sharply criticized Conrad and *Heart of Darkness* in a well-known essay in which he focuses on the racism he sees in Conrad's text. In Achebe's view, Conrad does not provide his African characters with humanness and "human expression." His argument holds that Conrad inscribes darkness on the black natives and Africa is portrayed as uncivilized and set in contrast to European civilization. Achebe calls *Heart of Darkness* "an offensive and deplorable book" and focuses on Conrad's representation of Africa and Africans. His claim is that Conrad "reduces" them to "props." One might investigate this argument and formulate one's own views. The writer may, like Achebe, focus on Conrad's representation of Africa and Africans. Does Conrad's text depersonalize the native characters? Or, are they indeed humanly rendered and situated in this place? To develop a good argument, it is necessary to read the text closely and to draw examples from it to support your viewpoint.

The writer can consider Achebe's view of Conrad's story from several angles. For example, one might consider how the "primitive" is set in contrast with European technology in *Heart of Darkness.* Is this technology implicitly regarded as "superior" to native life? Or is it indeed unable to exercise any power to conquer it? The writer may note how this technology is mired in the jungle. Does this suggest the inefficacy of the colonial enterprise or the limitations of European technology? Are the Africans stereotyped and demonized, as Achebe suggests? Or might you agree with critics like Robert Hampson, who claims that Achebe attacks "a grossly simplified version of *Heart of Darkness?*" This critic observes that Achebe does not discuss the difference between Marlow and Conrad or Conrad's distance from his narrator. Nor does he address Conrad's irony. The writer can show how Conrad is giving his readers Marlow's account of experiences in Africa, not his own. The writer may note that the character of Marlow lives in a specific cultural and historical situation, with its attendant prejudices and categories. Whereas Marlow's views are frequently racist, it does not necessarily follow that Conrad's are also.

Achebe claims that Conrad participates in the dehumanization of Africans, which was fostered by an "agelong attitude." However, the writer might argue that *Heart of Darkness* is about exposing European discourses of power. Kurtz's "breakup" and disintegration may reflect this. The writer might also consider the audience for whom Conrad was writing, as does Benita Parry, who argues that "Conrad in his colonial fictions does not presume to speak for the colonial peoples. . . ." In this critic's view, Conrad was addressing an audience "still secure in the conviction that they were members of an invincible power and a superior race" (Parry 1). Conrad knew that his readers were the readers of *Blackwoods* and that these readers were often civil servants. He wanted to make money with his story, and it is certainly possible that he did not wish to alienate those readers, who had their prejudices. Further, the writer could argue that Conrad was not writing a realistic account of life in the Congo. He was writing fiction. It is not "an image of Africa" in a sociological sense. Marlow's story is placed in context by a frame narrative. The writer may argue that this is a narrator who is coming to terms with imperialism. All of this suggests that Achebe's view needs to be placed in the context of other views. The writer can point out that Achebe tends to place this novel within our own times, not

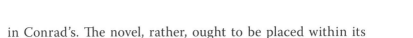

in Conrad's. The novel, rather, ought to be placed within its historical and cultural context.

Form and Genre

Form and genre are helpful ways of thinking about and describing literary works. Thinking about the form of *Heart of Darkness* can lead to writing an interesting essay. *Heart of Darkness* is a short novel. It is one that has elements of tragedy. A paper can question whether this novel meets our expectations of a tragedy and how it deviates from these expectations. How do these expectations affect how we write about this novel? *Heart of Darkness* is generally classified as a novelette. That is, it might be described as a long story or as a short novel. Could the story have been as effective if it were longer or shorter? It is sometimes helpful to view a story as a constructed work of art. When you read a Conrad story, it is essential to pay close attention to features of the work such as narration, point of view, and organizational scheme. Conrad was a very self-conscious technician in his writing. You should ask yourself why Conrad made the choices he did when constructing the work, and how the work would be different if he had made other choices. When studying *Heart of Darkness,* you will gain much by exploring the structure of the book—especially the ways in which the narrative weaves in and out of time. Marlow's narrative is discontinuous. It is a reflection based on memory. Perhaps Marlow is suggesting that storytelling is a way of making meaning.

Sample Topics:

1. **Narrative point of view:** How does the way this story is told affect how we read it and think about it?

   One of the most interesting features of Conrad's novelette is the shifting points of view from which this story is presented. Investigating this can lead to useful and interesting ways to write an essay. When reading *Heart of Darkness,* one should listen carefully to the narrator's voice. It is important to recognize that while we begin reading the account of a frame narrator, we encounter most of this story primarily through Marlow's perspective. Marlow himself appears to not believe that Africa is being redeemed through Western civilization. Instead, "a rapacious and pitiless folly" (65) occurs in which the so-called civilizers themselves appear devoid of any virtue or civilizing qualities. Marlow's confidence in the orderly progress of civilization withers and he experiences disenchantment.

A writer may ask how Marlow holds onto dignity, even as he expresses moral disgust with what he sees in some of the colonizers around him. By reading closely, one can hear sarcasm and irony in his voice. Yet, it is clear that he too is in the midst of this enterprise. He is driven by curiosity and determination to seek out Kurtz, only to have the mask of his pride and propriety torn off in this encounter. He is forced to confront whether he too has participated in barbarous destruction. The writer should explore Marlow's perspective and his values. As in other Conrad novels, the virtues of courage, honesty, and fidelity to the human community are challenged here. Marlow's code of conduct is confronted with a situation in which the land of the Congo and the character of Kurtz have life-changing effects on him. As Conrad once told his friend Edward Garnett, "Before the Congo I was just a mere animal" (See *The Congo Diary*). Western efficiency and rationality have participated in a "merry dance of death and trade." Marlow has a shocking encounter with evil. Of Kurtz, he concludes, "He was a remarkable man" (73). Yet, he has also seen a nightmare.

> The fact is I was completely unnerved by a sheer blank fright, pure abstract terror, unconnected with any distinct shape of physical danger. What made this so overpowering was—how shall I define it?—the moral shock I received, as if something altogether monstrous, intolerable to thought and odious to the soul, had been thrust on me unexpectedly . . .

2. **Literary history:** Do any of the themes of *Heart of Darkness* appear in other important works of literature?

The writer might consider intertextuality and literary history. Does Conrad recall earlier literary sources as he writes *Heart of Darkness?* If the writer looks at *Heart of Darkness* as a moral journey, it may be compared with the descent of the heroic narrator of Dante's *Inferno*. Similarly, it may reflect the sixth book of Virgil's *Aeneid*, as Lillian Feder has pointed out: a journey into "the depths of his own and his nation's conscience" (1955, 280–81). Like Dante's *Inferno*, *Heart of Darkness* is an often symbolic tale of a journey into a cosmic nightmare. Marlow might be compared with the character that Dante creates in the *Inferno* who is on a moral journey. In each case, the geography of the journey is representative and significant. (Here this awareness occurs before he reaches the Inner Station.) Marlow's account considers his personal responsibility and the collective responsibility of Western civilization. On the other hand, whereas Dante emphasizes his narrator-protagonist's capacity for choice, repentance, and reform, Conrad's Marlow appears as an atom in an indifferent universe, a mere man within the system of Western imperialism. The writer might explore Marlow's position within this scheme. He has the ability to have moral judgment, yet he fears losing control. He tries to maintain his moral posture. He blames the suffering Africans, the dark, disturbing landscape. But has the foreign territory caused this corruption? Is Marlow an innocent victim? Or is he part of the system of victimizers? As in Dante's *Inferno*, we may say that there is a journey inward into the darkness of the self. The writer ought to remember that this outward journey by Marlow also involves an inward journey, or a psychological-spiritual journey, as well.

If the writer wishes to further consider Conrad's story intertextually, he or she might consider the character of Kurtz alongside the famous story of *Faust*. One might explore how Kurtz, like Faust, goes beyond social conventions and seeks to be powerful and godlike. How does Marlow portray Kurtz's decline and utter degradation? What "horror" has each of these characters struggled with?

3. *Heart of Darkness* **and film:** How would *Heart of Darkness* look as a movie?

The writer might also explore the filmic possibilities of *Heart of Darkness*, a story that has yet to be adapted into the form of a full-length feature film. Film director Orson Welles's first film project for RKO Pictures was to be *Heart of Darkness* but this project ran out of funds and was never completed. Francis Ford Coppola based his Vietnam War film *Apocalypse Now* (1979) on Conrad's story. The writer of a paper on Conrad's *Heart of Darkness* might make a comparison of this film with the novel. Several critics, such as J. Hillis Miller, E. N. Dorall, and Linda Cahir, have considered Conrad's methods in his fiction alongside comments on this film.

Language, Symbols, and Imagery

By analyzing the language, symbols, and imagery of Conrad's story you can gain new insights and a new interpretation of the text. Look for Conrad's lengthy descriptions. Listen for how language is used in dialogue. As you read, highlight passages in which Marlow reflects on an important issue, event, or someone he has met. The environment is filled with symbols and images you might want to give attention to. In your essay, provide your own interpretation of Conrad's story in which you analyze these symbols.

Sample Topics:

1. **Heart of darkness:** What does the heart of darkness represent?

   Is this title referring to something more than Africa or King Leopold's Belgian enterprise in the Congo? The writer might reflect on Conrad's title and ask whether it is symbolic. Is Marlow's search not only a scramble for wealth in Africa, or for the sources of the Nile, but also what one critic, Peter Firchow, has called "the quest for the final symbolic answer to the question of who we are"? The writer's essay can explore the story's title, as well as the story's language and symbols, for this broader meaning. How is Conrad's novella a metaphor for a psychological exploration of Marlow's inner self?

2. **Explore objects as symbols:** What attention does Marlow give to specific objects?

   The writer might also consider the way in which Marlow observes objects. The junk of abandoned machinery has apparently been overtaken by the environment. The boiler wallows.

The truck is upended. The machinery is decaying, and the nails are rusty. We hear of "a heavy, dull detonation" for the blast to build a railway in this jungle. Marlow hears a "slight clanking" and notes that black men wearing iron collars are climbing a hill as if their joints were twisted "like knots in a rope." What is the interaction here of nature and machinery? How does imprisoned humanity fit into this scene? There are particular things here, points of contact with persons, however dehumanized. There is what F. R. Leavis calls an "overwhelming sinister and fantastic atmosphere." The writer might explore these surroundings.

Marlow's arrival at the company station is set within a context:

> I came on a boiler wallowing in the grass, then found a path leading up the hill. It turned aside for the boulders, and also for an undersized railway truck lying there on its back with its wheels in the air. One was off. The thing looked as dead as the carcass of some animal. I came on more pieces of decaying machinery, a stack of rusty nails. To the left a clump of trees made a shady spot, where dark things seemed to stir feebly . . .

The jungle itself acts as a symbol for all of nature:

> I tried to break the spell—the heavy, mute spell of the wilderness—that seemed to draw him to its pitiless breast by the awakening of forgotten and brutal instincts, by the memory of gratified and monstrous passions. This alone, I was convinced, had driven him out to the edges of the forest, toward the gleam of the fires, the throb of drums, the drone of weird incantations; this alone had beguiled his unlawful soul beyond the bounds of permitted aspirations . . .

3. **Setting:** How is the time, place, or geography in which the story is set significant?

Conrad's fiction provides an imaginative description of a setting that is African. Through research, the writer might distinguish this from the physical geography, or the historical and sociological makeup, of this region in the time in which this story is set. Conrad's fiction does not work factually. It works symbolically, through narrative and characterization. For example, Marlow has taken command of a steamboat in the Congo. We see how this boat runs aground and gets stuck in the mud, suggesting, perhaps, that the entire colonial enterprise has done so.

The theme of journey and navigation is central in *Heart of Darkness.* How does this quest myth unfold in a symbolic way within this setting? As the first section of the story moves toward a close, we have a strong sense of the surrounding geography. The narrator is a steamer captain who will bring "civilization" to the Congo. This place is a wilderness in which Marlow becomes aware of himself as having an uncertain relationship to his surroundings. He navigates his ship through the fog. There is a native attack. The ship—or perhaps civilization itself—is stuck in the mud: immobilized by the "dark" geography of this place. How might you interpret this symbolism?

4. **Sights and sounds:** What sensory imagery does Conrad use in the narrative?

As one investigates Conrad's uses of symbolism, one may also see the many places in which Conrad brings our attention to the senses, particularly those of sight and sound. The writer may examine the story for all of those places where sights and sounds evoke a strong impression. Can Marlow ever make the reader "see" what has occurred, or is this impossible? Marlow asks his listeners, "Do you see him? Do you see the story? Do you see anything? It seems to me I am trying to tell you a dream—making a vain attempt" (30). He suggests that his listeners, through his story, have a clearer vision now than he once did as he was experiencing the events: "You fellows see more than I could then. You see me, whom you know" (30). As one follows the visual imagery of *Heart of Darkness,* one also ought to listen to Marlow's narrative, like Marlow's listeners on the deck of the *Nellie.* The initial narrator intervenes:

"It had become so pitch dark that we listeners could hardly see one another. For a long time already he, sitting apart, had been no more to us than a voice" (30).

We hear from Marlow:

"A voice. He was very little more than a voice. And I heard him—it—this voice—other voices—all of them were so little more than voices—and the memory of that time itself lingers around me, impalpable, like a dying vibration of one immense jabber, silly, atrocious, sordid, savage, or simply mean, without any kind of sense. Voices, voices—. . ." (49).

There is an auditory quality to this story that one should pay attention to. The African adventure is full of sounds. One may inquire where in the text we hear the voice of the native. Is it a feared voice or a compelling voice? We hear African drumming:

This alone, I was convinced, had driven him out to the edge of the forest, to the bush, towards the gleam of fires, the throb of drums, the drone of weird incantations; this alone had beguiled his unlawful soul beyond the bounds of permitted aspirations. (65)

What voices can be heard in this novel? What do these voices suggest about the interaction between African and European cultures? When Marlow offers his story, this is not entirely a monologue. The writer may first recognize that Marlow's story is framed by the introduction of another narrator. Then the writer can demonstrate how within Marlow's tale we hear dialogue from many different perspectives. We see gestures that characters make in an effort to communicate. How many voices besides that of Marlow appear? The writer might look for these, as Robert Hampson has done in his article on "the speech that cannot be silenced" in Conrad's story. Several European languages announce themselves within the text. The writer may also investigate the ways that natives speak or whether they can be heard behind the voices in the foreground of this story. Are their voices subsumed by others in the text?

Compare and Contrast Essays

A common way of writing a paper on a literary work is to compare or contrast elements of the work. This way, the writer can discover similarities and differences between certain aspects of the novel or story and then comment on the resonance of those comparative or contrasting elements and what it contributes to the work overall. This approach can help a reader focus on oppositions in the text and may bring into sharper detail the elements that need to be more closely observed.

It is important that the essay do more than merely list these similarities or contrasts. Thoughtful commentary helps to make your paragraph something more than just a list. Good writing is descriptive and thoughtful. Make sure to provide detail. Through critical thinking and analysis, a writer can look at differences among characters or patterns of imagery in the work. The writer might start by defining who each character is—as conveyed through his or her traits or behavior—or how each image is defined and presented. The differences or the ways Conrad alters or changes his representation can then be explored.

When you compare or contrast elements of Conrad's story, it is a good idea to use either a block method or a clear point-by-point method. In the block method, you will define each of your terms in separate "blocks." First you write about "A." Then you write about "B." After this, you can bring these two characters, places, or ideas together in more immediate contrast or comparison. When you are writing about the likenesses or the differences of these items point by point, make sure that your reader can clearly distinguish between them. Point-by-point comparison or contrast must proceed in an organized way. Don't let your readers feel like you are playing ping-pong by going rapidly back and forth between these two elements. Develop your discussion carefully. Use your observations and analysis to make an argument, using comparison and contrast that gives your readers a unique and interesting interpretation of the text.

The challenge of this type of essay is determining what the differences between these characters, places, concepts, or images mean. It is the writer's purpose to explore these meanings. By asking questions, the writer will arrive at some answers. These notions will usually be individual to the writer of the paper. The questions will lead to the writer's own conclusions. That is what will make the paper interesting and original. To accomplish this effectively, it is best to go directly to the text of the novel to explore the similarities and differences. It is not enough to only state them. Rather, you must consider how those similarities and differences work in this text and what points they make.

Sample Topics:

1. **Marlow and Kurtz:** Compare and contrast Marlow and Kurtz.

What if the writer wishes to analyze the ways in which Marlow reflects Kurtz? What do we know about Kurtz? Most of what we know is through Marlow's narrative and involves Marlow's viewpoint. Many critics have suggested that there are some similarities between them. If so, what do you think that these are? Why does Marlow feel a powerful connection with Kurtz? Why does he regard Kurtz as "remarkable," when he is also repulsed? In contrasting these characters, the writer can first observe how Marlow approaches his expedition. Then the writer can demonstrate how it appears that Kurtz has approached his own mission. At this point, the writer will contrast these two characters, showing that Marlow's way is an alternative to the ways that Kurtz has approached his engagement with his mission, the jungle, and its natives. The question could be raised about whether Marlow could have become as deranged as Kurtz.

2. **Characters in Conrad novels:** Compare Conrad's characters in two different works.

If the writer has read other works by Conrad, a comparison and contrast might be developed concerning the "double" in *Heart of Darkness*, *Lord Jim*, and "The Secret Sharer." How does the writer view the image of the "double" that appears in each of these stories? In *Heart of Darkness*, Kurtz may be viewed as a double for Marlow. In *Lord Jim*, Jim struggles with his inability to admit his own cowardice, or the falsity of his romantic vision. He meets a ruthless character, Gentleman Brown: a man of egoism who is angry with the world.

In "The Secret Sharer," the captain meets the murderer Leggatt and tries to hide and protect him. Marlow's narrative in
Heart of Darkness might also be contrasted with his narrative in "Youth." Marlow's listeners to his tale in "Youth," have
mixed reactions. What might be the responses of his listeners
to *Heart of Darkness?*

Bibliography and Online Resources for *Heart of Darkness*

Achebe, Chinua. "An Image of Africa," *The Massachusetts Review* 18.4 (Winter
1977): 782–94.

Baines, Jocelyn. *Joseph Conrad: A Critical Biography.* London: Weidenfield and
Nicholson, 1959. Rpt. Westport: Greenwood Press, 1960.

Bhaba, Homi K. "How Newness Enters the World: Postmodern Space, Postcolonial Times and the Trials of Cultural Translation," *The Location of Culture.*
London: Routledge, 1994, p. 212.

Bloom, Harold, ed. *Heart of Darkness.* Modern Critical Interpretations. New
York: Chelsea House, 1987.

———. *Heart of Darkness.* Bloom's Notes. New York: Chelsea House, 1996, pp.
5–6.

———. *Joseph Conrad.* Modern Critical Views. New York: Chelsea House, 1986.

Cahir, Linda Costanzo. "Narratological Parallels in Joseph Conrad's *Heart of
Darkness* and Francis Ford Coppola's *Apocalypse Now,*" *Literature/Film
Quarterly* 20, no. 3 (1992): 182–87.

Conrad, Joseph. *Heart of Darkness,* ed. Robert Kimbrough, 3rd edition. New
York: Norton, 1988.

Dorral, E. N. "Conrad and Coppola: Different Centres of Darkness," Ed. Robert
Kimbrough, *Heart of Darkness.* New York: Norton, 1988.

Feder, Lillian. "Marlow's Descent into Hell," *The Art of Joseph Conrad: A Critical Symposium.* Ed. R. W. Stallman, East Lansing: Michigan State University
Press, 1960, pp. 162–70.

Firchow, Peter Edgerly. *Envisioning Africa: Racism and Imperialism in Joseph
Conrad's Heart of Darkness.* Lexington: University Press of Kentucky, 2000,
pp. 18–30.

Gogwilt, Christopher. *Joseph Conrad and the Invention of the West.* Stanford:
Stanford University Press, 1995.

Hampson, Robert. "Heart of Darkness and the Speech That Cannot Be Silenced,"
English 29, no. 163 (Spring 1990): 15–32.

———. Introduction. *Heart of Darkness.* New York: Penguin, 1995.

Harkness, Bruce. "An Old Fashioned Reading of Conrad; or, 'Oh No! Not Another Paper on Heart of Darkness!" *Conradiana: A Journal of Joseph Conrad Studies,* 32.1 (Spring 2000): 41–46.

Heart of Darkness Study Guide http://www.personal.ksu.edu/-lymax/english320/sg-Conrad-HD.html

Karl, Frederick R. *A Reader's Guide to Joseph Conrad.* New York: Farrar, Straus and Giroux, 1969.

———. *Joseph Conrad: The Three Lives, A Biography.* New York: Farrar, Straus and Giroux, 1979.

Knowles, Owen and Gene M. Moore. *Oxford Reader's Companion to Conrad.* Oxford: Oxford University Press, 2000.

Leavis, F. R. *The Great Tradition: George Eliot, Henry James, Joseph Conrad.* New York: George W. Stewart, 1948.

Meyers, Jeffrey. *Joseph Conrad: A Biography.* New York: Charles Scribner's Sons, 1991.

Miller, J. Hillis. *Poets of Reality: Six Twentieth-Century Writers.* Cambridge, MA: Harvard University Press, 1965, pp. 13–39.

———. "Heart of Darkness Revisited" in *Conrad Revisited: Essays for the Eighties.* Ed. Ross C. Murfin, pp. 31–50. Tuscaloosa: University of Alabama Press, 1985.

Moore, Gene M. ed. *Conrad on Film.* Cambridge: Cambridge University Press, 1997.

Moser, Thomas C. *Joseph Conrad: Achievement and Decline.* Cambridge, MA: Harvard University Press, 1957.

Najder, Zdzislaw. *Joseph Conrad: A Chronicle.* Trans. Helena Carroll-Najder. Cambridge: Cambridge University Press, 1983.

———. *Conrad in Perspective: Essays on Art and Fidelity.* Cambridge: Cambridge University Press, 1997.

Palmer, John A. *Joseph Conrad's Fiction: A Study in Literary Growth.* Ithaca, NY: Cornell University Press, 1968.

Parry, Benita. *Conrad and Imperialism.* London: Macmillan, 1983.

Perry Castenada Map Library, University of Texas. www.lib.utexas/index/.html Maps of Africa, Belgian Congo.

Stape, J. H. ed. *The Cambridge Companion to Joseph Conrad.* Cambridge: Cambridge University Press, 1996.

Stewart, Garret. "Coppola's Conrad: The Repetitions of Complicity," *Critical Inquiry* 7, no. 3 (1981): 455–74.

Swisher, Clarice. ed. *Readings on Joseph Conrad.* San Diego: Greenhaven Press, 1998.

Watt, Ian. *Conrad in the Nineteenth Century.* Berkeley: University of California Press, 1979.

———. "Impressionism and Symbolism in *Heart of Darkness*," *Joseph Conrad.* Bloom's Modern Critical Views, ed. Harold Bloom. New York: Chelsea House, 1986, pp. 83–99.

White, Andrea. "Conrad and Imperialism," *The Cambridge Companion to Joseph Conrad,* ed. J. H. Stape. Cambridge: Cambridge University Press, 1996.

THE NIGGER OF
THE "NARCISSUS"

READING TO WRITE

*T*HE *Nigger* of the *"Narcissus"* is one of Conrad's strongest early novels. It is not often read in classes today because of its title. The book, however, was among Conrad's most often read novels at the turn of the twentieth century. As a reader, you will find that this story is one that enables you to travel imaginatively across the sea to other parts of the world. The critical questions that you raise about the story will help you prepare to write. There are many different kinds of papers that may emerge from the topics that this story raises. Here we will look at some themes that are present in the novel. Then we will consider some strategies for developing essays about the major themes, characters, and issues in this story.

The story begins in Bombay (present-day Mumbai), India, where a crew assembles for a return journey to England on a ship named the *Narcissus*. James Wait claims to be sick and unable to participate in his duties on board. The men, who are unsure whether to believe he is really ill or not, respond to him caringly or with disdain and resentfully. The reader should pay special attention to Wait and to Donkin, another crew member. It should soon become apparent that Wait and Donkin never appear to fulfill their duties. Is Conrad saying something by contrasting the disciplined and dutiful sailors with those who do not have these traits? The ship is beset by a storm as it rounds the Cape of Good Hope, at the southernmost tip of Africa. As the ship nearly capsizes in the waves, the crew tries to save Wait in his cabin, and they nearly die in the effort. What does this say about heroism and solidarity among the sailors? After the storm, the ship is able to continue on its voyage. Wait is confronted by the ship's cook, Podmore, who attempts to save his soul. In response, concerned by his recent brush with death, Wait announces that he, at last, is ready for duty. What might the reader make of this change? Captain Allistoun, for one, rejects this and the crew reacts to this angrily. Much more of Wait's story unfolds before the ship can arrive in England. The reader may follow Wait's story with a hunch that Wait might be symbolic in some way. The influence of Wait on the crew is worth paying close attention to.

TOPICS AND STRATEGIES

This section of the chapter will discuss possible topics for essays on *The Nigger of the "Narcissus"* and will offer some general approaches to these topics. This is a series of suggestions intended to inspire your own inquiry. You may find a topic that follows a useful place from which to start your essay. Use this material to prompt your thinking about the novel. After you jot down your ideas and analyze relevant passages in the novel, you should formulate your claim, the argument you want your essay to make. Then, you can go back to your notes and begin to provide the evidence for your claim, organizing and arranging your thoughts into a persuasive essay.

Themes

A novel's themes are those major ideas or issues that the story is considering. There are several key questions that Joseph Conrad reflects on in his works. Each work expresses a distinctive perspective on the themes with which it deals. Your job as a writer is to discover and articulate this perspective in your essay. Identify a central theme in the work and then think about how it is addressed in the narrative. In your view, what is being said about the theme? If you read closely and ask questions about what you have read, you will develop your own line of argument. Focus on close reading and what you think the work is saying about a particular issue. This will help you to develop a claim on which to build your essay. Always make sure to write to express the point that you have to make about the themes that you see in this novel. Clearly define the main points that you want to make. You do not need to write about the entire novel; stick to your main

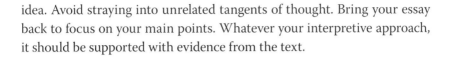
idea. Avoid straying into unrelated tangents of thought. Bring your essay back to focus on your main points. Whatever your interpretive approach, it should be supported with evidence from the text.

Sample Topics:

1. **A novel of the sea:** How are Conrad's settings of the sea and his images of a voyage significant in this novel?

   Foremost, this novel is about an adventure at sea. This is a story about the lessons that the sea teaches. By working through the text, the writer may wish to explore what these lessons might be. Conrad, in *A Personal Record,* recognized this novel as one of his two "exclusively sea books," along with *A Mirror of the Sea* (xiv). Novelist Henry James called it "the very finest and strongest picture of the sea and sea-life that our language possesses—the masterpiece in a whole class" (Simmons introduction xvii). How does Conrad use the sea to bring life to his story? How does he make us feel as if we are there?

2. **Human isolation and community:** What questions does this novel raise about the importance of individual choice and conduct within a community of people?

   Conrad's novel is not primarily concerned with race but with psychology. The story raises issues about human isolation and individualism and about solidarity or community. A reader will gain some insight into this novel by carefully considering how the crewmen live amid this environment of the sea. One might reflect on these crewmen, seeing them as much like children who have something to learn about life from the sea. What are they learning? How does this perspective affect how we view this novel? Good papers include the use of examples. So prepare to look carefully at Conrad's text for examples that can help you to make the points you want to make about this story.

3. **Shifting point of view:** Like currents in an ocean, the point of view from which we see this story often changes. Why does Conrad use this technique?

You may find reading this novel challenging. Conrad does not restrict himself to the mind of any single narrator. This means that point of view is fluid in this novel. We see the action from different vantage points. A reader has to adjust to these different perspectives. Read carefully and think about how the story is being told. A viewpoint character is the character that we are seeing the action through at any given point in the novel. Pay close attention to the narration. This is a story about a voyage and it is filled with motion. The storytelling likewise may have a sense of motion to it. Look for verbs and scenes of action, and think about the pace of these scenes.

4. **A pilgrimage or journey:** What is the journey that these characters are on? How is this an internal passage of character and learning as well as an external journey?

The Nigger of the "Narcissus" takes the form of a pilgrimage:

> On her lived truth and audacious lies: and, like the earth, she was unconscious, fair to see—and condemned by men to an ignoble fate. The august loneliness of her path lent dignity to the sordid inspiration of her pilgrimage. She drove foaming to the south as if guided by the courage of a high endeavor.

The writer might wish to examine this path and journey of the *Narcissus*. From the time of Chaucer's *The Canterbury Tales*, pilgrimage and journey have been central devices for storytelling. It might be possible for someone writing about Conrad's story to compare this form with other stories of journeys that he or she has read. A journey often is an adventure and is also representative of a character's development. Where are Conrad's characters going? What are they experiencing? What might they be learning? Is there a thesis that can be developed about their journey and what they learn from it?

5. **Loyalty:** Where is loyalty or disloyalty in the characters in this story?

Conrad writes that they are "a group of men held together by a common loyalty and a common perplexity not with human enemies, but with the hostile conditions testing their faithfulness to the condition of their own calling." What do you think is their vocation or "calling" as sailors? How are they bound together by a code of honor and the discipline of seamanship?

In preparing to write, jot down your main ideas about Conrad's story. You will want to keep coming back to these ideas. As you build your essay, think critically about Conrad's story by asking questions about it. It is important to show evidence from the text of the novel that supports your position.

Character

Investigating the qualities of characters in a story is often a good way to gain a stronger grasp of a story. As you write, pay careful attention to the unique qualities and differences in the characters that Conrad portrays. What are their motivations? At the center of this novel is the crew of the *Narcissus.* The writer can investigate this community of sailors. What joins them? What would threaten to break this community apart? The novel begins with some attention to the crew. It concludes on a note of comradeship and solidarity: "Good-bye brothers! You were a good crowd. As good a crowd as ever fisted with wild cries the beating canvas of a heavy foresail; or tossing aloft, invisible in the night, gave back yell for yell to a westerly gale." How is this group of sailors "a good crowd," and what energy did they bring to their voyage?

Sample Topics:

1. **James Wait:** How does Conrad develop the character of James Wait? What influence does this character have on the other men on the ship?

A writer should look carefully at how Conrad develops the character of James Wait, who is West Indian. There is an allure about him that you might examine. How does Wait's gentle power over the men set the stage for Donkin's malevolence and manipulation? How will Donkin lure the men away from their focus on "the craft of the sea?" Wait prompts sympathy among the men. There is pity and self-identification with him. They wonder if he will survive and whether they also will. Is this an irrational self-identification with him? This sentimental concern is not a good trait. It connects with the egoism of this character. We read:

> Falsehood triumphed. It triumphed through doubt, through stupidity, through pity, through sentimentalism. . . . The latent egoism of tenderness to suffering appeared in the developing anxiety not to see him die. . . . He was demoralizing . . .

In an essay, the writer can examine Wait's qualities and the responses of the crew to him. What does Wait's presence on this ship mean? If Wait is a force, what is this force? Why is this sympathetic identification of the sailors with Wait a problem? Is Wait the subconscious or a regressive force, causing the crewmen to lose their focus? What influence does Wait have over the crewmen? How does James Wait draw up their egoism, their fear, or dissolve their solidarity? James Wait is charismatic. How does Wait captivate the crew? How is his voice part of this, as well as his words? How does Wait use rhetoric or make use of language? If the writer looks carefully at how Wait's speech is described, some of his persuasive quality becomes clear:

> He enunciated distinctly, with soft precision. The deep, rolling tones of his voice filled the deck without effort. He was naturally scornful, unaffectedly condescending, as if from his height of six feet three he had surveyed all the vastness of human folly and made up his mind not to be too hard on it. . . . [His] words spoken sonorously, with an even intonation, were heard all over the ship . . ." (XXIII 18–19)

2. **The crew:** What differences are there between James Wait and the crew?

A writer can effectively examine the differences between James Wait and the crew. Joseph Conrad commented in his introduction to a biography of Stephen Crane that his own novel is about "the crew of a merchant ship, brought to the test of what I may venture to call the moral problem of conduct" (*Last Essays* 95). Considering the figure of James Wait in relation to the crew, the writer might consider the psychology of both. The crew, collectively, can be looked at as an important character in this novel. Toward the end of this novel, the narrator says, "Haven't we, together and on the immortal sea, wrung out a meaning from our sinful lives?" Have the characters wrung out a meaning? If so, what is it? This search for meaning may be one of the motivations for this novel. How does Conrad's novel represent a quest, not simply geographically but also in the spirit and character of humanity? The writer may trace back through Conrad's novel to indicate the ways in which the crew represents this journey. What are their struggles and their goals?

3. **Donkin:** Is Donkin an evil antagonist? What affect does he have on James Wait and on the crew?

The writer might explore how Conrad's portrayal of his antagonist, Donkin, represents a critique of men he met who lack the honor, poise, and character that he so valued. Conrad sailed in the British Merchant Service from 1878 to 1894. His career as a novelist immediately followed this. It seems likely that the character of Donkin was developed to reveal abuses in the navy. This character is inefficient and lazy; he has no honor. We read: "Is there a spot on earth where such a man is unknown?" (299). In his works, Conrad appears to oppose characters who agitate for revolutionary change. Instead, he appears to seek values of permanency, stability, and tradition. Conrad's fiction suggests that he wishes that society would have a code like that of the sailor: a disciplined value structure. A merchant seaman should be a man in whom the concern for his fellows is regularly put into practice. Donkin, in contrast, is selfish. He is subversive and has a divisive effect on the crew. He might be regarded as more a man of the land and the shore than as a man of the sea. You can write an essay that demonstrates this.

An examination of the relationship between Wait and Donkin also can provide you with material for an essay. Is Wait faking illness to gain the attention and sympathy of the crew? He asks Donkin: "Why are you so hot on making trouble?" A writer could explore possible answers to this question. You can investigate the answer that Donkin gives. Donkin says: "Cos it's a bloomin' shayme. We are put on . . . bad food, bad pay. . . . I want to kick up a bloomin' row, a blamed 'owling row that would make 'em remember!" (112). What does this say about Donkin or about the turbulence he injects into the crew and their journey? Conrad invests his characters with the power of language. What is Donkin's verbal power? Do the men believe his ideas and views? Donkin desires to "tear the veil." How is Donkin separated from "all the surrounding existences, that to him shall remain forever irrealisible, unseen, and enviable"?

4. **The rescue:** Why do the members of this crew go out of their way to rescue Wait, when it would be much easier not to?

Wait is rescued by the crew. The writer should examine whether this rescue is central to the novel. The sailors risk their lives to save him. This includes both the "good" and the "bad" characters. Do they like or hate the person they are working to save? "A rage to fling things overboard possessed us." The rescue is perilous. Why would they risk their own lives?

Do the men participate in their own potential destruction? Does their reason "fall" and sprawl on board? Has something instinctual taken over? Their return is described as "like the return of wanderers after many years amongst people marked by the desolations of time." Wait is locked in his cabin. What does this rescue show about the character, loyalty, solidarity, or commitments of the crew?

5. **Singleton:** Do the names that Conrad has chosen for his characters signify anything? If so, what does the singleminded purpose of Singleton mean?

The chapter in which we read of the perilous rescue ends with Singleton, a navigator who has been at the wheel for 30 hours: ever steadfast and enduring. The first great challenge of the storm is over and so is the first half of the novel. Some critics have said that the character of Singleton exemplifies the code of the sailor that Conrad so highly values. The writer might investigate this code of honor and discipline as it appears in Singleton, in contrast with Wait and Donkin.

Singleton appears to have a single-minded devotion to his ship and to being a sailor. He has always been at sea and is said to be a remnant, a "bizarre relic" from a "monstrous antiquity." He is as "old as Father Time himself" and is part of a great generation of seafarers:

> Singleton's generation lived inarticulate and indispensible, without knowing the sweetness of affections or the refuge of a home—and died free from the dark menace of a narrow grave. They were the everlasting children of the mysterious sea. Their successors are the grown up children of a discontented earth. They are less naughty, but less innocent; less profane, but perhaps also less believing; and if they have learned how to speak they have also learned how to whine. But the others were strong and mute; they were effaced, bowed and enduring, like stone caryatides that hold up in the night the lighted halls of a resplendent and glorious edifice. They are gone now—and it does not matter (25).

It is Singleton who faces the storm at the wheel of the ship. We see him confronting the storm:

> His hair flew out in the wind; the gale seemed to take its lifelong adversary by the beard and shake his old head. He wouldn't let go, and, with his knees forced between the spokes, flew up and down like a man on a bough (60).

We read that, "He steered with care" (89). This care is also much like the writer's attention to his craft. The writer of an essay on Conrad's novel has to exercise attention to the details that Conrad is using. The writer, like the sailor, has tenacity and a love of craft. Singleton has a love of the sea and demonstrates thoughtful seamanship. Singleton faces the elements of the sea and sees it as "an immensity tormented and blind, moaning and furious, that claimed all the days of his tenacious life, and, when life was over, would claim the worn out body of its slave" (99). What meaning do you see in this character?

6. **Different generations:** Is Conrad critiquing the younger generation of sailors, who are not as steadfast as Captain Allistoun or Singleton? How do different generations—the young and the old—interact in this novel?

When you are writing on this novel, you may think about the crew on board the *Narcissus*. How well are they prepared for their journey? What are the ages of these sailors? What experience do they have? The ship sails out of Bombay and summons them with a "call to unquiet loneliness, to inglorious and obscure struggle" (15). These men are put to the test and this bonds them. How are they men of service and action? How do they show this in their response to the captain's urgings as the storm comes up? The *Narcissus* receives "a merciless buffeting" (55) and the topsails are furled "in attitudes of crucifixion." How is it that the captain "could count the real sailors amongst [them] on the fingers of one hand"? (126) What would a "real sailor" be?

History and Context

One approach to *The Nigger of the "Narcissus"* is through Conrad's biography. Conrad said he was "striving for the upmost sincerity of expression." The writer may investigate how this novel intersects with Conrad's experience as a sailor. How is Conrad dealing with his own experiences here?

This novel was finished in January 1897 and appeared in book form in early December. It emerges from the English colonial experience. The story begins in India and largely concerns a man of African heritage. In Conrad's early novels, *Almayer's Folly, An Outcast of the Islands,* and in *The Rescue,* which was completed 25 years later, the setting is Malay and an island archipelago in the Pacific. These are set in the last years of what has sometimes been called the Victorian era, after the long-reigning monarch, Queen Victoria. By reading about this transitional period in British culture, you can gain some insight into some of the social and cultural issues that Conrad was dealing with.

Sample Topics:

1. **Home and community:** Explore the ideas of home and community. How are the sailors away from home? How do they make a home while at sea?

   In this novel, we join a voyage back to England from the East. What is it like to be away from home? Students at some distance from home might reflect on their own current experience of their environment and consider the ways in which classroom communities must be forged, as a microcosm of the larger world. You might explore what it is like for these sailors to be away from home or to make a new home on board a ship on a voyage.

2. **Autobiography and fiction:** How do the elements of this novel derive from Conrad's own experiences as a sailor?

   By looking at Conrad's writings, or at biographies about Conrad, we can learn something about his experiences as a young man at sea. Conrad writes that he sought "the vibration of life in the great world of waters, in the hearts of the simple men who have for ages traversed its solitudes" and "the objects of their care." He acknowledges that "every novel contains an element of autobiography" because a writer expresses himself in his creation. G. Jean-Aubrey claimed that the novel was a record of Conrad's experience in 1884. The *Narcissus* sailed from Bombay to London, and the characters were based on actual crewmen. However, the novel covers far more than a factual account. How does Conrad create fiction out of his experiences or news items that he has heard of?

3. **Psychology and time:** What does time have to do with how
   Conrad organizes his fictional narratives?

While it is set in a historical context, Conrad's novel also concerns the psychology of human motivation, moral principles,
and the tensions of human interaction. History is transposed
in a Conrad story. Chronological time often disappears into a
style of storytelling that wanders across time, recalling events
out of sequence. You might ask why Conrad does this. How
do his shifts in time affect how you are reading this story? It
is likely that Conrad fuses his many voyages at sea into this
novel, as well as into his other novels. You can make a conscious effort to mark out where shifts of time occur in Conrad's novel.

Philosophy and Ideas

The idea of human isolation and human connection in a community is
present throughout this novel, as it is in much of Conrad's work. The
community on board ship represents the human community. It is a
microcosm of the larger world in which people help each other out and
provide safety or else are in conflict with each other. However, on a
ship at sea, these men are quite isolated from civilization on land. They
are largely strangers and they have to work with one another on this
ship. Conrad inquires into how human beings are challenged to work
together in an indifferent universe and by the necessity of this interaction learn how to build a community. It is only by the difficult forging
of a community of cooperation, amid the contradictions of danger,
ambition, suspicion, and hostility, that people can bring meaning to
their lives. Through mutual cooperation they are able to face existence
and gain companionship. In this respect, narcissism is set against this
mutuality. Wait and Donkin show selfishness and threaten the solidarity of this community on board ship. Wait, who claims he is sick or
dying, is a constant reminder to the men of their own mortality and
death and how the community needs to work together for survival. It
is interesting that Wait is of African heritage. He is an outsider. While
the men will protect him and risk their lives for him, they are also
remote from him, or resistant to him, because he is of another place
and race.

Sample Topics:

1. **Individualism and community:** What is the contrast between isolation and solidarity here in this novel? What struggle is there between the individual and society?

   Which of Conrad's characters seem isolated to you? How are they separate individuals? How do they join together? The third chapter of this novel dramatizes a storm at sea. The writer, looking into the storm scene, may see the men struggling to help Wait. How is this action an expression of human solidarity? The writer can explore whether he or she finds heroism in this scene. What does this togetherness of men coming to the assistance of the lone individual mean? Conrad wrote that the objects and people presented in fiction should "awaken in the hearts of the beholders that feeling of unavoidable solidarity; of the solidarity in mysterious origin, in toil, in joy, in hope, in uncertain fate, which binds men to each other and all men to the visible world." How does this author draw readers into this sense of solidarity? How do we identify with these men on board this ship? We see that Singleton is vigilant and "He steered with care." The crew assists Wait. How do their lives depend on one another? What might Conrad be saying about human interdependence?

2. **Moral ambiguity:** How does the crew seek honor and decency? How is this compromised as they are affected by Donkin or by Wait?

   The writer can evaluate the moral ambiguities that arise in this novel. These are intertwined with the characters. How might one evaluate the presence and attitude of Captain Allistoun. In what respects does he represent an ideal for men at sea? How is he heroic? This captain keeps his "gaze fixed ahead, watchful, like a man looking out for a sign" (62). How might Conrad's ideal of the sturdy captain who is devoted to his ship be related to watchfulness, to a clear, focused gaze, or to "seeing" clearly? Do you think that Conrad might hope for his readers to develop a similar way of seeing clearly and acting with honor and courage?

3. **Effort and focus:** What ideal of effort and discipline is required to be a sailor or a writer, according to Conrad?

The disciplined and focused man often appears to be a good man in many of Conrad's stories. For example, Allistoun has found within himself "a taciturn serenity in the profound depths of a larger experience" (125). Is this Conrad's own ideal for himself as a writer? This captain is able "to hold the ship up in a superhuman concentration of effort" (65). How does Captain Allistoun preserve discipline on board his ship? What might this have to do with a writer's discipline? What might it have to do with the moral discipline that Conrad appears to seek?

4. **Staying on course:** How does the captain encourage his men to stay on task after the storm? Who gets in the way of this and why?

The captain urges his men to keep on their task, but they are persuaded otherwise by Donkin and by Wait. What is to be done with Donkin, who refuses to do his part? Allistoun says, "I will brain you with this belaying pin if you don't catch hold of the brace" (86). How does the captain insist on a response to the work to be done? How is the *Narcissus* resurrected? Follow the course of the ship and the story's plot. Can the captain keep the emotions of his men from submerging? He has been "one of those commanders who speak little, seem to hear nothing, look at no one—and [yet] know everything, hear every whisper, see every fleeting shadow of their ship's life" (125).

Form and Genre

The novel's narrative technique has drawn attention. There is movement at times from an apparently third-person omniscient point of view to a first-person narrative. The narrator then seems to have information that only a third-person omniscient narrator would know. Given Conrad's later work, this may be intentional experimentation with viewpoint. Give some thought to these changes in point of view.

The first-person narrator here is unnamed. His narration alternates with that of the omniscient narrator. What do you think of this movement of the narrative? Does it suggest anything about the changing moods of the sea? Or is Conrad suggesting that different characters have different perspectives?

Sample Topics:

1. **Perspective and point of view:** By often changing the point of view in this novel, what is Conrad suggesting about perspective and how we see things?

    Some critics have seen an instability in Conrad's story that looks to them like a fault. Through a close reading of the text, the writer might consider how the narrating voice shifts between a detached third-person voice and a first-person narrator who is a member of the crew. The writer should look for those moments when the omniscience of the third-person narrator appears restricted. Perspective is one of the central concerns of Conradian criticism. In this novel we have Wait's two interior monologues (107). An essayist may carefully assess this shifting point of view, offering a personal response to whether Conrad sustains the drama as he handles point of view.

    There has been some criticism that Conrad was wandering in his presentation of point of view and editorializing about how we ought to think about life. There are inconsistencies in the point-of-view narration, these critics say. For some critics, this narrator's voice is ever changing, like Proteus, the god of the sea. The writer on Conrad might ask questions about point of view and how this story is told.

2. **The narrator:** Who is this narrator? How does his voice change over the course of the novel?

    Listen carefully to the voice of each narrator that tells you the story. You will find that the narrator sometimes changes. What attitudes toward the characters or their situations are presented by these narrators? The ship and the crew are the focus of this story, rather than this narrator. Yet, sometimes this narrator is a participant observer, as in when he is apparently one of the five men who rescue Wait. How does this narrative voice maintain distance in his narration? How does this narrator express an ironic tone?

3. **Use of choral techniques:** When is Conrad's narrator like a chorus? When is this narrator ironic?

Conrad's narrators may remind some readers of a Greek chorus. In Greek tragedy, the Chorus often spoke grandly, recalling tradition, seeking some moral stance on the issue at hand. Their collective voice was lofty, presenting the dramatic theme. Often they represented the tradition, its myths and memories. A writer might inquire into how Conrad's narrator is sometimes similar—and why.

Language, Symbols, and Imagery

In Conrad's preface, he says that he wants to direct his readers toward their senses. A writer can investigate the many ways in which Conrad does this. Conrad writes, "My task which I am trying to achieve is, by the power of the written word to make you hear, to make you feel—it is, before all, to make you *see.*" What details does he use to help us to do this? How does he characterize Donkin and Wait so that we can hear and see them? What are we drawn to feel because of the imagery that is presented to us? Conrad's preface suggests a method of impressionism. The writer might examine how objects and images appear to the senses in a fragmentary way. How does one put these impressions together to gain understanding?

Sample Topics:

1. **Symbols of the sea:** How does this novel express the endurance that humanity has in this struggle with the sea? How is the sea itself a symbol?

This early Conrad novel is a sea story through and through. How does man confront the sea in this novel? How is humanity touched and taught by the lessons of the sea? Singleton, with confidence, faces the sea, forever steering the ship, as a duty. His language is simple, straightforward, and stoic, as if to say that silent endurance is a virtue. In contrast, Donkin's language is wordy and boisterous; he is unpleasantly garrulous. The writer might explore this contrast both in their characters and their approach to life at sea. Listen carefully to the language that the characters use and look closely at the images of the sea that are presented. How do these characters relate to the sea? What do you think that they have learned from their past voyages? For example, you might consider the long-enduring character of Singleton. How has Singleton learned these lessons with honor, whereas Donkin has rejected these lessons?

2. **Figures of life and death:** Is James Wait a symbol of fate, of potential destruction, or death? Do characters like Singleton, or Donkin, symbolize anything?

One critic has seen James Wait and the sea as symbols of life and death (James E. Miller, *PMLA* December 1951, "Nigger of the Narcissus: A Reexamination"). If you think they are, you might explore how Wait and the sea act as symbols in this novel. This critic goes on to suggest that Singleton and Donkin are opposite attitudes toward life and death. Do you think so? Other critics have seen Donkin and Wait as symbols for evil. The writer may analyze this idea. After all, while Wait's actions may cause death, this does not necessarily mean that he himself is evil or representative of evil.

3. **Pilgrimage and journey:** Discuss the journey that the *Narcissus* is on and how this represents the journey of life.

The symbolic ship may represent the wandering of humanity. Albert Guerard calls it a vision of a "dark human pilgrimage" and observes the interplay of dark and light images throughout the novel. The writer may look for these and consider the symbolic interaction of good and evil. What are we to make of the indifferent sea on which they sail? How does laboring humanity find dignity in this? Is Conrad saying, like the novelist Albert Camus after him, that this is a matter of heroic endurance? What is the moral universe of these men?

4. **Symbolic blackness:** What does Wait's blackness mean symbolically and how is he the center of action on the ship and in this story?

The blackness of Wait is used symbolically, rather than racially. He emerges like a force from the deepest and most remote sources of the sea. Somehow he becomes a center for the men, a focal point around which much of the action occurs. In "To My Readers in America," Conrad called Wait "the centre of the ship's collective psychology and the pivot of the action." The writer ought to examine Wait as a center of the action. Is he an active force, as in a whirlpool? Is he a "nothing" or a void?

It may be difficult for contemporary readers to read this novel as anything other than "a parable" of racial attitudes, as Avrom Fleishman has pointed out. James Wait and Donkin are like "co-conspirators" trying to gain the attention and sympathy of the crew. If Wait is something more than a racial representation, what does he stand for? Is he "blackness" within the entire human race? Clearly, one can say that racial attitudes may have affected Conrad's presentation. Wait is "the other." He is mystery and threat. Yet, the physical pigment of his skin is seen as only a mask. The question is whether Wait is a good man or a dark soul.

Compare and Contrast

Through comparisons and contrasts, a writer brings out the uniqueness of a character, a place, an object, or a symbol. How are things alike? How are they different from each other? For example, by placing two characters side by side and examining their traits and patterns of behavior, a writer can provide further insight into each of them, as well as their relationship with each other. This novel offers many possibilities for comparison and contrast essays.

Sample Topics:

1. **Is humanity grand or insignificant?:** Does humanity appear heroic or insignificant, courageous or lost, in this world of the sea, with all of its changes?

   The writer can contrast humanity with the vastness of the natural environment of the sea. Or, the writer might choose to contrast the good in some characters with the evil, or darkness, in others. Conrad depicts the dignity of the human and the plight of the infinitesimally small human life: one is small against the vast sea and the universe. This sense of the force of the natural elements comes early in the novel. The third chapter deals with a momentous storm, and this is followed by an account of the turning upright of the boat. How does the storm test men? What is their dignity and their puniness before the forces of the universe? How do we see courage and endurance in these men? The writer might contrast that endurance and courage with the power of the sea.

2. **Adversity and endurance:** Which characters show courage and dignity in the way that they endure the storm and other problems they encounter on the ship? Which of them do not?

   The writer might inquire into how this is also a night journey inward into the heart of humanity. The storm tests the men. It draws forth their connection with one another, their mutual effort against it. Human dignity lives in endurance amid this indifferent sea. You can write an essay describing how these ordinary men, with weaknesses, are confronted with the storm, the vastness of the sea that would overpower them. Show how they hold out against it with courage. In contrast, you can demonstrate how some men, like Donkin, live outside this honor and courage and would have only selfish ends. One might contrast how Singleton is admirable while Donkin is contemptible.

3. **Images of men and women:** Would the interactions on board the *Narcissus* be different if this were a fictional world of women rather than one of all male characters?

This is a world of men at sea. There are no women on this ship. During the period that Conrad was writing this novel, there was a shifting of social classes and races, a discontent among some women that corresponded with the emergence of "the New Woman" in Great Britain. You might read something about the suffragists in Britain at this time and how women attained the right to vote in England. How might the women on land in Britain be contrasted with these men on the ship? Does Conrad investigate any gaps in the Victorian idea of masculinity as rough, rugged, strong, and stoical? The writer might research the rise of the New Woman movement in Britain at the turn of the twentieth century. Then, using the text of this novel, alongside this information, the writer can ask about what it meant to be a man, or to be a woman, in the society of Conrad's time. What characteristics do these male sailors on board the *Narcissus* have? Do you think that women would have any different characteristics?

Bibliography and Online Resources for *The Nigger of the "Narcissus"*

Allingham, Philip V. "Conrad and Classical Imagery in *The Nigger of the Narcissus.*" Victorianweb.org/authors/Conrad/pva37.5.html

Conrad, Joseph. preface to *The Nigger of the "Narcissus."* http:www.classic authors.net/Conrad/"Narcissus"/"Narcissus<0x2 01D>1.html

———. *The Nigger of the "Narcissus."* Electronic Text Library. University of Virginia. http:etext.virginia.edu/toc/modeng/public/ConNarc.html

———. *The Nigger of the "Narcissus."* Electronic Text. Gutenberg Project. www.gutenberg.org/etext/1773

Fleishman, Avron. *Conrad's Politics: Community and Anarchy in the Fiction of Joseph Conrad.* Baltimore, MD: Johns Hopkins University Press, 1967.

Guerard, Albert. *Conrad the Novelist.* Cambridge, MA: Harvard University Press, 1959.

Henthorne, Tom. *Conrad's Trojan Horses: Imperialism, Hybridity and the Post Colonial Aesthetic.* Lubbock: Texas Tech University Press, 2008.

Karl, Frederick. *Joseph Conrad: The Three Lives.* New York: Farrar, Straus and Giroux, 1979; London: Faber and Faber, 1979.

Kimbrough, Robert. *Nigger of the "Narcissus." Norton Critical Editions.* New York: Norton, 1979. Rpt. 1985.

Marcus, Miriam. "Writing, Race and Illness in *The Nigger of the 'Narcissus,'*" *Conradian* 23:1 (1998): 37–50.

Miller, James E. "The Nigger of the "Narcissus": A Reexamination." *PMLA,* December 1951.

Palmer, John. *Nigger of the 'Narcissus.'* Twentieth Century Interpretations. Englewood Cliffs, NJ: Prentice Hall, 1970.

Simmons, Alan H. "The Nigger of the 'Narcissus': History, Narrative, and Nationalism," *Joseph Conrad: Voice, Sequence, History, Genre.* ed. Jakob Lothe, Jeremy Hawthorn, and James Phelan. Columbus: Ohio State University Press, 2008, pp. 141–59.

Thorburn, David. *Conrad's Romanticism.* New Haven, CT: Yale University Press, 1974, pp. 27, 51–53, 81–84, 108–09.

Watt, Ian. *Conrad in the Nineteenth Century.* Cambridge: Cambridge University Press, 1981.

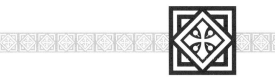

LORD JIM

READING TO WRITE

*L*ORD *JIM* is a psychological and moral fiction concerning how a character deals with lost honor. Writers may explore the sharp conflict between Jim's idealism and practical human relations. As a boy, Jim wants to go to sea to personally encounter the adventures he has read about in stories. He enters training school and goes into the merchant marines. He is selected as second mate on the *Patna*. However, Jim's experiences are just beginning and it is his development that writers may effectively examine. The *Patna* is a ship that is set to bring 800 Muslims on pilgrimage to Mecca. For the writer, pilgrimage and journey is another topic that can be investigated. Just as our lives encounter obstacles, so too does Jim's life. This is much like the encounter of the ship itself.

The beginning of Conrad's story hinges on a specific incident. The writer should pay special attention to this. The *Patna* crashes into an object at sea and the water starts coming in. Jim hurries below and soon recognizes that nothing can be done to save the ship. On deck, the officers have begun to prepare one of the lifeboats. They expect the inevitable sinking of the ship and plan to escape, regardless of the passengers, who will be left behind to their fate. Jim watches as they lower the lifeboat and decides to jump into it. When the officers reach land, they learn that the *Patna* and its passengers have been rescued. The ship did not sink. The officers and Jim have run away, but Jim is haunted by this and he is determined to stand trial. A writer may inquire into Jim's psychology. To ask questions about Jim's decisions and his responses may be a good starting point for a paper. We see how the court takes away his license and how he begins to wander from job to job through the ports of the Far East. Often his story of disgrace is recalled and his shame comes back to him. So he continually moves on, forever the character on a journey.

Marlow, a narrator of this story, becomes Jim's friend and he arranges through a man named Stein to have Jim given an appointment to be in charge of a trading post in Patusan. Once in Patusan, Jim leads a revolt against their oppressor, Sherif Ali. Jim becomes a hero to the Patusans. He is named Tuan Jim, or Lord Jim. Once disgraced, he has now become heroic and honored. You might explore this transition in Jim's social position. However, you might also look at how Jim is soon challenged. For Gentleman Brown, a renegade, comes up the river looking for whatever he can grab. After a conflict between Brown and the Patusans, Jim meets with Brown and Brown insists that Jim fight it out or let Brown leave without further trouble. Brown plays on Jim's memories of the *Patna* incident. By talking with the Patusans, Jim enables Brown to leave. Cornelius shows Brown another way out, and Brown ambushes a group of Patusan warriors. The son of Doramun, the leader of the Patusans, is killed in this ambush. Jim had pledged his honor and his life on this decision. At last, this pledge of honor is Jim's demise.

In chapter 7 we are given a description of Jim's youthfulness and apparent capability. However, we also know of the weaknesses in Jim's character. Marlow's narrative offers a complicated view of Jim:

> And all this time I had before me these blue boyish eyes looking straight into mine, this young face, these capable shoulders, the open bronzed forehead with a white line under the roots of clustering fair hair, this appearance appealing at sight to all my sympathies: this frank aspect, the artless smile, the youthful seriousness. He was of the right sort; he was one of us. He talked soberly, with a sort of composed unreserve, and with a quiet bearing that might have been the outcome of manly self-control, of impudence, of callousness, a colossal unconsciousness, of a gigantic deception. Who can tell! . . . I listened with concentrated attention, not daring to stir in my chair; I wanted to know—and to this day I don't know. I can only guess.

Follow the story and character of Jim carefully. How do you view this complex character and his motivation and actions through what Marlow tells you about him?

TOPICS AND STRATEGIES

This section of the chapter will discuss possible topics for essays on *Lord Jim* and will offer some general approaches to these topics. This is a series of suggestions intended to inspire your own inquiry. You may find a topic that follows a useful place from which to start your essay. Use this material to prompt your thinking about the novel. After you jot down your ideas and analyze relevant passages in the novel, you should formulate your claim, the argument you want your essay to make. Then, you can go back to your notes and begin to provide the evidence for your claim, organizing and arranging your thoughts into a persuasive essay.

Themes

A novel's themes are those major ideas or issues that the story is considering. There are several key questions that Joseph Conrad reflects on in his works. Each work expresses a unique perspective on the themes with which it deals. Your job as a writer is to discover and articulate this perspective in your essay. Identify a central theme in the work and then think about how it is addressed in the narrative. In your view, what is being said about the theme? If you read closely and ask questions about what you have read, you will develop your own line of argument. Focus on close reading and what you think the work is saying about a particular issue. This will help you to develop a claim on which to build your essay. Always make sure to write to express the point that you have to make about the themes that you see in this novel. Clearly define the main points that you want to make. You do not need to write about the entire novel; stick to your main idea. Avoid straying into unrelated tangents of thought. Bring your essay back to focus on your main points. Whatever your interpretive approach, it should be supported with evidence from the text.

Sample Topics:

1. **Jim and the issue of guilt:** Who is Jim and how does Jim deal with the issue of guilt? Does he atone for his mistake in leaving the *Patna*?

What sense of guilt can you see in Jim's story, as Marlow tells it? Clearly, Jim's future is affected by his choice to abandon the *Patna.* Perhaps Jim is "a simple and sensitive character." Yet, as Marlow can see, Jim is also morally complicated. How Jim's sense of guilt affects his future actions is a theme the writer can investigate by probing Jim's actions throughout the novel. In writing about *Lord Jim,* the writer should consider carefully what the characters say about Jim. Stein defines Jim: "He is a romantic— romantic. And that is very bad—very bad . . . Very good too." What might Stein mean? How is "romantic" both good and bad? It is Stein who makes Jim his agent in Patusan. By this, he hides Jim from public view. The writer can examine Stein's perspective.

Another approach is to consider what Jim thinks about his past actions. Does Jim carry a sense of guilt? Is he attempting to atone for this? Or, is he seeking to find other ways to escape or ways to be heroic?

2. **Marlow's point of view:** If we see the action of this novel mostly from Marlow's view, how does that affect what we are reading and how we see?

We see Jim, of course, from Marlow's point of view. So, when writing about *Lord Jim* we have to work through Marlow's analysis. What does Marlow think of Jim? We can gain a little further knowledge about Jim from other perspectives that are offered in comments by Cornelius, Stein, the French lieutenant, or Brierly. Stein asserts that Jim is a romantic. The French lieutenant says that his "honour is gone." Marlow recognizes that Jim has become part of the inner circle of sailors, "one of us," although he has not upheld the code Marlow believes they should live by. That is, Jim has lacked "a fixed standard of conduct." How is Jim's lack of a standard of conduct significant? Why is Jim's departure from what Marlow calls "the solidity of the craft" of such great concern to Marlow? How might this affect Marlow's view of Jim?

3. **Piecing together experience:** Do the fragments of stories about Jim add up to a clear image of him? What kind of a picture do we have of Jim?

When the reader comes to chapter 5, a wandering reverie begins. This may call for patience from the reader, who has to follow a story that is not always chronological. Marlow is patching together an image of Jim from many sources. How do we learn about each other from many different sources? We come to know each other gradually. What kind of picture do we arrive at about a person? How do we assemble the fragments of different testimony, reports, accounts, conjecture, and observations into our view of another person? How are Marlow's own hopes involved in the picture he forms about Jim? Marlow laments to Jewel: "he is not good enough. . . . Nobody, nobody is good enough" (chapter 33). How is Marlow's sense of human limitation part of his tragic view of life?

4. **Complexities of Jim's character:** How does Marlow feel about Jim? The writer may consider whether a reader is moved by Marlow's account to compassion for Jim or uneasiness about him.

On the one hand, Marlow affirms that "he was one of us." However, on the other, Marlow sees behind the surfaces of Jim and is disappointed with something about him. What do you think this is? The writer may inquire into this ambivalence in Marlow's position. What might Marlow be concerned about? What is this "impudence . . . callousness . . . colossal unconsciousness . . . gigantic deception" that Marlow speaks of? For the writer who is writing on *Lord Jim,* the conversations between Marlow and Jim that appear in chapters 7 through 17 are important to explore. What might we learn about them through their dialogue? How, as readers, do we come to also ask Marlow's questions? However alluring Marlow finds Jim, he feels that Jim has violated the code of ethics to which he has always subscribed. Jim has betrayed that code by running off from the *Patna,* when he should have stayed.

In Patusan, Jim appears as a man of action. He conquers his enemies. He is named Tuan Jim by the natives. He is able to marry the beautiful girl of his dreams. How is this "glory" deceptive? Is Conrad being ironic? The writer can probe into the various ways that Jim is vulnerable, rather than invincible, and how his pride may be another blind spot in his character. He sleeps while assassins plot to kill him, and only Jewel's awareness saves him. Jim is not prepared for the invasion of the island by Brown. In what ways is he still a self-preoccupied romantic? What forces Jim to go beyond his ego and this self-preoccupation? How can a writer interpret Jim's choices and actions toward the end of this novel?

Character

Characterization in this novel comes in impressionistic bits and pieces. Marlow is a narrator who sees the world from a certain angle. He gives us his perspective, his story, and he brings us into the life of the characters he describes. The narrative techniques are important for us to look at carefully. Marlow presents, decodes, or deciphers the reality he has encountered. The reader becomes a witness, using Marlow's eyes. In *Lord Jim,* the first four chapters appear fairly straightforward. They are not always chronological, but usually they are enough to give us Jim's history and the things that lead up to when he deserts the *Patna.* We see the voyage of the *Patna* and are led up to the incident on the fateful night. Jim appears secure. The pattern of the novel likewise appears secure, with its omniscient narrator. Suddenly, a problem appears:

> A faint noise as of thunder, of thunder infinitely remote, less than a sound, hardly more than a vibration, passed slowly and the ship quivered in response, as if the thunder had growled deep down in the water. The eyes of the two Malays at the wheel glittered towards the white men, but their dark hands remained closed on the spokes. The sharp hull driving on its way seemed to rise a few inches in succession through its whole length, as though it had become pliable, and settled down again rigidly to its work of cleaving the smooth surface of the sea. Its quivering stopped, and the faint noise of thunder ceased all at once, as though the ship had steamed across a narrow belt of vibrating water and humming air (26–27).

The changes are barely perceptible, but they are momentous. The student writer will see in this highly descriptive passage the careful noting of sensory images. You might pay close attention to them. Jim is still oblivious to the calamity that awaits him. There is an unseen reality here, a mystery that creeps up on him unexpectedly. The third-person narration is about to dissolve, concluding chapter 3. Suddenly, the narrative jumps to Jim's voice, as he gives his evidence at the inquiry a month later. The novel, like Jim's life, has abruptly changed.

Sample Topics:

1. **Jim's flaws:** Is Jim a hero or an antihero?

Jim looks like a romantic hero. However, he is vulnerable because he dreams of being a romantic hero. The writer might examine this flaw in Jim's character. As one writes, one may see further how the moral and psychological aspects of Jim are entwined with the ironic workings of this story. The writer might conclude that, in Jim, we have an antihero who is somehow also, perhaps, a hero. Jim's act of fleeing from the *Patna* is one of cowardice. How does this choice then put Jim to the test? Does Jim succeed and attain victory or does he fail? His act also represents a break from the human community. Is this break ever healed?

2. **Marlow's perspective on Jim:** How does Marlow view Jim? How is what we know about Jim affected by this?

We see Jim through the eyes of Marlow who "showed himself willing to remember Jim, to remember him at length, in detail and audibly." Following Marlow, we can see his narrative point of view as a subject for an essay. Marlow, in *Lord Jim*, has come some distance from the short story "Youth." A writer can consider Marlow's skepticism and his perceptiveness. Can Marlow's outlook be contrasted with Jim's? In what sense does Jim express the romantic wonder and inexperience of "Youth"? The writer may reflect on the image of Jim as fresh, in white apparel, and on the ways in which this contrasts with his adventurousness, his mistakes, and the tragedy of the *Patna* affair.

3. **Jim as every person:** Marlow says that Jim is "one of us." What might he mean by this?

The writer can elaborate on Marlow's statement by looking not only at the community on board the ship but to the wider human community. Does Marlow mean maritime officers, Western civilization, or people in general? Contact between Jim and Jewel is an example of community and relationship. So is Jim's contact with the officers early in the novel and with the Patusans later on. Jim jumps overboard early in the novel, abandoning his responsibilities, and then tries to make his way back to solidarity, to belonging and community. The writer might reflect on how people like Jim struggle with isolation and seek to belong. Is this a common human characteristic?

4. **The social world of the characters:** Discuss the social and ecological environment of the novel.

Conrad's main interest was not in the psychological development of his characters, one of his critics, Ian Watt, believes. Rather, Conrad is more of a social novelist. He is concerned about the way individual actions have an impact on society. "Conrad stands outside the main tradition of the novel of character," Watt says (269). Watt observes that Conrad's characters are far more connected with the social or natural reality of a place or a society than existing as isolated individuals. This critic sees the same environmental determinants in Conrad's work as we find in the student essay by Ryan Nardi earlier in this volume. You might take another look at that essay and see if you agree or disagree with the thesis there. How is the environment in which Jim lives and acts an important factor in this novel? Meanwhile, it is important to remember that Conrad is skeptical. He gives us fragments of evidence that may suggest something about his characters. It is to these fragments that the reader and writer on Conrad must look.

5. **Leadership:** Is Jim a capable leader or not? Does his character change during the course of this story and does Jim become a leader, or does he stay the same?

The writer on *Lord Jim* ought to examine whether the title "Lord" is deserved or whether it is mocking the title character. Is this an example of Conrad's irony at work? "Tuan" is said to mean "mister" or "sir" in Malay, and it is hardly the honorific title of "Lord." The character of Jim obviously went through what Conrad himself called "an expansion." Did his fundamental character change? The writer could argue that Jim, the romantic, never really changes much throughout the course of this long novel. Circumstances may challenge him, but Jim's ego has a kind of permanency. One could argue that he remains naïve, self-centered, airily romantic.

The writer may explore the theme of leadership by looking at the ways that Jim fails as a leader. How are Jim's youth and moral naiveté expressed in the situations that arise on Patusan? Why is he unable to see the evil in Brown? How do his choices and actions result in suffering for the islanders? Jim is a deeply flawed character. Does Jim develop a conscience? Does he, in your view, become a hero or not?

History and Context

The writing of *Lord Jim* was interrupted by Conrad's writing of his stories "Karain," "Youth," and *Heart of Darkness.* Marlow becomes the narrator in "Youth" and *Heart of Darkness,* along with his appearance in *Lord Jim.* The writer who has read all of these Conrad stories can make several connections between the themes present in them and can also compare Marlow's narration across these stories. *Lord Jim* appears to have been part of a very large project for him. Conrad explicitly linked the novel with his story "Youth" and *Heart of Darkness,* saying that "the three tales, each being inspired by a similar moral idea" would make "a homogeneous book" (Letters to Blackburn and Meldrum, 79). What do you think he is trying to achieve, or to understand, by writing these stories? The story "Youth" is where *Lord Jim* begins. Perhaps *Heart of Darkness* is where it ends. You might explore the connection between these stories through the character of Marlow, who is in each of them. Conrad wrote of *Lord Jim*, "It has not been planned to stand alone. H of D was meant in my mind as a foil, and Youth was supposed to give the note" (Letters to Blackburn and Meldrum, 63). Ian Watt, using William Blake's terms, likens "Youth" to a song of innocence and *Heart of Darkness* to a song of experience (269). You might read "Youth" and see if you can draw your own comparisons.

Sample Topics:

1. **The life story behind the story:** How did Conrad's own experiences offer him material for this story?

   Biographies of Conrad will give you information about his youth as a sailor. You can also explore the real story behind the incident that begins Conrad's *Lord Jim.* The source for Conrad's novel was, in part, the story of the *Jeddah.* This ship left Singapore on July 17, 1880, with 900 people who were going on a pilgrimage to Mecca, the Muslim holy city. The white officers of the ship abandoned the ship on August 8. They told a false story, believing that the ship had sunk. The *Jeddah,* however, had been towed safely into harbor. How did Conrad build a meaningful story on the basis of a few facts and incidents that he had learned of? How does his experience relate to this story?

2. **Jim as a composite of actual persons:** Where did Conrad get his idea of a character with romantic dreams? Are any of his characters based on actual people that he met?

   Like many characters in fiction, Jim is a composite of many possible influences. This fictional character is sometimes said to be based on Jim Lingard, the son of Tom Lingard of *Almayer's Folly.* Conrad had met a man named William Lingard in the Far East. Jim is a deserter and his character also emerged from the deserters of the *Jeddah.* One of these was Augustine Podmore Williams, the son of a clergyman, who was criticized but remained a sailor. Jim is likewise a development of Conrad's often naive Almayer of his first novel and of his reading in travel accounts about adventurers. Conrad clearly also drew on himself and his own experiences. He too was hit in the back by a spar and likely "spent many days stretched on his back, dazed, battered, hopeless, and tormented as if at the bottom of an abyss of unrest" (11). You can explore this through Conrad's writings about Jim. You might also look at what Conrad's biographers have to say.

Did the author see any aspects of himself in his characters? You can explore this by reading a biography about the author. Conrad was no romantic like Jim, whatever his early dreams of adventure may have been. Some critics suggest that *Lord Jim* expresses Conrad's disillusionment. Yet, it can be argued that *Lord Jim* is not entirely a novel of disillusionment: Jim still retains some illusions. Conrad, however, did not.

3. **A longer story than expected:** Why did this story grow into a large novel from a short story?

Lord Jim was initially supposed to be a short story, a "sketch." Instead, it turned out to be one of Conrad's most lengthy and powerful novels. A writer might consider why Conrad needed so large a canvas to present his story. What prompted Conrad to keep writing this tale and to turn it into a lengthy novel? Do you think that this could be as effective if it were a short story? The serial publication of *Lord Jim* began in October 1899 in *Blackwood's*. Finishing the novel in January 1900, Conrad then fell ill with bronchitis and a recurrence of malaria and gout. He continued to revise the novel in February 1900, working on the eighteenth chapter, as *Blackwood's Magazine* printed chapters 10 and 11. Conrad was now deciding that his story was not yet completed. Jim had not yet gotten to Patusan. Much to *Blackwood's* surprise, Conrad's story just kept going. Do you think that this just needed to be a long story? Is there a lot here that Conrad had to work out by writing a long novel?

On July 14, 1900, after 45 chapters, Conrad believed he had finally reached the end of his novel. He wrote to his friend, the novelist John Galsworthy: "The end of L. J. has been pulled off with a steady drag of 21 hours . . ." (*Letters* I, 295). The novel appeared in book form in October 1900 and the serialized version moved toward its conclusion in November. When an author engages for a long time on a novel, it is likely that the novel's characters and themes were of some importance to him. What in *Lord Jim* was so important to Conrad that he kept his story going for 45 long chapters?

Philosophy and Ideas

Sample Topics:

1. **Selfishness and altruism:** What might Conrad be saying about altruism and egoism, selfishness and love and tenderness? Do you think that these are reconcilable or not?

   Lord Jim is a novel that brings to mind the concerns of ethics. When Jim has romantic dreams of glory, how does his egotism meet accepted moral standards and what society requires of him? Marlow says, "he seemed to love the land and the people with a sort of fierce egoism, with a contemptuous tenderness." Can the writer reconcile these aspects of Jim's character? Is it possible for the same person to be self-centered and self-giving?

2. **Honor and disgrace:** What is the code of honor that Jim has violated? How is he affected by this?

   Jim is a complex character whose conflicts seem to remind us that nobody is perfect. In his romanticism, Jim appears to want to live up to chivalry and honor that the Western world has long esteemed so highly. The writer might explore how Conrad interrogates Western ideals of perfection and perfectibility in this novel. For example, the narrator says of Brierly: "He had never in his life made a mistake, never had an accident, never a mishap, never a check in his steady rise, and he seemed to be one of those lucky fellows who know nothing of indecision, much less of self-mistrust." In writing an essay, one might examine the paradox of Brierly, who "had saved lives at sea, had rescued ships in distress . . ." but lost hope in his own life. Or, one may look at Jim's romantic illusions and his tendency to make mistakes. Might Conrad be rejecting the idea that anyone can live up to the code's standards or the romantic ideal? Might Jim's downfall, like Brierly's, be the result of trying to measure up to this idealistic code?

3. **Ethical choices and actions:** Is Jim right or wrong in his actions when he jumps from the *Patna* or when, while on Patusan, he allows Brown to escape?

   Jim is surrounded by situations that are filled with moral choices. His abandonment of the *Patna,* to save his own life, was such a choice. Gentleman Brown places him in another problem situation. Jim cannot see ahead to how Cornelius will act or how things will lead to the ambush of the natives. Yet, Brown is evil and corrupt. Is Jim right to allow him to escape? If the writer considers the consequences of this, does that make Jim's action wrong? If Jim's neglecting his responsibility when he jumped from the *Patna* was wrong, is his accepting responsibility for the safety of the people of Patusan, in this case, right? An essay can be developed in which the writer weighs these complicated moral situations.

4. **Human nature and the divided self:** Is Jim a divided man or a complete man? Is it possible for him to become whole?

   In this novel, Conrad probes the nature of humanity. Jim is "one of us," says Marlow. The writer might argue that Jim appears to have a moral awakening. Or, the writer might argue that this moral awakening never comes. To make up your mind about this, examine Marlow's viewpoint toward Jim. What does Marlow hope for when he considers Jim? Perhaps Marlow seeks atonement not only for Jim but for all people, who, in their frailty, make mistakes. Marlow ponders the way that people deviate from the code he so admires. When human nature departs from standards of conduct, Marlow is concerned. As he considers human fallibility, he seems to search the sea and sky and the human heart for meaning. Marlow is a maritime man who has trained young men like Jim for service. He believes that honor and the craft of seamanship are essential. How is Jim a disappointment, as well as a hope, for him? How does his narrative reveal this?

5. **Fate and choice:** What is Marlow's perspective on fate and the choices that people make?

You can explore this novel to reflect on what Marlow thinks about fate and our choices. He positions Jim as a young man confronting death in those moments on board the *Patna*, when he thinks the ship is about to sink:

> He was not afraid—oh, no! he just couldn't, that's all. He was not afraid of death perhaps, but I'll tell you what, he was afraid of the emergency. His confounded imagination had evoked for him all the horrors of panic, the trampling rush, the piti-ful screams, boats swamped—all the appalling incidents of a disaster at sea he had ever heard of. He might have been resigned to die but I suspect he wanted to die without added terrors, quietly, in a sort of peaceful trance. A certain readiness to perish is not so very rare, but it is seldom that you meet men whose souls, steeled in the impenetrable armour of resolution, are ready to fight a losing battle to the last, the desire of peace waxes stronger as hope declines, till at last it conquers the very desire of life. Which of us here has not observed this, or maybe experienced something of that feeling in his own person—this extreme weariness of emotions, the vanity of effort, the yearn-ing for rest? Those striving with unreasonable forces know it well,—the shipwrecked castaways in boats, wanderers lost in a desert, men battling against the unthinkable might of nature, or the stupid brutality of crowds.

In what ways is Jim blind—unable, or unwilling, to see? Jim has daydreamed of "valorous deeds" and has assured himself that he would not flinch when others did. Of course, Jim flinches. He recognizes, "It is all in being ready. I wasn't; not—not then. I don't want to excuse myself but I would like to explain. . . ." Does Jim adequately explain himself to you?

What do you think Marlow's attitude is? Does he think that Jim has made bad choices or that Jim was destined to be in certain situations?

6. **Firm resolve or escapism:** When does Jim face the situations that he finds himself in? When does he run to escape from them? What does this say about Jim's character?

Jim seeks "a clean slate." However, Marlow states that he believes in a destiny that is inscribed on each person. "A clean slate did he say? As if the initial word of each our destiny were not graven in imperishable characters on the face of rock." The writer might look at this sense of destiny in Marlow's view. Alternatively, the writer may ask if Marlow's perspective is one of Darwinian natural selection. What qualities, abilities, or code is it necessary for a man of the sea to have in order to endure?

Jim appears to want to prove himself to the world. Yet, he also seems to be constantly on the run from his past. Perhaps his actions are a repetition of his escaping the *Patna* on that dark night. Rather than facing things, he runs from them. Marlow writes, "I could never make up my mind . . . whether his line of conduct amounted to shirking his ghost or facing it out." Which is the case? Is Jim facing things, or is he always trying to escape?

Form and Genre

Conrad challenges us with the way in which *Lord Jim* is narrated. It is easy for a reader to be confused by the narrative. This confusion may reflect the moral confusion in which Jim finds himself. The story is not chronological, and this shifting of time may baffle the reader. Multiple narrators tell different parts of the story. Some reflection on these perspectives may lead to a very good subject for an essay, because these varied views remind us that everyone sees the world a bit differently. Why would the writer tell his story out of sequence? Does this have anything to do with memory? We learn about events in this way, as different people tell us about them. We learn bits and pieces and then have to put these stories that people tell us all together. Marlow, one of our narrators, has had to piece together these fragments of the story of Jim's life. He only has a limited grasp of what happened. A reader soon recognizes that Conrad's narrative technique involves multiple narrators. He experiments with a story line that is not always chronological. You might think about how this technique expresses the novel's concerns.

Sample Topics:

1. **Multiple narrators and putting together the story:** Why does Conrad use several narrators? How does this affect how we read and how we learn about the events of the story?

   Jim's tale comes not only from an omniscient narrator but also from Marlow, Egstrom, Tamb' Itam, Stein, Jewel, and sometimes as a first-person narrative from Jim himself. Since these narrators each tell only a part of Jim's story, it becomes the work of the reader to put all of this together. Each narrator offers us some information, while expressing a particular point of view. This reminds us that we tend to get our information about events from many different sources and distinct points of view. As a writer, one has an individual point of view to offer. We encounter Jim as he appears to be through these narrators. Jim, however, is more than a composite of these various perspectives. Conrad suggests that what we make of Jim from this collection of sources may not add up to absolutely certain knowledge of Jim.

2. **The break from chronology:** Why does Conrad not write the story in chronological order, from the beginning to the end?

   The break from chronology is also significant. We tend to be most accustomed to narratives in a time sequence of beginning-middle-end. Because Conrad's method is so different, this can make for some difficult reading. Many readers approaching the novel for the first time may find it difficult to follow. The chapters told by the omniscient narrator wander in time. Multiple narrators tell their story nonconsecutively. When Marlow tells the story, his listeners know parts of Jim's story that the reader does not yet know. Why do you think Conrad orders his story in this way?

3. **The fractured mirror:** How do we learn about the people in this story from different angles? Why are we given those different angles?

We frequently learn about people and events from many sources, all of which have a partial view of their subject. These storytellers who discuss this person have met this person at different times. Conrad represents how we learn and accumulate information. Sometimes this is out of order or sequence. We see different sides of a person at different times. Likewise, we may see different sides of a situation on different occasions. This technique also reflects the moral confusion that is present in the story's main character, Jim. It is like a fractured mirror that reflects all the facts that Marlow has to put together. This assembling of the pieces provides an incomplete knowledge, a sense of what possibly occurred. In this way, this narrative method underscores the subjectivity of knowledge. It suggests an inability to know everything for certain. After you read through a few of Marlow's descriptions, jot down what you think he wants to let us know. As you turn this list into a paragraph, you will see how you are putting things together. You are establishing an order for your own essay. Writing, in this sense, is like putting the pieces together.

4. **Voice and language:** What can we learn by listening to the different voices of the characters in this novel?

To carefully consider the dialogue in this story, listen to what characters say to each other and what they say about their world. This novel is filled with multiple voices: Marlow's narration, his dialogue with Jim, the frame narrator's voice, and the voices of characters are all important. Voice and language become the tether between Jim and the lives on the *Patna*. They try to call him back. How do sound and language link us? How do voices of self-recrimination begin within Jim?

5. **What would you have done?:** If you were in Jim's position, what would your choices have been? Why?

Jim apparently struggled with his decision. We need to listen to Jim's voice as he recalls this. Suddenly, he discovers that he has left the boat: "I had jumped . . . it seems." Does this reflect a less than conscious decision? We do not always know in advance how we might act in a crisis. The writer may ask, are we like Jim, or are we different? Marlow asks, "What would you have done? . . . Do you know what you would have done?" The writer might consider that question. When you listen to Jim's explanation of his choices and actions, do you believe him? You can write a self-reflective essay on what you think that you might have done if you were in Jim's situation. Or, if you are asked to be objective in your writing, you might reflect on how people in similar situations would act.

Compare and Contrast Essays

Marlow's view of Jim is complex. On the one hand, he sees the promise in him and, on the other hand, he is disturbed by the moral lapse in Jim's character. When you write an essay of comparison and contrast about this, you might interrogate the conflicting sides of Marlow's view of Jim. In abandoning the *Patna*, Jim has violated the ethical code that Marlow lives by. Yet, Marlow likes something about him. As the writer examines the character of Jim, he or she might also look at the contrasting perspectives and attitudes that Marlow has toward him. The writer might also choose to compare or contrast Jim as he appears on the *Patna*, early in the novel, with his manner and actions in the latter part of the novel.

Sample Topics:

1. **A two-part novel?:** In one of Conrad's letters to his friend Edward Garnett, he expressed some concern that there are two parts to this novel: the *Patna* episode and the Patusan experience. Do you think there are two parts that are different? Do these parts of the novel attempt to tell the same story or different stories? The writer might reflect on the structural unity, or disunity, of this novel. If you think that there are two parts to this novel, you might contrast them with each other. How are these two parts of the novel related?

Some critics who view *Lord Jim* as a two-part novel see Marlow's interview with Stein in chapter 20 as a dividing point between the two parts of the novel. You might look at this scene and say whether you agree with this view or not. A writer could argue that the main incident of the first part (Jim's abandonment of the *Patna*) has everything to do with the second part. Starting with this thesis, a writer can build an account of how Jim's decisions in Patusan are emotional responses to how he was treated earlier on, following the *Patna* incident. Or, the writer might recognize continuity between the proud, romantic self of Jim as a young sailor on the *Patna* and the kind of romantic dreams that continue while he is living at Patusan.

2. **Exploring changes in Jim's character:** Does Jim change during the course of the story?

   The writer might explore whether there have been any changes in Jim from the beginning of the novel, on the *Patna,* to the last part of the story in Patusan. After the *Patna* incident, the romantic Jim feels like he is a victim of circumstances. He has yet to take responsibility for what he has done. Seeing himself as a romantic hero, he yearns for another opportunity to show the world that he is heroic. However, he has to face his failure. Do you think that he does? The maritime code has a fixed standard of conduct and its rulings are a clear reprimand of his misconduct. Does this make a difference in Jim's behavior? The writer can look at how the romanticism in Jim develops through the novel, beyond this incident. Does this character gain more awareness and maturity? Does he ever see clearly?

3. **Jim's romantic nature and aspirations:** Jim has been at times described as a character that is caught in a romance of his own making. Is he?

   This novel grew from a sketch, "Tuan Jim," and what Conrad called "the pilgrim ship episode." Looking at the first chapters of this novel, the writer can think about Jim's choice to abandon the *Patna.* Looking at a later part of the novel, you can look at Jim's choice to exile himself "from the haunts of white men." Follow how Jim moves from scene to scene. As he is affected by events, how are Jim's romantic dreams, or his sense of invincibility, challenged?

How does Jim remain a romantic? In what ways does he act on a fantasy of conquest, of overcoming his enemies, and of achieving the respect and honor of his people in Patusan? Jim has high aspirations and it appears that Marlow wishes to applaud this. Even so, Marlow is critical of the cowardice he sees in Jim. The writer might examine the ambiguity of Jim's character. How are we to see him: as heroic, or unheroic?

4. **Exploring Jim's mistakes at Patusan:** Why does Jim act the way he does when he encounters Gentleman Brown?

When Brown invades Patusan, his actions destroy Jim's dreams. You might investigate how this happens. Why is Jim unprepared for Brown? Is he overconfident or too little wary of the evil that may lurk in others? In response, Jim does not kill Brown. Instead, he goes to face him and then gives him a path out of this place. In your view, should he have done so? Do you see this action of kindness as a lack of strength in standing up to a villain? If Jim is kind when he should be strong and decisive, what does this say about Jim? Might Jim's past action of fleeing the *Patna* make him more merciful than he should be on this occasion?

Bibliography and Online Resources for *Lord Jim*

Baines. Jocelyn. *Joseph Conrad: A Critical Biography.* London: Weidenfield and Nicholson, 1960, pp. 241–52.

Bloom, Harold, ed. *Lord Jim.* Modern Critical Interpretations. New York: Chelsea House, 1987.

Conrad, Joseph. *Lord Jim.* London: J.M. Dent and Sons, 1917.

Dryden, Linda. *Joseph Conrad and the Imperial Romance.* New York: St. Martin's Press, 2000.

Ghent, Dorothy. "On Lord Jim," *The Art of Joseph Conrad: A Critical Symposium.* East Lansing: Michigan State University Press, 1960, pp. 140–53.

Gillon, Adam. *Joseph Conrad.* Boston: Twayne, 1982, pp. 84–91.

Gordon, John Dozier. *Joseph Conrad: The Making of a Novelist.* Cambridge, MA: Harvard University Press, 1940.

Guerard, Albert. *Conrad the Novelist.* Cambridge, MA: Harvard University Press, 1958, rpt. 1969, pp. 126–74.

Karl, Frederick. *A Reader's Guide to Joseph Conrad.* New York: Noonday Press, 1960, pp. 120–31.

———. *Joseph Conrad: The Three Lives.* New York: Farrar, Straus and Giroux, 1979, pp. 445–508.

Krieger, Murray. *The Tragic Vision: Variations on a Theme in Literary Interpretation.* New York: Holt, Rinehart and Winston, 1960, pp. 165–79.

Kuehn, Robert, ed. *Lord Jim.* Twentieth Century Interpretations. Englewood Cliffs, NJ: Prentice Hall, 1969.

Martin, Ross C. *Lord Jim: After the Truth.* Boston: Twayne, 1992.

Moser, Thomas and Norman Sherry. *Lord Jim.* Norton Critical Editions. New York: Norton, 1996.

Najder, Zdzislaw. "Lord Jim: A Romantic Tragedy of Honour," *Conrad in Perspective: Essays on Art and Fidelity.* Cambridge: Cambridge University Press, 1997, pp. 81–94.

Paris, Bernard J. *Conrad's Charlie Marlow: A New Approach to Heart of Darkness and Lord Jim.* New York: Palgrave Macmillan, 2006.

Parry, Benita. "On Lord Jim," *Marlow.* Bloom's Modern Literary Characters. New York: Chelsea House, 1992.

Simmons, Alan H. and J. H. Stape. *Lord Jim, Critical Essays.* Atlanta: Rodopi, 2000.

Spittles, Brian. *How to Study a Joseph Conrad Novel.* New York: Macmillan, 1990.

Thorburn, David. *Conrad's Romanticism.* New Haven, CT: Yale University Press, 1974, pp. 53–56, 116–21, 130–35.

Wake, Paul. *Conrad's Marlow: Narrative and Death in "Youth," Heart of Darkness, Lord Jim, and Chance.* Manchester: Manchester University Press, 2008.

Watt, Ian. *Conrad in the Nineteenth Century.* Berkeley: University of California Press, pp. 254–356.

Wiley, Paul L. *Conrad's Measure of Man.* Madison: University of Wisconsin Press, 1954, pp. 50–60.

Winner, Anthony. "Lord Jim: Irony and Dream," *Marlow.* Bloom's Modern Literary Characters, ed. Harold Bloom. New York: Chelsea House, 1992.

"YOUTH"

READING TO WRITE

"**Y**OUTH" IS one of Conrad's most significant short stories. It is in this story that he introduces Charlie Marlow as the primary narrator. "Youth" is the first time we meet Marlow, who is also a narrator for *Heart of Darkness, Lord Jim,* and *Chance.* In this story, Marlow tells his story to several listeners, one of whom writes down that story and becomes the frame narrator. As a reader gets to know Marlow and his manner of telling stories, the reader gains a very important aspect of Conrad's method. The reader sees the actions through Marlow's viewpoint. So it is necessary to be aware that Marlow, while usually reliable, has his own values and his own way of looking at the world. With this manner of telling a story, a reader gradually gets to know characters. Our knowledge of people comes to us in fragments. We learn about them a little at a time. Sometimes we just have peoples' stories about the people we might get to know. In this story, characters and events unfold for us through Marlow's recollections. It is important that the reader realize that Marlow has a limited point of view, even while it is an interesting one. Marlow's perspective tells us as much about Marlow himself as about the people and events he discusses.

As "Youth" begins, Marlow is looking back in time some 20 years. Back then he had joined the *Judea* as second mate. The ship was sailing for Bankok (as Bangkok was then spelled), carrying a cargo of coal. However, the journey was difficult. Setting out from London for Newcastle, they encountered rough weather and were delayed. Further on, the *Judea* was hit by another ship. It was three months before they could set sail from London. Once again there was poor weather in the English

Channel. The *Judea* began leaking and this again delayed the ship's voyage. Marlow remembers that after several months of work on repairs, the *Judea* cast off again for Bankok and sailed to the Pacific Ocean. At Java Head, the ship and crew faced a fire in the cargo hold. Water was rushed in to try to save the ship but the vessel exploded. As a mail boat attempted to tow the *Judea*, the fire became more turbulent. The crew had to abandon ship, escaping in lifeboats, with Marlow at the helm. From afar, tossed on the waves, they watched the ship sink. Finally, after hours at sea, they reached land. Marlow ends his story by recalling how he awakened to a new morning in the Far East.

The reader is drawn into Marlow's tale, which is one of memory. In a sense, the reader joins Marlow, as if he or she is part of that crew from long ago. To write effectively about "Youth," one does well to let Marlow's memories come alive and to follow them closely. Marlow's associations and connections with his past say much about what he believes and values, what he regrets, and how he sees life and his profession as a man on the sea.

TOPICS AND STRATEGIES

This section of the chapter will discuss possible topics for essays on "Youth" and will offer some general approaches to these topics. This is a series of suggestions intended to inspire your own inquiry. You may find a topic that follows a useful place from which to start your essay. Use this material to prompt your thinking about the novel. After you jot down your ideas and analyze relevant passages in the novel, you should formulate your claim, the argument you want your essay to make. Then, you can go back to your notes and begin to provide the evidence for your claim, organizing and arranging your thoughts into a persuasive essay.

Themes

This story is about the hopes and challenges of youth and the dreams and ideas of a young sailor. Conrad's irony is at work as he has Marlow, now an older sailor, tell us the story of his own youthful adventure. In some ways, this story is a tribute to youth, as Marlow recalls youth as a vital, enthusiastic time. Conrad recalls the wonderful energy of youth. The *Judea* asserts "Do or Die" as its motto. Marlow says, "I remember it took my fancy immediately. There was a touch of romance in it, something that made me love the old thing—something that appealed to my youth!" (5). The story evokes the romance and wonder of the exotic East. Charlie Marlow remarks, "But for me all the East is contained in that vision of my youth. It is all in that moment when I opened my young eyes on it" (42). In this sense, this tale is a fond recollection of the wonder he once felt as a young man. However, this story is also an examination of the ignorance and naiveté of youthful dreams and ambitions.

Sample Topics:

1. **Memory and youth:** What does this story say about what we remember from the past and how we recall yesterday?

   This story recalls a time that will never come again, for these thoughts and emotions are of their own time and place. They can only be recovered in memory. Marlow says, "And this is how I see the east. I have seen secret places and have looked into its very soul; but now I see it always from a small boat, a high outline of mountains, blue and afar in the morning; like a faint mist at noon; a jagged wall of purple at sunset . . ." (37). Marlow now sees how naïve his youthful view was and he feels some sadness: "I remember my youth and the feeling that will never come back any more—the feeling that I could last for ever, outlast the sea, the earth, and all men; the deceitful feeling that lures us on to joys, to perils, to love, to vain effort—to death . . ." (36). You might give some thought to how the past is shaped through memory. How is immediate experience different from past experience that is recalled? What is the gap between living events and recalled ones? What is the difference between living and experiencing things and telling about them?

2. **Change:** What is Marlow saying about change? Is he nostalgic for his youth?

   In this story, youth is set alongside a sense of change and mutability. Conrad reflects on the movement of a life toward age and dying. We see an aging captain and his wife, a first mate who is growing older, and a creaky, old ship. Youth is set in contrast with this process of aging. Marlow tells us that now all of these people have died and that "youth, strength, genius, thoughts, achievements, simple hearts—all die. . . . No matter" (7). Yet, he recalls his joy on the day he joined to sail: "How time passes! It was one of the happiest days of my life" (5). The frame narrator, who recalls Marlow's tale, is similarly nostalgic. He begins his story by saying, "You fellows know there are those voyages that seem ordered for the illustration of life, that might stand for a symbol of existence" (4). He ends the story by recognizing how the past drifts away like the sea: "our faces marked by toil, by deceptions, by success, by love; our weary eyes looking still, looking always, looking anxiously for something out of life, that while it is expected is already gone—has passed unseen, in a sigh, in a flash—together with the youth, the strength, with the romance of illusions" (42). How does this story illustrate life or the passing of success, love, or "the romance of illusions"? Do you share this attitude, or do you feel differently about what life may bring?

Character

Marlow's tone, as well as his words, reflect his attitude toward his past. In writing about "Youth," the writer should pay close attention to Marlow's narration. How does he convey his memories to us? Conrad explores the adventurous wonder of youth and perhaps its naiveté. The older Marlow recalls his own youth in a kind of communal pass-the-bottle gathering on deck. He remembers the time fondly as one of vigor and hopeful energy. However, this is also memory recalling a time that once was and will never be again. So there is nostalgia in the memories. There is also a sense of aging and death in the aging ship. You might explore how the ship the listeners are on, or the *Judea* of Marlow's story, reflect this sense of age. Speaking of the *Judea*, Marlow says, "I remember it took my fancy immensely. There was a touch of romance in it, something that made me love the old thing—something that appealed to my youth!" (5). Even so, there is a sense of passing and change that pervades the atmosphere of this story. Marlow asserts, "youth, strength, genius, thoughts, achievements, simple hearts—all die . . . No matter" (7). How do people, like Marlow, hold memories or express nostalgia for a time gone by? In what sense do our memories of our experiences make us what we are?

Sample Topics:

1. **Regrets and memory:** What might Marlow regret as he recalls his youth?

    Marlow's narration recalls the vision of youth but also regret. "I remember my youth and the feeling that will never come back any more . . ." (36). Marlow's listeners on deck may also have similar emotions—and perhaps some of Conrad's readers may too. The writer should take some time to investigate these emotions. In the first pages of the story, you will see many references to memory: "It was altogether a memorable affair" (4). Of the Judea, he says, "I remember it took my fancy immensely" (5). Conrad refers to "Youth" as "a feat of memory . . . a record of experience" (xi). How does memory operate in this story?

2. **Marlow looks at his younger self:** How does Marlow view youth and his yesterdays?

    You can build a paper by asking questions about Marlow and the characters he remembers. How does the young Marlow view adventure on the sea? Consider his references to youth: "O youth! The strength of it, the faith of it, the imagination of it!" (12). What do you make of the enthusiasm in this exclamation? Marlow says, "As for me there was also my youth to make me patient" (18). How does the older Marlow view his younger self as engaged in an egotistic and self-preoccupied focus on adventure? In what sense does he recall youth fondly, when he says, "Ah! The good old time—the good old time. Youth and the sea. Glamour and the sea!" (42).

3. **Recalling youth:** How do the listeners to the story recall their own youths?

    It is implied that the listeners to Marlow's story are also "old." How might these listeners also recall their own youths while listening to Marlow's story? Toward the end of this story, the reader is given the image of the faces of the listeners reflected on a tabletop. The frame narrator returns:

> We all nodded at him over the polished table . . . our weary eyes
> looking still, looking always, looking anxiously for something
> out of life, that while it is expected is already gone, has passed
> unseen, in a sigh, in a flash—together, with the youth, with the
> strength, with the romance of illusions. (42)

Mirrored images are reflections—not the thing itself but representations of it. These reflections are like blurs on the table
surface. How might the memories of these men be looking
back across the distance of time? How do you view Captain
Beard or the other elder sailors on the voyage that is described?
What challenges do Captain Beard and his crew face? How
does life bring unpredictable problems? In what ways does this
story about their experiences suggest this?

History and Context

In "Youth," *Heart of Darkness,* and *Lord Jim,* Marlow appears as a narrator. A writer is likely to develop new insights for writing on *Heart of
Darkness* and *Lord Jim* by looking carefully at the short story "Youth."
Here Marlow looks back on a period in his own life. It was a time when
the sea itself was a glamorous destination. He recalls the fiery enthusiasm of his youth with fondness and regret:

> Oh, the glamour of youth! Oh, the fire of it, more dazzling than the
> flames of the burning ship, throwing a magic light on the wide earth,
> leaping audaciously to the sky, presently to be quenched by time, more
> cruel, more pitiless, more bitter than the sea—and like the flames of the
> burning ship surrounded by an impenetrable night.

This short story is part of the context from which those major works by
Conrad emerged. So a close look at the themes and techniques used in
the short story is important. "Youth" is a story that deserves your careful
attention, if you want to learn more about Conrad's craft.

Sample Topics:

1. **The romance of youth:** If you have also read *Lord Jim,* how does
   Marlow's romantic view of himself as a youth reflect the romantic view of Jim?

"Youth" emerged in May and June of 1895 and appeared that September in *Blackwood's,* a British magazine. *Lord Jim* was begun when Conrad had completed "Youth." If you have read *Lord Jim,* how does Marlow's narration in that novel compare with his narration in "Youth?" Locate sections in each text in which youthful enthusiasm is apparent. You may find lines that suggest that Marlow still treasures his memory of youth and sees life itself in it.

Toward the end of his narrative, Marlow says:

> I remember my youth and the feeling that will never come back any more—the feeling that I could last forever, outlast the sea, the earth, and all men; the deceitful feeling that lures us on to joys, to perils, to love, to vain effort—to death, the triumphant conviction of strength, the heat of life in the handful of dust, the glow in the heart that with every year grows dim, grows cold, grows small, and expires—and expires, too soon, too soon—before life itself (37).

Is Marlow admiring youth, or is he critical of youth?

2. **The British Empire:** How was the "youth" of Britain in its imperialist enterprise like the youth of a young, idealistic sailor?

Is Conrad making any comment in this story on Britain? In the latter part of the nineteenth century, the British colonial empire was approaching its greatest extent. The sea served as a path to the world. The writer might evaluate the importance of the sea for the British, whose homeland is surrounded by water. Marlow says, "And I thought of men of old who, centuries ago, went that road in ships that sailed no better, to the land of palms and spices, and yellow sands, and of brown nations ruled by kings more cruel than Nero the Roman and more splendid than Solomon the Jew" (18). This paragraph ends on an image of the ship and the words inscribed on her stern: "Judea, London. Do or Die." What is this ship and its enterprise's place in the long scope of history?

Philosophy and Ideas

Sample Topics:

1. **The voyage of life:** How does the voyage Marlow describes illustrate life or symbolize existence?

   As Marlow begins his recollection, he makes what appears to be a philosophical comment: "You fellows know there are those voyages that seem ordered for the illustration of life, that might stand for a symbol of existence. You fight, work, sweat, nearly kill yourself, sometimes do kill yourself trying to accomplish something—and you can't." What was Marlow seeking to accomplish? How does his first voyage represent this? What do you think that Marlow is saying here?

2. **Stages of life:** How is youth different from other stages or phases of life?

   Sometimes when a person is young, that person looks forward to the future. Here, Marlow is looking backward. You might give some thought to the difference in these perspectives. What does Marlow's narrative suggest about memory or about time and experience? Do you think that the listeners, who are mostly older men, miss their youth, have regrets, or have fond memories of it?

Form and Genre

"Youth" is a frame narrative. This way of framing a story was an important innovation made by Conrad, and it is something that the writer on "Youth" should attend to carefully. Following the introduction by an omniscient narrator, we meet Charlie Marlow, who tells us the story. The writer can investigate Marlowe's narrative and ask what this has to do with memory. Marlowe's memory goes back about 20 years, to the time he had just joined the *Judea* as second mate on a voyage bound for Bankok. What were his emotions and his dreams then? What is his attitude now? You will see that the ship faces difficulties and then is hit by another ship and has to pause for repairs. Later at Java Head, there is a fire in the hold and the crew has to pump water. How do the men respond to these problems? What does Marlow, the narrator, think of this and in what terms does he remember these events? You can explore the form that his narrative takes. Ask questions about his attitude and how this attitude colors the story that he tells.

Sample Topics:

1. **Narrative:** How does the story develop through the frame narrator and through Marlow's narration?

"Youth" is subtitled "A Narrative." The writer can develop an essay by reflecting on the qualities of narrative and the story's narrators. "Youth" begins with a frame narrator who recalls that "We were sitting around a mahogany table. . . ." This "we" includes Marlow, whose subsequent narration of the story calls for careful attention. Marlow becomes Conrad's new technical device: a participant observer. Marlow tells most of this story to the four other men on deck and he thereby brings us, Conrad's readers, into their company. These men are joined in "the strong bond of the sea, and also the fellowship of the craft" (3). What do you think that Marlow's story says about this fellowship and this craft of seamanship? "Youth" is mostly told in a chronological fashion. However, experiences come in a fragmentary way. Apparently irrelevant details are mixed with more significant incidents. The writer may notice that Marlow's tale seems to start several times.

2. **What genre is this story?:** Is "Youth" a chronicle, a romance, or "a symbol for existence"? Might the story be all of these?

"Youth" appears to have some autobiographical elements from Conrad's own life at sea. How is this story a kind of autobiography? Marlow retraces his life from the fragments of experience. Adventure stories have shaped the young Marlow's imagination. In fact, it may seem to the writer as if the young Marlow was trying to live a romance adventure story. Marlow recalls himself at the age of 20: "And there was somewhere in me the thought: By Jove! This is a deuce of an adventure—something you read about . . ." (12). The writer can observe incidents recalled by the older Marlow in which his younger self looked at the world as if it were a storybook drama. For example, when burning coal explodes, he wonders: "What next? I thought, Now, this is something like. This is great. I wonder what will happen next. O youth!" (26) Is this story a romance, or an adventure story? Is it an autobiography or recollection? You can write an essay about which genre you think this story might be categorized in.

3. **Life as an adventure story:** In what ways does the young Marlow desire to have his life be the plot of a romance of adventure?

The writer might look at the way that Marlow recalls his youthful anticipation of further adventures. Once he looked to the East as an imagined place of adventure. For him, the reality of the old ship he was aboard was cast into illusions and dreams: "To me she was not an old rattle-trap carting about the world a lot of coal for a freight—to me she was the endeavor, the test, the trial of life" (12). Later, we read: "I was steering for Java— another blessed name—like Bankok, you know" (36). How, for the young Marlow, is the East an idealized dream more than a destination? What does the older Marlow think about this now?

Language, Symbols, and Imagery

By looking carefully at the language and imagery of this story, you can gain some insight into what Conrad is attempting to convey. "Youth" begins: "This could have occurred nowhere but in England, where men and sea interpenetrate, so to speak." This emphasis on the sea occurs throughout Conrad's stories. Consider the sea imagery in "Youth": "the vast night lying silent on the sea" (35). Look at the images of water and of fire. "I could see the circle of the sea lighted by the fire" (31). "The ship trembled, the mass of flame swayed as if ready to collapse, and the foretop gallant mast fell. It darted down like an arrow of fire . . ." (32). Are these symbols that suggest something primal and elemental?

Sample Topics:
1. **The sea and its influence:** The writer might examine the impact of the sea on these lives. Does the sea have a symbolic role here in this story?

We have seen that the sea is a constant presence in Conrad's early stories. You might explore its impact on Conrad's own life. How does he bring this to his fictional world and his characters? What does his story say about the influence of the sea on the lives of these characters? Trace the imagery of the sea that you find in this story. In your essay, you might consider how choosing a life of sailing has affected the characters in this story or its listeners. What might Marlow's story mean to the men who are sitting on deck listening to it?

2. **Encountering Asia:** How is the Far East viewed by Marlow? What role does it play in Marlow's life?

The writer can follow Marlow's reflections on his journey to Asia. The Far East was an exotic place where Marlow once dreamed of going. Marlow says, "And this is how I see the East. I have seen its secret places and I have looked into its very soul" (35). If he has done this, what has he seen? What do you think is the importance of the East for Marlow? Is it an actual place, or a dream, or the destination of a quest? Has Marlow's vision of it changed since the time of his youth?

3. **The lifeboat as a symbol:** How is the first ship that Marlow is in charge of symbolic?

Marlow's first command is of a lifeboat. The writer might consider how this may be symbolic. The boat is small, ancillary to the main ship. Yet, it is a "life" boat, a boat of rescue. When the ship goes down, Marlow drifts away on his lifeboat—alone. What has become of the solidarity and community of shipmates bound by a code and forged into a unit by facing common adversity? The writer might examine how this "me" becomes "us." How does Marlow learn what he is called to within his responsibility to the other crew members? How does he learn to coordinate his command of his little craft with the greater enterprise?

Compare and Contrast Essays

The obvious comparison and contrast that can be made is Marlow's own one of how his youth, which is past, is different from his adult maturity in the present. Following Marlow's narrative, a writer can compare Marlow's recollection of himself as a young man with the older Marlow, who is the teller of the story. Marlow announces a list of youthful ambitions:

> And do you know what I thought? I thought I would part company as soon as I could. I wanted to have my first command all to myself. I wasn't going to sail in a squadron if there were a chance of independent cruising. I would make land by myself. I would beat the other boats. Youth! All youth! The silly, charming, beautiful youth.

Consider carefully Marlow's youthful ambitions and the ways that he recalls his attitudes. Reflect on Marlow's selection of details of what he recalls when he thinks back on his experience as a young man.

Sample Topics:

1. **Past dreams and present realities:** How does Marlow celebrate youth, even while critiquing youth?

   This narrative is Marlow's reflection back on an earlier time. How does Marlow now assess these earlier dreams and ambitions? What is he nostalgic for? What is he critical of? How does Marlow's experience and attitude now compare with his experience and attitude toward adventure on the sea in his youth? What cynicism or pessimism might there be in the older Marlow's account? What disenchantment is present here that contrasts with the young Marlow's early enchantment with adventure and the sea? He recalls how the ship was destroyed. His crew "slept in the careless attitudes of death (41)." What has become of the romantic dreams or the momentary vitality of youth?

2. **Youth and age:** What differences of attitude are present in the characters in this story? If the older sailors have a code of con-

duct and have inherited standards, are these standards no longer meaningful to a younger generation?

Marlow says, "It was twenty-two years ago; and I was just twenty. How time passes! It was one of the happiest days of my life." How is this story a meditation on the passage of time and of change? His youth is contrasted in this paragraph with the age of the mate: "The mate looked me over carefully. He was also an old chap, but of another stamp. He had a Roman nose, a snow-white long beard, and his name was Mahon, but he insisted that it should be pronounced Mann."

Ancient as Rome, sporting a white beard, this Mann may be everyman. You might write on the contrast here between the youthful and somewhat naïve Marlow and the figures like Mann who surround him. Of the captain, he writes: "He was sixty, if a day." The ship, the *Judea,* is also old, its name recalling an ancient society. Why might Conrad be setting up this contrast between youth and age early in this story? The writer might also reflect on the contrast between Marlow's memory of youth and the listeners to his story in the present: men whose faces are marked by age and experience. Is there some ethic, or background of order, that the older Marlow, our narrator, looks back on?

3. **How Marlow's vision of the world has changed:** How, in Marlow's view, has the world changed?

As Marlow tells his story, it becomes clear that he is looking back on a time that is no more. Has the world changed? Has Marlow's vision changed? Could it be that Marlow once felt a grand sense of possibility and now has a seasoned awareness of limitations? How does he consider his youthful self, the mate who sailed on the *Judea?* You may notice that there is intensity to Marlow's tale, as if the energy of his youth is returning to him as he recalls it. Yet, his romantic expectations are now seen for the illusions they were. How does some of the past seem absurd to Marlow now?

Bibliography for "Youth"

Bloom, Harold, ed. *Marlow.* Bloom's Modern Literary Characters. New York: Chelsea House, 1992.

Erdinast-Vulcan, Daphna, Alan H. Simmons, and J. H. Stape. *Joseph Conrad: The Short Fiction.* Atlanta: Rodopi, 2004.

Spittles, Brian. *How to Study a Joseph Conrad Novel.* New York: Macmillan, 1990.

Wake, Paul. *Conrad's Marlow: Narrative and Death in "Youth," Heart of Darkness, Lord Jim, and Chance.* Manchester: Manchester University Press, 2008.

THE SECRET AGENT

READING TO WRITE

*T*HE *SECRET Agent: A Simple Tale* looks like a detective story. The writer may, of course, examine this novel as one. However, because Conrad shifts the order of his story, it is unlike the carefully plotted chronological police story that we may be accustomed to. This is not written in the manner of a suspense novel. The arrangement of the story does not promote and build suspense in the manner of a "page turner." The reader may soon see that the anarchists themselves are not a formidable antagonist and the chase after them is not the most important element of this story. When writing on Conrad's *The Secret Agent,* the writer may consider the wider theme of corruption. How does it spread through the city life of this novel like a plague, so that it infects different characters?

The Secret Agent would probably be more of a thriller if it were plotted like one. Instead, Conrad plays with chronology and sequence. In addition, Conrad employs dramatic irony. The writer might recognize a mock-heroic comedy at work here in Conrad's story. This is more a story of antiheroes than of characters that possess the qualities of courage, wisdom, or honor that would distinguish a character as a hero. The revolutionists of *The Secret Agent* (1907) have conspiracies, move toward disaster, ruin a woman and a mentally challenged boy named Stevie. The story is set in the city. There is no movement or escape to the sea, as in other Conrad stories. Why? Russian politics becomes Conrad's subject. Yet, the story itself is not about Russia. Nor is it like the Russian stories of Tolstoy or Dostoevsky, in which characters explore moral issues. Adolf Verloc and Winnie Verloc are not going to explore moral questions.

Political anarchism is not the primary theme, despite the idea that anarchists are planning to blow up the Greenwich Observatory. The writer might explore how Conrad develops *The Secret Agent* as an indictment of the city or of the modern world. Here the city appears to alienate humanity. *The Secret Agent* is filled with large plans that have small results. Expectations fall apart here. Characters are small, bumbling, and alienated. The novel seems to say that life is messy and cannot be so neatly planned.

TOPICS AND STRATEGIES

This section of the chapter will discuss possible topics for essays on *The Secret Agent* and will offer some general approaches to these topics. This is a series of suggestions intended to inspire your own inquiry. You may find a topic that follows a useful place from which to start your essay. Use this material to prompt your thinking about the novel. After you jot down your ideas and analyze relevant passages in the novel, you should formulate your claim, the argument you want your essay to make. Then, you can go back to your notes and begin to provide the evidence for your claim, organizing and arranging your thoughts into a persuasive essay.

Themes

A novel's themes are those major ideas or issues that the story is considering. There are several key questions that Joseph Conrad reflects on in his works. Each work expresses a distinctive perspective on the themes with which it deals. Your job as a writer is to discover and articulate this perspective in your essay. Identify a central theme in the work and then think about how it is addressed in the narrative. In your view, what is being said about the theme? If you read closely and ask questions about what you have read, you will develop your own line of argument. Focus on close reading and what you think the work is saying about a particular issue. This will help you to develop a claim on which to build your essay. Always make sure to write to express the point that you have to make about the themes that you see in this novel. Clearly define the main points that you want to make. You do not need to write about the entire novel; stick to your main idea. Avoid straying into unrelated tangents of thought. Bring your essay back to focus on your main points. Whatever your interpretive approach, it should be supported with evidence from the text.

Sample Topics:

1. **The city:** How is the city portrayed in this novel? How does this environment affect the characters?

   The Secret Agent is a novel in which the action is concentrated and focused within the city of London. It is not as sprawling as *Nostromo* or as varied as *Lord Jim*. *The Secret Agent* begins in its urban setting with Verloc marching to the embassy, entering a grimy street. It is "a street which could with every propriety be described as private. In its breadth, emptiness, and extent it had the majesty of inorganic nature, of matter that never dies" (13–14). The street is "an immensity of greasy slime and damp plaster interspersed with lamps and enveloped, oppressed, penetrated, choked and suffocated by the blackness of a wet London night" (150). Here children play with "joyless, rowdy clamour" (151) and "lonely" pianos play in the public houses. We come to a spot where amid "the grimy sky, the mud of the streets" one sees that "A dismal row of newspaper sellers standing clear of the pavement dealt out their wares from the gutter" (79). How do environment and character intersect? How are characters related to this city? In what ways in this setting filled with brutality or loneliness or the fear that we see in Winnie Verloc? If the London of this story is clouded, muddy, hungry, and filled with shadows, in what ways are the characters part of this?

2. **Irony:** How does Conrad use irony in this novel?

   An ironic attitude permeates this novel. Conrad writes: "The practice of his life [. . .] had consisted precisely in betraying the secret and unlawful proceedings of his fellow-men" (245). In reading this story, observe the strong ironic tone. It is often important to give attention to Conrad's uses of irony. The ironic method is a way of emphasizing the theme. For example, explore Conrad's attitude toward the police and how they interact with the criminal elements of this society. The irony implicit in the book is that the police, who should serve the law, are evidently as morally corrupt as the anarchists. You can explore how the police and the criminals are in a relationship, in which each needs the other to exist.

3. **Order and anarchy:** How are order and anarchy blurred in this novel?

Order and anarchy ought to be opposites. They are blurred here. The Professor claims, "The terrorist and the policeman both come from the same basket." As you read, you may notice that Conrad's police in this novel are as shady as his terrorists. Given this pervading corruption, what is he saying about the public moral order? How is this social condition reflected in the faces of these characters? You might write an essay in which you point out how his descriptions of the characters suggest their moral turpitude. Even Inspector Heat is "marred by too much flesh" (116). You might also examine how characters like Adolf Verloc, Michaelis, or the Professor reflect their environment. Do you think that Conrad is critical of the order of the society in his novel, as well as of the anarchy that he portrays?

Character

When you write about Conrad, consider character development and how he employs and pursues it in his work. As you read his novels and stories, observe how the characters act. Do his characters change? Do they reveal themselves as the story progresses? Your paper can focus on questions of character development or the author's method of characterization. It is helpful to investigate how we come to know the characters. In Conrad's work, this is particularly tricky at times because of the shifting of viewpoint narrators. So read closely. Characters in Conrad's work often use language and mannerisms of speech peculiar or specifically matched to them. The way in which a character speaks or inhabits a space can offer clues to his or her inner workings and motivations.

Sample Topics:

1. **Winnie Verloc:** Winnie Verloc's story and her problems are central to the novel. In an author's note, Conrad pointed to this. Her story is filled with "Utter desolation, madness, and despair." She feels no love for her husband, a mysterious and insecure man. Her mother is crippled. Her brother is mentally handicapped. The life of the Verlocs participates in the desolation of the city. You might explore how. Winnie and Adolph Verloc have married not for love but for convenience and security. Yet, there is an atmosphere of insecurity in their lives. The writer can describe this uneasy atmosphere of Winnie's life and the emptiness of her relations with her husband. One may describe how Winnie Verloc is surrounded by moral and physical decay and how her despair is conveyed.

   Winnie is nonpolitical and poor. The narrator says, "The visions of Mrs. Verloc lacked nobility and magnificence." This is another way of saying that she tends to be ignorant and that her mental life is a bit limited. She has no great dreams or range of mind. Rather, there is devotion, but she is short-sighted. How do you view Winnie Verloc and the role she plays in this novel?

2. **Stevie:** How is Stevie a sympathetic character?

   The relationship between Winnie and Stevie is also important. Conrad sets these two characters side by side. She is Stevie's protector. You might make a list of Stevie's qualities and his limitations and think about how other characters treat him. Take notice of the ways in which Winnie Verloc relates to Stevie. The closeness of this relationship has consequences, and this leads to the conclusion of the novel. The writer might reflect on how the relationship between Winnie, Stevie, and Winnie's husband, Verloc, and his dealings lead to this ending. Why is Stevie chosen to be a victim in this story? Is Conrad suggesting that people like Stevie are victimized by society?

3. **Adolf Verloc:** Adolf Verloc moves in anarchistic circles, where he is not known by name. What does this anonymity have to do with this story and with him as a character?

We see Adolf Verloc sitting at the back of his store, a "square box of a place," with "eyes naturally heavy" and "an air of having been wallowed, fully dressed, all day long on an unmade bed." If Verloc is alienated and lost in this big city, what is being suggested here about the city's indifference to the fate of the individual? Do you think that Verloc is anonymous in every area of his life? Verloc is a member of the proletariat who harbors "a rather inimical sentiment against social distinction" (245). How is he a man of false appearances and of duplicity? How is he idealistic? What does this result in? Verloc is a gray, idle, enervated character. We read: "His idleness . . . suited him very well . . . He was too lazy for even a mere demagogue, for a workman orator, for a leader of labour. It was too much trouble" (12). This passivity pervades his environment—from his parlor to the city. Verloc is a vacuum of vice and degeneracy, and there is about him "the air common to men who live on the vices, the follies, or the baser fears of mankind; the air of moral nihilism common to keepers of gambling halls and disorderly houses; to private detectives and inquiry agents . . . (13). You might write an essay describing this character and his motives, considering him in relation to Winnie Verloc and Stevie or to the anarchists.

4. **The Professor:** How does the Professor represent alienation and evil?

The Professor is a cold character who always carries a bomb around that is strapped to him. He is immediately characterized as stiff, unfeeling, and stoic:

> The Professor turned into the street to the left, and walked along, with his head carried rigidly erect, in a crowd whose every individual almost overtopped his stunted stature. It was vain to pretend to himself that he was not disappointed. But

that was mere feeling; the stoicism of his thought could not be disturbed by this or any other failure. Next time, or the time after next, a telling stroke would be delivered—something really startling—a blow fit to open the first crack in the imposing front of the edifice of legal conceptions sheltering the atrocious injustice of society.

The extreme, almost ascetic poverty of his thought, combined with an astounding ignorance of worldly conditions, had set before him a goal of power and prestige to be attained without the medium of arts, graces, tact, wealth—by sheer weight of merit alone. On that view he considered himself entitled to undisputed success. (73)

Do you see here a portrait of a terrorist? One might consider the Professor psychologically. The Professor's anarchism and aggression cover a neurosis, a struggle with being an outcast. Indeed, the writer could view the Professor as psychotic. His inner disorder prompts his outer quest for disorder. The Professor advocates a society in which "the weak" ought to be eliminated. He supports a racial hygiene or eugenics, which was in the air of scientific discussion at the time this novel was written. The Professor says: "First the great multitude of the weak must go, then the only relatively strong. You see? First the blind, then the deaf and the dumb, then the halt and the lame—and so on. . . ." What do you think of this attitude? The Professor, despite all his inner lameness, asserts, "I remain—if I am strong enough." In this world, the Professor is a "deadly . . . pest in the street full of men" (311). For Conrad, self-interest like this is poor behavior. How is Conrad criticizing the nihilism of this view?

5. **Characterization through setting:** How are characters in this story characterized through the settings in which they live?

The writer can explore how Mr. Verloc's environment reflects his personality. Why does Conrad set Verloc in a tiny shop in London? How does his manner of conducting business reflect his personality? The novel introduces Mr. Verloc within the confines of his shop:

> The shop was small, and so was the house. It was one of those grimy brick houses which existed in large quantities before the era of reconstruction dawned on London. The shop was a square box of a place, with the front glazed in small panes. In the daytime the door remained closed; in the evening it stood discreetly but suspiciously ajar.

You can follow Mr. Verloc as chapter 9 begins with him in a darker mood:

> Mr. Verloc, returning from the Continent at the end of ten days, brought back a mind evidently unrefreshed by the wonders of foreign travel and a countenance unlighted by the joys of home-coming. He entered in the clatter of the shop-bell with an air of somber and vexed exhaustion. His bag in hand, his head lowered, he strode straight behind the counter, and let himself fall into the chair, as though he had tramped all the way from Dover.

The writer might contrast certain moments of Mr. Verloc's life with others, as his demeanor and environment change. For example, chapter 2 begins:

> Such was the house, the household, and the business Mr. Verloc left behind him on his way westward at the hour of half-past ten in the morning. It was unusually early for him; his whole person exhaled the charm of almost dewy freshness; he wore his blue cloth overcoat unbuttoned; his boots were shiny; his cheeks, freshly shaven, had a sort of gloss; and even his heavy-lidded eyes, refreshed by a night of peaceful slumber, sent out glances of comparative alertness (9).

History and Context

In his introduction to the novel, Conrad said he "began this novel impulsively and wrote it continuously" (xxi). The idea came "in the shape of a few words uttered to a friend in a casual conversation about anarchists or rather anarchist activities" (xiii). Anarchism was in the air during the time Conrad and his wife lived at "the Pent," Ford Maddox Ford's summer home. Conrad mentions that he was struck by the "criminal futility" of the anarchists.

Today we live in a world in which terrorism is a harsh reality. Conrad's tale has been recognized as important for our reflections. However, even if we recognize terrorist activity in Conrad's novel, his story is very much of its own time and context. The writer can investigate the historical context in which Conrad wrote. Conrad studied the history of these anarchists and argued against their premises.

At the beginning of chapter 3, we hear Michaelis: "History is made by men, but they do not make it in their heads. The ideas that are born in their consciousness play an insignificant part in the march of events. History is dominated and determined by the tool and the production— by the force of economic conditions." (41)

This is a view of history that follows the thought of Karl Marx, who wrote that economic forces of production were fundamental in the historical process. For Marx, the dialectic, a tension of opposing economic forces or classes, is responsible for history. How does this philosophy lie behind the action promoted by Michaelis? How is Conrad arguing against this view with his novel?

Sample Topics:

1. **Anarchism:** Conrad set out to explore the attraction of anarchy and revolution in the late nineteenth century. What was this attraction?

   The problem of anarchism was often on the mind of Conrad, who tended to be politically conservative. In a letter to Cunninghame Graham in February 1899, Conrad distinguished between an anarchist and a "peace man" who urges that men be brothers and some day can be. A writer might explore how anarchism in this novel is very different from the kind of nonviolent reform that was advocated by Gandhi in India.

   Anarchism displayed a violent side in the last decades of the nineteenth century. In 1881, Czar Alexander II and American president James Garfield were assassinated by anarchists. In 1901, President William McKinley was shot by an anarchist born of Polish immigrants. Anarchism was a great concern in the 1890s during the proletarian growth in Russia that led to worker strikes. It also emerged in the syndicalist movement in France, a workers' movement for which George Sorel advocated violence. In London, on February 15, 1894, Martial Bourdin blew himself up with a bomb in a London park and Conrad read reports of this.

Revolution was occurring in Russia, even as Conrad wrote his novel. Marxist parties, the Bolsheviks and the Mensheviks, split in 1905 and a revolution swept across that country. In 1904–05, the defeat of Russia by Japan encouraged Conrad to write a political essay and reflection on Russian politics. He wondered if there might be political "rational progress" inside of Russia. "I am greatly moved by the news from Russia," he wrote to Ada Galsworthy on November 2, 1905. "Certainly, a year ago, I never hoped to live to see all of that." Instead, what emerged were violence and revolution.

In an essay, the writer can explore this history and Conrad's response to it with his novel. Conrad will not defend anarchism as a political stance, observes Eloise Knapp Hay, who has written about politics in Conrad's novels (242). In fact, Conrad is very critical of anarchism. In *The Secret Agent*, the Professor, a violent anarchist, is seeking shelter from a humanity he distrusts and he would destroy anything. The chief inspector is cool and wise and upholds "what is normal in the constitution of society" (93). You can write on which position Conrad favors and why.

2. **Class and social circumstances:** Investigate the culture of London at the turn of the twentieth century.

This novel is filled with images of the city, where some people live in material conditions of poverty. By reading carefully through the novel, you can trace some of these images. You can then write about the impact that this environment may have on people who live in it. Some research into the lower class culture of London at the turn of the century would provide a context for illustrating your paper with greater detail. For example, you might locate information on lodging houses. Or you might consider the social treatment of people like Stevie, who is mentally challenged. The Salvation Army was started only a few years before to assist poor people. Early sociologists, like Charles Booth, were writing about the life of London laborers and the poor. Some people who were well off had gone "slumming" to identify with the poor by living among them. There were efforts by ministers and social workers. You might set your thoughts about Conrad's portrayal of this class alongside some of these sociological and historical accounts.

Philosophy and Ideas

Conrad can be explored for his political and philosophical beliefs. We find in Joseph Conrad's work themes of isolation and community, meditations on death, concerns with guilt and shame, reflections on language, admonitions to see clearly and avoid illusions, understandings of human interaction with nature, and assertions of individuality, the power of love, and the value of hard work. As you read through his novels, you will see that Conrad offers his readers characters and situations that compel us to think about moral decision making, human sympathy and pity, the value of restraint and moderation, and the importance of honor. In Conrad's life and works, there is an emphasis on ethics, inquiries into colonialism, opposition to anarchism, and reflections on romance, marriage and family, science, and the emerging modern world.

In writing about a Conrad novel you might examine a few of the philosophical ideas that arise. With Conrad, you will have to spend some time reflecting on issues of identity, isolation, community, subjectivity and individuality, knowledge and skepticism. He was a writer who was concerned with ethics and responsibility and with knowledge and subjectivity. To inquire into ideas or problems such as these, you can look at the questions that the characters themselves ask. One might also work to identify themes that move through the novel.

Sample Topics:

1. **Modern science:** What might Conrad be suggesting about modern science in this novel?

Science grew in prestige and social importance in the last decades of the nineteenth century. Its connection with technology was indisputable. Is Conrad making a comment in this novel about the admiration and adulation of science? Chemistry is involved in the anarchist's scheming. One might write on the elements of science that are here. You might look at the dialogue from characters, like Ossipon, who claim to speak for science but show little or no feeling. Is Conrad suggesting that science is unable to communicate with human emotion? When Ossipon "scientifically" points out Cesar Lombroso's study of criminality, he implies his own ignorance, since such studies based in scientific materialism cannot encompass human emotions. You might research Lombroso's specious "science," in which he claimed that physical characteristics pointed to criminality.

Conrad casts his irony toward dehumanizing science or instrumentality. The plan to bomb the Greenwich Observatory is a plot hatched ironically as an attack on science. Vladimir says, "A bomb in the National Gallery would make some noise. But it would not be serious enough. Art has never been their fetish. . . ." Therefore, they will attack science, which is. In your essay, you might explore the reasons why the anarchists attack the observatory. What does it symbolize?

2. **Alienation:** How do the anarchists express alienation and moral corruption?

The larger picture in which the anarchists move is one of immorality and alienation. Conrad does not emphasize the anarchists because political anarchy itself is not the theme of the novel. Rather, the main theme is the overshadowing moral corruption that affects every character here. The writer can look at specific scenes and dialogue among the anarchists or the police that shows that Conrad is not intending a realistic treatment of forms of anarchism. Instead, he is showing how this moral corruption touches everyone: the anarchists, the police, and the Verlocs.

The anarchists appear to have an overall indifference to life. They are shams and are not formidable forces that anyone can take seriously. Ossipon, the Professor, Karl Yundt, and Michaelis are treated ironically, as "would be" terrorists who express an utter lack of humanity. They are ciphers, or hollow men. Critics say that Conrad does not depict anarchists historically. You can write on why you think that Conrad portrayed these anarchists as ridiculous.

3. **Communications breakdown:** How does communication break down between the people in this story?

Interpersonal relations are built and strengthened through communication. However, here in Conrad's novel there is a breakdown in communication. Follow the conversations that occur in this novel. What do these conversations suggest about the relationships between the characters? Winnie Verloc and Adolph Verloc engage in a communication that is a bit strained and distant. Winnie and Ossipon are unable to communicate with each other. In Frederick Karl's view, Conrad is saying that failing to communicate and to be honest with each other reflects a failure of morality. What do you think? How is Conrad suggesting that people need to have respect for one another and a sense of ethical conduct to recognize one another's needs? How does the interaction between Winnie Verloc and Ossipon, for example, show the opposite of this capacity to listen and understand?

Form and Genre

Sample Topics:

1. **Irony in storytelling:** Why does Conrad tell his story in an ironic way?

Conrad often makes use of irony in his writing. This is a device by which he is able to treat his story in a detached manner. The way the story is told "is to make very large the distance between the way things appear to the persons in the story and the way they are made to appear to the reader," says E.M.W. Tillyard. The characters in this story have little self-awareness. They are all caught up in something that we, the readers, can begin to see. Verloc covers up a great deal from others and from himself. He wears a hat and a heavy overcoat indoors. What correlation can the writer make between the city's materialism and the shadow of despair that is lingering over these characters' lives? What are these characters unaware of that we, the readers, can see in their lives and actions?

2. **Social analysis:** How is Conrad analyzing his society, while also critiquing it through satire?

There is a turn to dark comedy and satire in *The Secret Agent.* You can explore the narrator's tone throughout this story. Satire is a means for critiquing a society and its flaws. It holds up human folly, vices, and shortcomings to view by using irony, dark comedy, or other means. The mode of satire has a long history. It appears in the eighteenth century in the work of Jonathan Swift in *Gulliver's Travels* and Alexander Pope in *The Dunciad.* In the nineteenth century, we see satire in the writing of Charles Dickens, who was one of Conrad's favorite authors. You might investigate how Dickens's satire and London settings perhaps served as models for some of Conrad's London scenes in this story. What social critique do you see in this story? Who, or what, is Conrad critiquing?

Language, Symbols, and Imagery

In a novel in which setting is such an important factor, you can expect that some of the images and objects that you see as you read are also symbolic. Read carefully through the passages that describe this city landscape. How does this environment reflect the preoccupations of the characters or their issues in life? Pay close attention to specific objects that are focused on in the narration.

Sample Topics:

1. **The cab:** How does the cab act as a symbol in this story? Does it bring the characters anywhere or only in a kind of circle, like the circles that Stevie draws?

The cab ride to the charity home that is taken by Winnie, Stevie, and their mother is among the most arresting scenes of this novel. The city looms around them with a sense of "impending chaos." This scene takes about 16 pages. Following the cab ride closely, a writer can examine the ways in which symbolism is at work here. The cab has the qualities of a torture chamber or a death cab pulled along by a horse that is a figure of doom. The cab, Conrad writes, "was so profoundly lamentable, with such a perfection of grotesque misery and weirdness of macabre detail, as if it were the Cab of death itself." The grotesque extends to objects, as in the cab ride. We see the cab "like a medieval device for the punishment of a crime, or some very new-fangled invention for the cure of a sluggish liver" (163). Read the scene closely and try to develop some thoughts about the images that you see.

2. **The horse:** How is the horse symbolic of animals and people being mistreated?

The horse is an object of sympathy for Stevie. How is this a reflection of man's inhumanity? How do the horse and Stevie reflect each other? Stevie urges the driver not to whip the horse. The simple, mentally challenged person is faced with the harsh, impersonal city. The driver responds: "'Ard on 'osses, but dam sight—on poor chaps like me." The writer may wish to explore how the theme of moral corruption, or insensitivity, might be related to this. We see in Stevie much sensitivity as he tries to replace indifference with care for innocent creatures. He, too, is an innocent creature in a grimy city that is caught in a web of crime. He pleads for kindness and humanity in a world that seems deprived of this. He is lost in a world of expediency, cruelty, and callousness:

> Stevie was staring at the horse, whose hind quarters appeared unduly elevated by the effect of emaciation; a little stiff tail seemed to have been fitted in for a hearty joke; and at the other end the thin, flat neck like a p___ covered with old horsehide, drooped to the ground, under the weight of an enormous

bony head. The ears hung at different angles, negligently; and the macabre figure of the mute dweller on the earth seemed straight up from the — and backbone in the muddy stillness of the air.

3. **Stevie's drawing circles:** As the writer examines the character of Stevie, attention should be given to his curious habit of drawing circles. What might Conrad mean by this?

The circle is a geometrical figure that has a kind a kind of completion: Wherever one begins it comes around into a whole. There is a kind of order in this. How is this order in contrast with the disorder of the city or Stevie's own imperfections? Stevie is a simple and beautiful soul in a city of misshapen grotesques who clash over materialistic ends. How does this novel critique insensitivity?

4. **Grotesques:** The writer might explore how Conrad's characters are grotesques. What is excessive or macabre in these descriptions? Do they suggest a distorted world?

A grotesque is an odd, deformed character. This exaggeration of a character's peculiar traits is often used in satire. Verloc is "burly, in fat-pig style" (13). We see in Yundt that "an extraordinary expression of underhand malevolence survived in his extinguished eyes." He thrusts forth a hand "deformed by gouty swellings" that suggests murderous intent (42). Michaelis has "an enormous stomach and distended cheeks of a pale, semi-transparent complexion, as though for fifteen years the servants of an outraged society had made a point of stuffing him with fattening foods in a damp and lightless cellar" (41). Ossipon has "a flattened nose and prominent mouth in the rough mould of the negro type" (44). One gets the sense that this is not a favorable appearance. The Professor is clearly a miserable grotesque. We read that "his flat, large ears departed widely from the sides of his skull." His cheeks are "flat" and he is "of a greasy, unhealthy complexion" (62). Why are these characters so misshapen? Does the way they appear suggest the state of their souls? What eccentricity, contradictions, or inconsistencies do you see in these characters?

Bibliography and Online Resources for *The Secret Agent*

Bethoud, Jacques. *"The Secret Agent." Cambridge Companion to Joseph Conrad.* Cambridge: Cambridge University Press, 1996.

www.booth.lse.ac.uk, Charles Booth Library, maps and information on London, 1885–1910.

Eagleton, Terry. "Form, Ideology and *The Secret Agent*," *Joseph Conrad.* Ed. Elaine Jordan. New York: St. Martin's Press, 1996.

Gillon, Adam. "The Desperate Shape of Betrayal: An Intimate Alliance of Contradictions," *Joseph Conrad.* Twayne: Boston, 1982.

Najder, Zdzislaw. "Joseph Conrad's *The Secret Agent*, or the Melodrama of Reality," *Conrad in Perspective: Essays on Art and Fidelity.* Cambridge: Cambridge University Press, 1997, pp. 110–18.

Panichas, George A. *Joseph Conrad: His Moral Vision.* Mercer University Press, 2005.

Ross, Stephen. *Conrad and Empire.* Columbia: University of Missouri Press, 2004.

Schauder, Ludwig. *Free-Will and Determinism in Joseph Conrad's Major Novels.* Amsterdam: Rodopi, 2009.

Simmons, Alan H. ed. *The Secret Agent: Centennial Essays.* Amsterdam: Rodopi, 2007.

Spillers, Brian. *How to Study a Joseph Conrad Novel.* New York and London: Macmillan, 1990.

Tillyard, E.M.W. "*The Secret Agent* Reconsidered," *Essays in Criticism* (July 1961): 309–19.

www.victorianlondon.org/frame/maps.html, historical maps of London.

"THE SECRET SHARER"

READING TO WRITE

"THE SECRET Sharer" is another of Conrad's best-known short stories. The narrator is a young captain in his first command of a ship. As you begin to read, you will likely have the sense that the captain is not trusted by the crew and that he has begun to feel like a stranger on his own ship. The reader is soon introduced to the captain's double: a fugitive who appears mysteriously and is given refuge on his ship. Alone one night, the captain sees a man floating in a glow on the bottom of a rope ladder. Leggatt is this man, and he was the first mate of another ship. He has killed a man and was being taken to Bangkok for trial when he escaped. The reader soon recognizes that the captain feels sympathy for Leggatt, as he hides him in his cabin. When the officer seeking him, Captain Archbold, visits the next day, he is shown the ship without any word being said about Leggatt. The captain plans the fugitive's escape by sailing close to the islands, claiming that he wants to get more of the land breezes into his ship's sails. Leggatt escapes overboard, his hat blowing back on the waves. The captain shifts the helm to save the ship and gains the respect of the crew.

When writing on "The Secret Sharer," the writer has to come to terms with the symbolic nature of the story. The darkness, the ocean, the headless figure, and the secret self all suggest the unconscious. Does the captain come to terms with his own dark nature through his encounter with Leggatt? In what way is Leggatt his "double" or his "other self?" The writer can observe that these words occur often in the story. How does Leggatt inspire boldness in the captain?

170

As the story opens, there is loneliness about the ship and the man on deck. The narrator is a stranger on a vast ocean, under a dark sky. The captain wonders whether he will measure up to the "ideal conception of one's personality every man sets up for himself secretly." The writer might examine the anxiety and self-consciousness in this statement. Does this reflective captain, who wonders if he will be able to face this challenge, indeed meet the challenge?

TOPICS AND STRATEGIES

This section of the chapter will discuss possible topics for essays on "The Secret Sharer" and will offer some general approaches to these topics. This is a series of suggestions intended to inspire your own inquiry. You may find a topic that follows a useful place from which to start your essay. Use this material to prompt your thinking about the novel. After you jot down your ideas and analyze relevant passages in the novel, you should formulate your claim, the argument you want your essay to make. Then, you can go back to your notes and begin to provide the evidence for your claim, organizing and arranging your thoughts into a persuasive essay.

Themes

A novel's themes are those major ideas or issues that the story is considering. There are several key questions that Joseph Conrad reflects on in his works. Each work expresses a unique perspective on the themes with which it deals. Your job as a writer is to discover and articulate this perspective in your essay. Identify a central theme in the work and then think about how it is addressed in the narrative. In your view, what is being said about the theme? If you read closely and ask questions about what you have read, you will develop your own line of argument. Focus on close reading and what you think the work is saying about a particular issue. This will help you to develop a claim on which to build your essay. Always make sure to write to express the point that you have to make about the themes that you see in this novel. Clearly define the main points that you want to make. You do not need to write about the entire novel; stick to your main idea. Avoid straying into unrelated tangents of thought. Bring your essay back to focus on your main points. Whatever your interpretive approach, it should be supported with evidence from the text.

Sample Topics:

1. **Motives:** A writer may explore the captain's motives and his responses to the secret guest, the fugitive. He hides Leggatt from the law. Isn't the captain supposed to represent leadership and uphold the law?

   "The Secret Sharer" concerns the individual's ethical choices. This is an important focus in Conrad's fiction, across many of his novels and short stories. The alter-ego, or other self, appears here. The issue of sympathy and self-identification with this other character is present in this story. The young captain's authority is not yet tested by command of a ship at sea. There is some insecurity, or self-doubt, as he faces this challenge. "I was somewhat of a stranger to myself," the captain thought. "I wondered how far I should turn out faithful to that ideal conception of one's own personality every man sets up for himself secretly."

   In writing about "The Secret Sharer," the writer might consider the ambiguities of the moral plot. The writer can write about whether the title refers to a hidden double or a sharer of secrets. Alternatively, an equally strong essay can lay bare the captain's motives. Filled with sympathy for the escaped prisoner, he makes choices that contradict his role as a captain. What might the captain's reasons be? Do you agree with his reasoning?

2. **Loyalty and standards:** Why does the captain conceal his double from the crew?

   The captain and the fugitive seem to mirror each other. The captain believes that there were mitigating circumstances behind Leggatt's action. Rather than following the code of law, he risks his own reputation. He conceals the fugitive. The writer may examine this deception and how this violates the moral core of the captain. What issues of loyalty and standards are at stake? The captain is aware of what is happening to him as he perpetrates this. One can write about whether the captain would have done the same thing if he were in Leggatt's position. You can examine the choice that the captain is making as one between loyalty to the community's law and standards and his own conscience.

3. **Leadership:** Is this captain a capable leader? Does he properly exercise his leadership role?

Observing that this is the young captain's first voyage in command of a ship, the writer might ask what this story suggests about leadership or about a rite of passage or a kind of initiation. How does a person new to an important job face his or her task? How does this character approach decision making? Has he given up on his responsibility for leadership? What qualities ought a sea captain to have? After identifying these qualities, such as courage, trust, and fidelity to the crew and the voyage, one might write on leadership. Is this captain lacking in personal ethics? What qualities does he need to develop as a leader?

Conrad confronts us with the practical imperatives of seafaring. If Leggatt is being pursued as a murderer, why is Leggatt being concealed? Is this ethical? Is it necessary? Must a captain of a ship be ethical? If difficulty emerges on board the ship, may a life be sacrificed if it imperils the safety of those on board the ship? Is such a practical solution called for? Is this stronger than codes of law? In your paper you might investigate whether this captain makes good choices.

Characters

When you write about Conrad, consider character development and how he employs and pursues it in his work. As you read his novels and stories, observe how the characters act. Do his characters change? Do they reveal themselves as the story progresses? Your paper can focus on questions of character development or the author's method of characterization. It is helpful to investigate how we come to know the characters. In Conrad's work, this is particularly tricky at times because of the shifting of viewpoint narrators. So read closely. Characters in Conrad's work often use language and mannerisms of speech peculiar or specifically matched to them. The way in which a character speaks or inhabits a space can offer clues to his or her inner workings and motivations.

Sample Topics:

1. **The captain:** What is implied here about the character of the captain?

   This story suggests that Leggatt is somehow the captain's double. What is it that they have in common? How is Leggatt reflective of an aspect of the captain's personality? To write about this, explore where in the text connections are made between the captain and Leggatt. How are these men characterized? Are they mirrors of each other? If the captain comes to depend on something about Leggatt, what is it? What psychological struggle is going on in the captain?

2. **Leggatt, the fugitive:** Describe Leggatt. What are Legatt's characteristics? Does a lawless self exist in Legatt? What relationship exists between the captain and Legatt?

   Leggatt is discovered to be a criminal. The captain describes Leggatt as intelligent and sane, but perhaps he is more a creature of the irrational unconscious. What do you think? You might explore how Leggatt is an instinctual creature, full of appetites and abruptness. Leggatt's language reflects this. "He told me the story roughly, in brusque, disconnected sentences" (131). You might show how Leggatt provokes anxiety. What kind of personality do you detect in him?

   Some critics have suggested that Leggatt represents the criminal aspect of the narrator's life. Other critics have turned this around and suggested that Leggatt actually represents a higher self, rather than a fallen one. Leggatt is the captain's ideal. You might also write about this. However, it is clear that, whatever identification the captain feels, he and Leggatt are quite different. In your writing, you might explore this difference and contrast Leggatt and the captain.

3. **Doubling:** How are the captain and Leggatt doubles of each other?

   This is one of the central questions that this story raises. The captain risks everything for Leggatt, to ensure his survival. We read that Leggatt "followed me like my double on the poop" (100). How are the captain and Leggatt mutually interconnected? We read, "the shadowy dark head, like mine, seemed to nod imperceptibly" (101) and Leggatt has become "my double" (102), "my own grey ghost" (103), "my other self" (111), and "the secret sharer of my life" (114). The captain says, "I felt dual" (112). We read: "The double captain slipped past the stairs" (138). How is Leggatt the captain's double? In the story's final sentence, we hear of "The secret sharer of my cabin and of my thoughts, as though he were my second self . . ." (143). We read, "Their hands meet and clasp for a second. . . . No word was breathed by either of us when they separated" (138). Your essay might explore the ways in which Legatt and the captain seem inseparable. What is it that they share?

4. **Archbold:** Is Captain Archbold, the man who is looking for Leggatt, a good man or a bad one?

As part 2 begins, Leggatt hides only a few feet away, as the captain greets Archbold, a man who is looking for Leggatt. Then the captain, pretending deafness, leads Archbold around the ship and away from the object of his search: Leggatt. In considering this scene, the writer may ask about the captain's deception or about Archbold's weaknesses of character. If Archbold is portrayed as stubborn rather than charitable, how is Archbold the enemy or villain here? The writer may also wish to probe the loyalties that emerge between the captain and Leggatt, the fugitive.

5. **Rites of initiation:** What initiation does the captain experience in this story? Is there any initiation for Leggatt?

Observing that this is the young captain's first voyage in command of a ship, the writer might ask what this story suggests about a rite of passage or a kind of initiation. How does a person new to an important job face his or her task? How does this character approach decision making? Has he given up on his responsibility for leadership? What qualities ought a sea captain to have? After identifying these qualities, such as courage, trust, and fidelity to the crew and the voyage, one might write on leadership. Is this captain lacking in personal ethics? What qualities does he need to develop?

What about Leggatt? Has he received an initiation and learned something? What will be Leggatt's future? Based on what you have read, you may speculate on the future of Leggatt beyond this story. In the final lines of the story, Leggatt is referred to as "a free man, a swimmer striking out for a new destiny." Is he? If Leggatt is a fugitive, does he have much of a future? On what qualities would this exile from humanity build this future?

Philosophy and Ideas

The psychologist Carl Jung has written about the shadow self, an undiscovered self that includes qualities or attributes that we might deny because they are unpleasant. The writer may probe "The Secret Sharer" for this shadow in the character of the captain. Are people so complex that there are shadow sides to them? Jung frequently spoke of the need to integrate the self. Can the captain, in facing what Leggatt means for him, overcome things within himself and be a more whole person? The Germans have spoken of the doppelganger, or the double. This is a figure that often appears in late nineteenth-century literature, from Stevenson's Dr. Jekyll and Mr. Hyde on through Oscar Wilde's Dorian Gray. How are Conrad's captain and Leggatt a development of this? How does it reflect the search for unity and psychological wholeness in the early years of the twentieth century?

Sample Topics:

1. **The shadow:** What is the shadow side of the captain's personality? How does Leggatt reflect this?

   In writing on "The Secret Sharer," one can explore the darker sides of the self in these characters. How is there a division of the respectable self and what Albert Guerard calls the "interior outlaw self that repudiated law and tradition?" (*Conrad the Novelist*, p. 26). Psychologist Robert Lifton theorized a similar divide in the psyche of the Nazis engaged in the so-called "Final Solution" of the Holocaust. Many readers have suggested that Leggatt represents the darker side of the captain's own life and mind. How is the captain a divided self? What is the ideal captain? Is this character a failure in this role? What interferes with leadership, or with wholeness? Albert Guerard says, "in broad terms 'The Secret Sharer' concerns the classic night journey and willed descent into the unconscious" (*Conrad the Novelist*, p. 26). In his view, we have to "subdue those selves which interfere with seamanship" (31). Does this captain experience his own complexity and realize some acceptance of his shadow side? If so, is there any psychic integration? Can this captain become a whole person?

2. **The unconscious:** How does "The Secret Sharer" probe the unconscious mind?

Psychologically, is the captain a partial man rather than a whole one? How is Leggatt's action on board the ship instinctual? Early in the twentieth century, psychologists like Sigmund Freud and C. G. Jung probed the unconscious. The writer might consider whether this story has anything to do with this. Does the captain encounter his own unconscious in the form of Leggatt and confront primitive aspects of human nature? What is the captain's self-image? How is the captain forced to face his own actions? What does the captain feel is dark or unacceptable? How is the captain threatened by the emptiness? How does he deal with the instinctual or his knowledge of the irrational in the human? Does he share in Leggatt's crime?

3. **Moral ambiguity:** In writing about "The Secret Sharer," one might consider the ambiguities of the characters and the plot. Does the title refer to a hidden double or a sharer of secrets?

A central concern of this story may be whether the letter of the law should take precedence over the spirit of the law. A writer may explore the captain's motives and his responses to the secret guest, the fugitive. The captain is supposed to represent leadership and law. He has an obligation to support Captain Archbold and to pursue justice in the matter of the fugitive. However, filled with sympathy for the escaped prisoner, he makes choices that contradict his role as a captain. The captain believes that there were mitigating circumstances behind Leggatt's action. Rather than following the code of law, he risks his own reputation. One can write about whether the captain might feel that he would have done the same thing if he were in Leggatt's position. The writer can examine the choice that the captain is making as one between loyalty to the community's law and standards and his own conscience. If Leggatt is being pursued as a murderer, why is Leggatt being concealed? Is this ethical? Is it necessary?

4. **The secret self:** What is the connection between these two men, the captain and the fugitive?

If a writer considers these two characters doubles, or mirror images of each other, he or she can probe the psychology of the captain further. There have been many psychoanalytic approaches to the story. Likewise, there have been numerous interpretations of the moral character of the individuals Conrad has created here. Is the fugitive evil? Is the captain lured by and involved with evil? Or, is the sympathy that guides the captain's action a good thing? This sympathetic identification with an outlaw is central in this story. How might the captain be dealing with something inside of him: his own secret self? Does this captain experience his own complexity and realize some acceptance of his shadowside?

Language, Symbols, and Imagery

In "The Secret Sharer," Conrad carefully controls his structural devices and symbols. This more or less realistic story is able to integrate and support the symbolic elements the author interjects. The symbolism is structured in a way that is nearly allegorical.

Sample Topics:

1. **The sea as symbol:** If the sea is a microcosm of the world for Conrad and it acts as a symbol, how is the stormy sea nonrational and the quiet sea reflective of what is rational?

How is the sea symbolic in this story? If you have ever looked out on the ocean, you have seen that sometimes it appears peaceful. At other times, the waves are rough and stormy. The atmosphere of night and sea surrounds the issue of moral responsibility in this story. The writer may examine how the quiet sea symbolizes rational self-confidence. This is disrupted by something from below the sea: the "unearthing" or uprising of the second self. There is "a blue sea that itself looked solid, so still and stable did it lie below my feet" (91).

One might explore the sea captain's logic. How does reason meet with anxiety, doubt, or the nonrational? Can the individual save himself in the midst of difficulty? In much of Conrad, people are impenetrable to one another. In the case of "The Secret Sharer," what does this captain see of himself in Leggatt? Why this self-identification?

2. **The unconscious:** How do the sea, or the ship, represent the unconscious?

"The Secret Sharer" has sometimes been called a psychological masterpiece. You might explore questions about Leggatt in your paper. What is Leggatt's symbolic nature? Does he represent the captain's moral consciousness? How does he, like the sea, represent our unconscious lives? Is he a criminal aspect of the narrator's life, as Albert Guerard has suggested? If you write from this perspective, you will consider how the sympathetic identification that the narrator feels with Leggatt may be detrimental and how the captain has to overcome this secret self.

Compare and Contrast Essays

Often in writing a paper on literature, one may compare or contrast aspects of the story. Here there appear to be similarities and differences between the captain and Leggatt. You might establish your definition of each of these characters first. Avoid simply listing these similarities or differences. Offer your commentary and apply critical thinking and analysis. Look for what the similarities, or differences, between these characters might mean. You can go to the text of the story for this. Consider the work and what point these similarities between the captain and Leggatt might suggest to you.

Sample Topics:

1. **Comparison with other literary works:** One might compare and contrast "The Secret Sharer" with other literary works.

In Charles Dickens's *Great Expectations*, Magwich, Pip's benefactor, is a criminal and a fugitive at large. Might there be a parallel here between the captain's protection of Leggatt with Pip and his protection of Magwich? Magwich's own double is another criminal who is being pursued. This image of the double appears often in British fin de siècle literature—in Stevenson's *The Strange Tale of Dr. Jekyll and Mr. Hyde* and in Oscar Wilde's *The Picture of Dorian Gray*, and in other works. If the writer is familiar with these stories, the doubling of the captain and Leggatt may be interestingly placed alongside an examination of these other characters.

Bibliography for "The Secret Sharer"

Bloom, Harold ed. *Heart of Darkness and The Secret Sharer.* Modern Critical Interpretations. New York: Chelsea House, 1996.

———. *Joseph Conrad.* Bloom's Major Short Story Writers. New York: Chelsea House, 2001.

Erdnast-Vulcan, Daphna. *The Strange Short Fiction of Joseph Conrad: Writing, Culture, and Subjectivity.* New York and Oxford: Oxford University Press, 1999.

Erdnast-Vulcan, Daphna, Alan H. Simmons, and J. H. Stape, eds. *Joseph Conrad: The Short Fiction.* Atlanta: Rodopi, 2004.

Hansford, James. "Closing, Enclosure and Passage in The Secret Sharer," *The Conradian* 15:1 (1990).

Harkness, Bruce. *Conrad's Secret Sharer and the Critics: A Casebook.* Belmont, CA: Wadsworth, 1962.

Hawthorn, Jeremy. "Symbolism in The Secret Sharer," *Readings on Joseph Conrad,* Ed. Clarice Swisher. San Diego: Greenhaven Press, 1998.

Jones, Michael. "Conrad, The Sea, and The Secret Sharer," *Readings on Joseph Conrad.* Ed. Clarice Swisher. San Diego: Greenhaven Press, 1998.

Moser, Thomas. *Joseph Conrad: Achievement and Decline.* Cambridge, MA: Harvard University Press, 1957.

Schwartz, Daniel R., ed. *The Secret Sharer.* Case Studies in Contemporary Criticism. New York: Bedford/St. Martin's Press, 1997.

Steiner, Joan E. "Conrad's The Secret Sharer: Complexities of the Doubling Relationship," *Conradiana* 12 (1980): 173–86.

Watts, Cedric. "The Mirror Tale: An Ethico-structural Analysis of Conrad's The Secret Sharer," *Critical Quarterly* 19: 3 (1977): 25–37.

Zabel, Morton Dauwen. "Conrad, the Sea, and 'The Secret Sharer,'" Introduction to *The Shadow Line and Two Other Tales.* Ed. Morton Dauwen Zabel. New York: Doubleday, 1959.

NOSTROMO

READING TO WRITE

*N*OSTROMO WAS inspired by a story that Conrad heard while on the Gulf of Mexico on a shipping run in 1875–76. It was also prompted by Ford Maddox Ford and by Conrad's reading of news clippings. The story, which is in three parts, came 26 or so years later. This is a large canvas, one that F. Scott Fitzgerald called "the greatest novel" and "the one I would have rather written . . . than any other novel." *Nostromo* is considered one of Conrad's most important novels. F. R. Leavis called *Nostromo* "one of the great novels of the language." He recognized it as Conrad's "most considerable work." Robert Penn Warren said that the ideal was to read all of Conrad's major works and to set *Nostromo* as "central" to them (x–xi). *Nostromo* may be challenging to read. In *Nostromo*, Conrad shifts time sequences. This novel is not written chronologically. So one of the challenges of *Nostromo* for a reader is determining where we are in the chronology of events.

The writer who is working on *Nostromo* can consider the many ways in which this novel prompts reflection on money, commerce, and politics. In Eloise Knapp Hay's view, the novel is a political one in which moral principle is cast aside for material interests that are considered good for the nation. *Nostromo* is the story of a mine, the community of people affected by this mine, and the character of Nostromo. Nostromo, the story's central character, is employed by the Oceanic Steam Navigation Company at Costaguana, where this story is set. Here in Costaguana, a silver mine is owned by the Gould Concession. Charles and Emily Gould have inherited this mine and plan to make it financially successful. They claim to have the interest of the entire community in mind. Of course, a profitable mine will make the Goulds wealthy. Mr. Gould makes arrangements to have the silver from the mine shipped out of Costaguana. The plan is to have a lighter intercept the O.S.N. steamer and to get the cargo of silver to the United States. Instead, the silver is hidden on an island and the lighter is sunk.

Nostromo and Martin Decoud have been entrusted with the silver. But they have their own plans for it. They steal the silver. Nostromo and Decoud are caught in a moral dilemma. If the silver belongs to the Costaguana community as a whole, how can they justify taking it for personal gain? Each of them sees a different way of putting the silver to use.

TOPICS AND STRATEGIES

This section of the chapter will discuss possible topics for essays on *Nostromo* and will offer some general approaches to these topics. This is a series of suggestions intended to inspire your own inquiry. You may find a topic that follows a useful place from which to start your essay. Use this material to prompt your thinking about the novel. After you jot down your ideas and analyze relevant passages in the novel, you should formulate your claim, the argument you want your essay to make. Then, you can go back to your notes and begin to provide the evidence for your claim, organizing and arranging your thoughts into a persuasive essay.

Themes

A novel's themes are those major ideas or issues that the story is considering. There are several key questions that Joseph Conrad reflects on in his works. Each work expresses a specific perspective on the themes with which it deals. Your job as a writer is to discover and articulate this perspective in your essay. Identify a central theme in the work and then think about how it is addressed in the narrative. In your view, what is being said about the theme? If you read closely and ask questions about what you have read, you will develop your own line of argument. Focus on close reading and what you think the work is saying about a particular issue. This will help you to develop a claim on which to build your essay. Always make sure to write to express the point that you have to make about the themes that you see in this novel. Clearly define the main points that you want to make. You do not need to write about the entire novel; stick to your main idea. Avoid straying into unrelated tangents of thought. Bring your essay back to focus on your main points. Whatever your interpretive approach, it should be supported with evidence from the text.

Sample Topics:

1. **Ethical issues:** How might one find a moral position in this story from which to look on the actions of these characters? What is Conrad suggesting about the need for moral principles?

   It is often challenging to deal with ethical issues. There are many perspectives. The ethical issues that arise during the course of the novel appear to urge the reader to find a moral standpoint from which he or she can evaluate the action. The writer might explore the choices that these characters make. How does Conrad's novel critique greed or poor decision making? What business development might be good for the nation of Costaguana? How ought this to be structured? The writer can reflect on the silver mine and its impact on the community. Going beyond Conrad's text, the writer might research and reflect on modern business practices that have proved to be both ethical and commercially successful. The writer can then contrast these with unethical practices and with the cases that he or she finds in *Nostromo.*

2. **Silver and material interests:** What is the importance of silver and how is it connected with the material interests that drive the mine?

   Silver is present in the imagery of this novel and it stands for capital. Silver is mined. It is not drawn from manufacture, agriculture, or commerce. Rather, like ivory in *Heart of Darkness,* silver is a raw material from the "heart" of the land. Profits from silver here are built on cheap labor and the metal's value. It symbolizes material interest and represents seeking profit. Foreign investment—British and American— is involved in this society. Does this create progress or well-being? Or is this system built on domination and material interests "inherently unstable?" (Najder 237). What does this political system produce? Does it create misery or promise? Charles Gould says, "I pin my faith to material interests. Only let the material interests once get a firm footing, and they are bound to impose the conditions on which alone they can continue to exist. . . . Money making is justified because the security which it demands must be shared with an oppressed people. . . . A better justice will come afterward" (*Nostromo* 84). What do you think of his statement? How can a better justice emerge from principled actions, considered judgments, and solid principles?

3. **Postcolonial approaches:** How is colonialism criticized in this novel?

This novel is sometimes marginalized from the postcolonial discussion, which tends to focus on *Heart of Darkness* or *Lord Jim.* Yet, there is a powerful argument here against exploitation. How might the writer make use of *Nostromo* in a postcolonial discussion? A postcolonial discussion is one that is about the culture and life of countries after colonial rule. The student of history may be interested in investigating what happened in colonized countries. Might Costaguana be compared with any of these places? Conrad has sometimes been look on as a critic of colonial enterprises, although some would argue against this position. In *Nostromo,* imperialism is capitalism abroad. The characters are involved in the economic changes of Costaguana. Charles Gould owns a silver mine near Sulaco. He was born there of English background. Before Gould develops his mine, the gorge is in a tangle. Capitalism affects the area. What do you think that Conrad is saying about this enterprise?

4. **Ecological issues:** How are concerns about nature and the environment expressed in this novel?

Conrad includes before-and-after images of the gorge at San Tome. We see destructive energy at work. The gorge is "a paradise of snakes" sustained by a waterfall that flashes "bright and glassy throughout the dark green of the heavy fronds of tree-ferns." After human intrusion, the gorge becomes "a big trench half filled up with the refuse of excavations and tailings." The stream has been dammed up. Human energy is drawn away from cultivating virtues into the pursuit of profit. What does this say ecologically? Is the mine being exploited? Is the land being destroyed? Can the project bring hope and income to the area of Costaguana?

5. **Isolation:** Where in this story do you see characters that are isolated? What are the consequences of this isolation?

In many of Conrad's stories, characters are isolated, whether on a boat at sea or on land. In these stories a segment of humanity is isolated from the rest of the world, while forced to live as a working community in the company of one another. In the coastal province of Sulaco in *Nostromo* people are confined to a region where they must work out their destiny. The natural seascape and landscape inevitably have an impact on the characters.

Conrad's characters stand out from society, much like the heroes of Greek tragedy. They act in isolated worlds, dealing with their inner problems. Conrad gives us tragic heroes who struggle to work out their relationship with society. Unlike the Greek heroes, they are not highborn, and there is little glory that they move toward. They have moral issues to contend with; call them inner issues, if you will. These inner problems are mirrored in the external landscape, or in events. How is this exemplified in *Nostromo?* What is being said in this novel about the heroic and the nonheroic? How does the outer landscape reflect the inner disposition of Conrad's characters? In what ways do these characters deal with isolation?

Character

An exploration of character offers the writer a strong approach to *Nostromo*. While this novel is often considered in terms of its politics, it is helpful to remember that these politics come out of the interaction of the characters in this novel and emerge from their situations and objectives.

The writer may want to explore the questions that arise from this: In what ways is *Nostromo* a study of identity? How are ideas of the self contrasted here?

Sample Topics:

1. **Nostromo:** The character Nostromo (Gian Battista) is a protagonist whose integrity is to be doubted. Jacques Berthoud remarks that Nostromo is "the fragility of an integrity founded on vanity" (124). Nostromo is characterized by what others say about him. How does this affect how we see his tragedy? Nostromo, says Najder, "gets lost in his own conflicting impulses." The writer may explore these conflicts in this character. How is he concerned about his reputation and how is this reputation affected? How do Nostromo's passions and interests lead him to his fall?

   Conrad describes the moral weakness of his characters: "A transgression, a crime, entering a man's existence, eats it up like a malignant growth, consumes it like a fever. Nostromo had lost his peace; the treasure was real. He clung to it with a more tenacious, mental grip . . ." (429). Nostromo says, "The silver has killed me. . . . It holds me yet" (Nostromo 559). How is this like the cry of Kurtz in *Heart of Darkness:* "the horror! the horror!" What are Nostromo's issues? How does he change during the course of this novel?

2. **Heroes and antiheroes:** Who, in your view, are the heroes of this novel?

   Could Nostromo have been a hero? From the ancient Greek heroes of the Trojan War to the superheroes of comic books, television, and film, we have inherited many notions of the heroic. Some have said that a hero is one who acts on behalf of the community. A hero, many have said, is someone who has courage and character. In what ways does Nostromo fall short of these ideas of the hero? How is he an antihero? Captain Mitchell says, "This Nostromo, sir, a man absolutely above reproach, became the terror of all the thieves in the town"

(Nostromo 11). How does this image of the moral man contrast with what Nostromo becomes? Can you find any heroes here? The writer might consider his or her idea of hero and apply this to the characters that Conrad draws. In the traditional novel, such heroism is often linked with chivalry, virtue, or personal character. Is there anywhere in Conrad's novel that we meet with people who embody these qualities?

Is the individual respected in the society portrayed in this novel? Who are the heroic individuals? The writer can examine throughout the novel the conflict between individuals and society. How does this affect how they act? Conrad rejects "the mob." Which passages show that he finds it violent, unstable, inhuman, and mobilized by greed? This society is backed up by force. "There was not one of them that had not, at some time or other, looked with terror at Nostromo's revolver poked very close to his face" (12). How does the individual succumb to this force? What does peer pressure have to do with this?

3. **Don Martin Decoud:** How is Don Martin Decoud connected with nature or with the material processes of the mine?

You might, like some critics, see Decoud as too compromised a character to ever be heroic. You might examine how Decoud sees the world around him. We read that he "beheld his universe as a succession of incomprehensible images."

Is Decoud weighed down mentally and emotionally by the silver? Has he been overwhelmed by it? As Decoud comes to his end, the narrator says, "Don Martin Decoud, weighted by the bars of San Tome silver, disappeared without a trace, swallowed up in the immense indifference of things" (560).

4. **Charles Gould:** What is Charles Gould's personal stake in the silver mine? Is it possible that Charles Gould may be seeking some order in the mine so that he can also find order in his own life?

Charles Gould attempts to revive the silver mine that has destroyed his father. Obviously he seeks to make the mine profitable. He says that he seeks to bring stability to his home-land. In Gould's view, the silver mine will drive progress. "What is wanted here is law, good faith, order, security. Any-one can declaim about these things, but I pin my faith to mate-rial interests . . ." (Nostromo 150). Gould sees the mine as a beneficent influence. Silver will generate profit and contribute to civilization. Do you think that Gould is sincere?

Surely, he seeks silver and recognizes the need for politi-cal stability. However, Charles Gould is not a political man. He thinks often about the silver mine in connection with his own life. A writer can develop an essay exploring this. Gould thinks that perhaps the mine would not have caused the death of his father if his father had been a more disciplined man. Sometimes he goes off at night to spend the night in the mine. Is there some psychological interest in this for him, as well as material interest? Charles Gould wishes to change the "moral disaster" of the mine that his father experienced into a "moral success" (66). He thinks often of his father. "He was afraid I would hang on to the ruinous thing, waiting for just some such chance, and waste my life miserably" (72). Does Gould have to justify this pursuit of silver? How does he idealize this quest? How is Charles Gould's search something more than simply a materialistic quest?

5. **Emilia Gould:** Describe Emilia Gould's role and her relation-ship with Charles.

Is Emilia an independent woman? How is she different from her husband? Why does the mine become their mutual goal? In your essay, you can probe the relationship between these characters. Conrad writes, "It was as if they had been mor-ally bound to make good their vigorous view of life against the unnatural error of weariness and despair" (82). Charles Gould's father has succumbed to weariness and despair and so Charles and Emilia refuse to be similarly overcome.

Emilia supports Charles in this endeavor: "And at once her delight in him, lingering with half-open wings like those birds that cannot rise easily from a flat level, found a pinnacle from which to soar up into the skies" (65). Emilia idealizes the mine and her marriage and is affected by the gradual corruption of Charles. How is Charles separated from Emilia? Is his egotism to blame? Is Conrad implying anything about the value of restraint? What sort of vision do the characters lack as they tumble blindly to their ruin?

6. **Observing how characters change:** How do Nostromo, Gould, Decoud, or another character of your choice change over the course of the story?

A valuable approach to Conrad's fiction is to observe how characters are transformed during the course of the novel. You can look carefully at how Nostromo changes. Does he lose a sense of identity as he swims ashore and falls asleep in the fort? In what sense does he "awaken"? He emerges from his "lair in the long grass . . . natural and free from evil in the moment of waking as a magnificent and unconscious wild beast" (458). Nostromo is now in a dilemma. He needs to keep a secret about what he has done. He finds that he has "no intellectual existence or moral strain to carry on his individuality unscathed, over the abyss left by the collapse of his vanity" (466). How do both Nostromo and Charles Gould become more and more isolated, moving apart from the rest of mankind? How does their departure from community, toward their own material ends, affect them? In deciding to possess the treasure of silver, does Nostromo become absorbed by the silver? Can we say that he has become figuratively "swallowed up" by the mine and the material interest it represents? Has he lost himself to this?

7. **Hirsch:** How is Hirsch an antihero?

Several of the characters in *Nostromo* appear to lack the qualities that would constitute someone who is heroic. Some of them are decidedly antiheroes. You can write an essay about this. For example, in Part Two, Hirsch is discovered hiding onboard as they sail to the Isabels. We read: "Señor Hirsch's sensations as he lay there must have been those of extreme terror" (218). Soon we begin to learn that he is treacherous, fearful, without heroism. We read that Nostromo "reproached himself for not having stabbed and flung Hirsch overboard at the very moment of discovery without even looking at his face" (223). Decoud also sees that he should have done something about Hirsch: "Not to have bound and gagged him seemed to Decoud now the height of improvident folly" (227). Hirsch is vulgar, with only material interest. Decoud and Nostromo's mission is endangered by this proud and materialistic man. The writer might consider how Hirsch reflects the outside world coming in to this enclosed world.

You might contrast the antiheroic Hirsch with any of the other characters. For example, the writer can explore Conrad's characterization of Captain Mitchell. In examining Captain Mitchell, the OSN representative, you may find that Captain Mitchell is courageous, whereas Hirsch seems despicable. An essay can follow in which you explore how the text shows Captain Mitchell's strengths and his limitations and in which you compare these with the faults that you see in Hirsch.

8. **Dr. Monygham:** How does Dr. Monygham struggle with moral darkness? How does Conrad create in us sympathy for Dr. Monygham?

Dr. Monygham is a complex character. He appears bitter and has a deformity. We do not know until late in the novel that it has been caused by the torture of a political tyrant, Guzman Bento. Dr. Monygham is unhappy with himself and disillusioned with the world. He has made up lies to end the torture he was subjected to. He has been imprisoned in darkness. Now he struggles with a sense of moral darkness. We do not know the reasons for his cynicism or bitterness until late in the novel. He has suffered the torture of his interrogator, Father Beron. Now he regrets having confessed, and he struggles, heroically, to walk. He continues to suffer this regret. How are loyalty and idealism expressed by this character? How has he, through all of his trials, developed a moral sense?

People believed him scornful and soured. The truth of his nature consisted in his capacity for passion and in the sensitiveness of his temperament. What he lacked was the polished callousness of men of the world, the callousness from which springs an easy tolerance for oneself and others; the tolerance wide as poles asunder from true sympathy and human compassion. This want of callousness accounted for his sardonic turn of mind and his biting speeches. (520)

History and Context

How does Conrad think about history? *Nostromo* is a sprawling novel, a tale of revolution cast as a historical fiction. In his author's note to *Nostromo* in 1917, Conrad wrote: "it seemed somehow that there was nothing more in the world to write about." Conrad reworks and challenges historical fiction in this nonsequential novel. One might write on how this lack of chronology affects this historical novel or what it has to do with historical narrative, which is usually chronological.

Conrad has been regarded by some as a critic of imperialism, who saw its demise. Yet, he was also a man of his time, not ours. There were during Conrad's time humanitarian aspects to this opposition to African or Asian imperialism. There were also those who opposed the inevitable development of entangling alliances throughout the world and those who opposed the cost of maintaining the global sweep of empire (See Fleishman 81).

Sample Topics:

1. **Imperialism:** How does the mine represent the colonial enterprise?

   Conrad focuses on the moral effects of imperialism on the colonizers or the impact of colonization on the natives of a place that has been colonized. Conrad is critical of how these activities tend to dehumanize and demoralize the colonist. Conrad appears concerned with barbarity and the disruptions caused by colonization. There is a critique of the individuals and groups that engage in this. How did colonization decolonize the colonizer? Did this venture into unfamiliar regions and cultures make him instinctual? Do you think that Conrad is skeptical of this endeavor? The San Tome mine is the center of rapacious hostilities and conflict between social groups in Costaguana. Will this mine generate wealth? Will it create misery? You might analyze the problem of economics in Costaguana.

2. **Latin American history:** Are there any parallels between what happens in Costaguana and actual events in the history of Latin America?

Nostromo is a study of the politics and society of an imagined country. It is filled with power shifts between Ribiera, the presidential figurehead, Mestizo rebels like the Montreros, and Sir John of the railway. Some research on Latin American history would add depth to a paper on *Nostromo*. The writer might raise questions about the history of this country that never existed. How is it representative of the struggle of Latin American nations? Nostromo is a world away from the Malay of Conrad's first novels. However, a writer on Conrad could find parallels in his implications about the colonial experience in different parts of the world.

   Nostromo is framed as a historical novel. In what ways is this history also about the present of Conrad's time? Sulaco in the west breaks free from Costaguana in this story, which was written about the same time that Panama broke from Colombia. What can be said about the experience of the people in Costaguana in light of contemporary experience or through a postcolonial perspective?

3. **The idea of progress:** Is Conrad making a comment on the notion of progress? Do you think there is any progress in Costaguana?

Arguments on behalf of colonialism often drew on the notion of progress. In this view, the conquest and development of other cultures by the European nations would "improve" these places and benefit these cultures. Gould says something like this when he claims that a better time is yet to come. Yet, you could argue that no such future of progress emerges for Costaguana.

Conrad appears to point to a kind of regression in the imperialist experience. Jim went East. Marlow went to Africa. Neither went easily "forward." In the case of *Nostromo,* the novel itself revolves, repeats, and goes in circles like Friedrich Nietzsche's idea of history as eternal recurrence. The writer can trace the way that the circular structure of this novel may reflect the society that is depicted here: one that never seems to go anywhere or make any progress.

4. **Inhabitants of Costaguana:** How does Conrad portray the people of this imagined country?

You might write an essay noting the ways in which the natives of Costaguana are described. In response to *Heart of Darkness,* Chinua Achebe contends that Conrad characterizes Africans in a way that dehumanizes them. Is Conrad doing anything similar as he portrays the inhabitants of Costaguana? That is, are the people he portrays characterized in a fully human and sympathetic way or not? Are these portrayals suggestive of a point he wants to make about this society and this point in history? The writer may reflect on what Conrad may be saying about this culture and, more generally, about humanity in this novel.

Philosophy and Ideas

Throughout Conrad's novels we see concerns with sympathy, isolation, and community repeating. Common features and themes of the novels are fidelity and betrayal, individualism and community, honor, exile, loneliness, and commitment. *Nostromo,* however, is about an entire community. Whereas in *Lord Jim,* Conrad focuses on the ethical choices of one individual, in *Nostromo,* we see the relationship between ethics and the politics of a society. Conrad's chief modern Polish critic Najder points to "an emotionally charged ethical commitment" in Conrad's works (234). He also speaks of "a novelistic exercise in epistemology" (234). Conrad is thinking about thinking. The writer, considering this, might look for reflections on thought in this novel.

The philosopher Bertrand Russell once wrote of Conrad: "he thought of civilized and morally tolerable human life as a dangerous walk on a thin crust of barely cooked lava which at any moment might break and let the unwary sink into fiery depths" (82). What is this fragility of mankind that Conrad addresses? Might the San Tome mine in this novel represent that uneasy precipice on which humanity walks?

Sample Topics:

1. **Darwinism:** Is the theme of survival of the fittest at work in this story? Who is "fit" and who is not?

   Nostromo might be explored as an extended reflection by Conrad on Charles Darwin's theory of natural selection, which had, by Conrad's time, become a kind of "social Darwinism." The Darwinian concept of evolution by natural selection was appealed to by those who pursued self-interest and "civilization" in the name of "survival of the fittest." Thus, Darwin's scientific theory transmuted, becoming a social rationale. You might explore how "Darwinism" became a system of beliefs that was linked to the commercial, competitive environment. This view saw inequalities as a necessary stage in social evolution. Biological notions were transferred into "social Darwinism." Competitive expansion was thus justified, or rationalized, on evolutionary grounds. Thus, the science of the evolutionary position was used in support of colonial expansion. To survive and to rule was to show that one was the fittest.

   How does the situation in Costaguana reflect this? In what ways do the colonizers privilege efficiency and a notion of progress or claim inherent superiority over the natives? In some colonial enterprises, it was claimed that a "lower" race—that of the natives—needed "improvement." To "improve" the "subject races" was seen as a "moral duty." Meanwhile, forms of autocratic rule, often by law, were exercised. How could humanitarian impulses be reconciled with the quest of profit or with strategic political advantage? You might describe Conrad's ambivalence in this matter. As you go through the text, take note of any characters who express this attitude. You can then develop an essay in which you examine their motives.

2. **Nature:** Has humanity disrupted nature in Costaguana? What does the exploitation of the mine have to do with this? How is the mine a site of moral concern?

The mine at San Tome has disrupted the ecosystem and the "paradise of snakes." How might Costaguana represent the "fall of man" from a primeval Garden of Eden to a place in which the "snake" is a devilish human force? What inhumanity has come to this place? Does *Nostromo* affirm humanity and nature, or is it a dark vision of evil?

The writer may further explore the moral questions that the author is raising with this novel. Is Conrad writing about material interests and concerns here? If so, how is the mine the center of moral concern in this novel? We read: "The mine had been the cause of an absurd moral disaster; its working must be made a serious and moral success" (66). What kinds of moral or immoral behavior emerge in this interaction with the mine? How is Gould obsessed? Is the mine an end in itself for Gould? How is his material interest expressed? When the writer looks at characters like Holyroyd, Hirsch, Montero, or Sotillo, how do their motives and actions express material interest? How do they affect the people around them because of this interest? In what ways does this material focus supersede any care of the people in the community?

3. **The community:** How is the community at stake? Which characters are concerned with the public welfare?

You might contrast the self-interested characters in this story with another group of characters: Don Jose Avellanos, Mrs. Gould, the Sulacans. These characters all seem to be concerned with the public good. In what ways is the mine less important for them than the lives of the people of Costaguana? They appear to ask if the mine can be for the sake of the community of Costaguana. How can material interests be approached for the betterment of the community? In what ways does Don Jose Avellanos represent a moral norm? He has an orientation toward people that expresses concern. He acts with good intentions. These may not always have the results intended. How does Mrs. Gould show her concern for other people? How does she seem to be on both sides?

Form and Genre

Nostromo is told in an unconventional narrative style, one full of time shifts. The form of this story makes it challenging to read. In his *A Preface to Conrad*, Cedric Watts refers to "bewildering mobility," "a kaleidoscopic quality," irony, and "conceptual jaggedness" (150). Because of this, you will want to exercise care to make sure that you understand the sections of this novel and how they fit together. Conrad biographer Zdzislaw Najder calls *Nostromo* "Conrad's most ambitious and formidable artistic endeavor" and says that it has "epic scope and sweep"(*Conradian,* vol. 40, no. 3, 2008, "A Century of *Nostromo*" 233–46). This epic sweep makes it impossible to write a good essay about everything in this novel. You should focus on one major theme, rather than try to be comprehensive in your coverage of this novel. For example, you might examine this novel for its shifting of points of view and its departure from chronology. You could present just a few examples from the story to support your observation. Najder points out that in *Nostromo* we see the way that people gather information about events they have not witnessed. You might find a few examples of this. Your essay could explore the form of this novel and Conrad's use of innovative techniques.

Sample Topics:

1. **An imagined country:** What are the features of Conrad's imagined country of Costaguana?

   This story takes place in an imagined country. However, even with this external geography, there is also an element of interiority to this novel. You might try to describe some of the external features of the countryside and its people. However, you ought to go beyond this, to some thinking about how this environment affects the psychology of the characters. Here there is "a mixture of customs and expressions." The politics here are representative of many Latin American countries. This is a "synthetic product," says Conrad to R. B. Cunninghame

Graham (October 31, 1904, CL 3: 75). In Conrad we see that this world is still mysterious amid all of this modernization. In literary modernism, we at times see a movement from external space to interior space, as in the novels of Woolf or Joyce. We move toward something that is more memoir than travel narrative. The writer might explore how this novel moves into psychology and what is going on in the minds of these characters.

2. **Visual techniques:** In what ways are Conrad's novels cinematic?

While there have only been a few movies made from Conrad's novels, Conrad has a kind of cinematic writing because he insists on concrete sensory imagery. His work may be difficult for filmmakers because he has multiple narrators and develops stories in ways other than chronologically. Yet, Conrad's technique enables readers to see the action and his characters from many different sides at the same time. There is a disjunction between the order of events and the order in which they are told. The writer can write an essay on how Conrad's work is visual. Would this novel make for a good movie? Who might direct it or act in this story?

Language, Symbols, and Imagery

Joseph Conrad was Polish born, but he wrote in English. His style carries traces of his original language and of French, a language in which he was thoroughly fluent. Zdzislaw Najder points to Polish traces in *Nostromo*. He sees deviation from English idiom and grammar "under the impact of Polish usage." Najder points out that Conrad uses the phrase "from under" and "from over," which is strained in English and natural in Polish. A writer might examine Conrad's style, the craft of his prose, for unusual sentences. The quality of his writing is unmistakable. An entire essay could be written on how he writes. What makes Conrad an effective writer? How are the qualities of good writing present in his prose?

Sample Topics:

1. **Ships:** How do ships and boats function as symbols in this story? What is each boat symbolic of?

The ships in which Conrad's characters sail are sometimes symbolic, or representative. You can write an essay noting the differences in these boats and what you think they represent. For example, Nostromo and Decoud board a small lighter as they seek to move the silver in their possession. Their sailboat collides, as if by chance, with General Sotillo's steamer as they approach Sulaco and its port. We read: "The steamer had struck the lighter obliquely" (254). Might these sailing vessels be symbolic? What if the lighter, or sailboat, is romantic heroism? Might the steamer represent commercial greed? Its size overpowers the smaller boat, which is on a romantic adventure. Romance is affected by its impersonal force. The writer can inquire into the way these vessels act as symbols for the larger themes of the novel.

2. **The mine:** What is the significance of the San Tome mine, economically, ecologically, and symbolically, in this story?

The San Tome mine stands at the center of this story. One might look at the images of house, cave, and nature as well as references to animal imagery. The San Tome mine looms amid the mountain ranges. One might relate this to the Congo of *Heart of Darkness* and the ivory in that novel to silver in this one. How does the environment itself affect the characters? The writer can inquire into how the mine reflects the human heart. In what ways is it welcoming? How is it savage and violent? The mine is the center of Charles Gould's desire. If this at first corresponds to his marriage, how does the mine begin to destroy his domestic life? How is the force of the mine personified? Conrad writes: ". . . its yield had been paid for in its weight of human bones. Whole tribes of Indians had perished in the exploitation; and then the mine was abandoned . . . no matter how many corpses were thrown into its maw" (55).

3. **Disease and corruption:** How does silver become like a disease that corrupts some of the characters?

A disease metaphor moves through this novel and this is often associated with the silver. How is silver a curse? Decoud sees that "the possession of this treasure is very much like a deadly disease for men situated as we are" (222). Nostromo makes similar remarks toward the end of the novel, in which we hear of the "lost treasure of the San Tome mine" (424). How does the silver motivate the characters? How does it affect them? Does it symbolize their destruction? The narrator says of Mr. Gould: "The mine had corrupted his judgment by making him sick of bribing and intriguing merely to have his work left alone from day to day" (303). As the story moves toward its conclusion, Mrs. Gould whispers to Nostromo, "I too have hated the idea of that silver from the bottom of my heart" (420). How are characters corrupted? Which of them do you believe are free from corruption?

4. **Seeing clearly:** The writer can also investigate how seeing or not seeing clearly are important in this novel.

Joseph Conrad's effort to help his readers to "see clearly" appears to continue in this novel. How are some characters "blind" here, while others have vision? Often you will find references to sight and vision. For example, we read that as far as Decoud could see, "Everything had vanished but the light of the lantern. . . ." But he hears Nostromo's feet: "The two men unable to see each other, kept silent till the lighter, slipping before the fitful breeze, passed out between almost invisible headlands . . ." (211). Sometimes the theme of seeing is marked by symbols. Mrs. Gould buys Giorgio Viola a pair of spectacles. We read that "he had consented to accept the present of silver-mounted spectacles from Señora Emilia Gould" (38). Giorgio, a "Genoese with a shaggy white leonine head," lacks vision in other ways and this affects his daughters and the community of Costaguana. You can write an essay in which you point to the ways that the characters in this story see, or neglect to see, the truth of their situation. How well do they see one another?

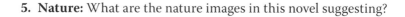

5. **Nature:** What are the nature images in this novel suggesting?

The environment of Costaguana and Sulaco has a quality of wildness about it. Azuera is a "wild chaos of sharp rocks" (17). There is aridity here, for the rocks are "utterly waterless" and the place is "as if blighted by a curse" (17). We read of the region: "Then, as the midday sun withdraws from the gulf the shadow of the mountains, the clouds begin to roll out of the lower valleys. They swathe in somber tatters the naked crags of precipices above the wooded slopes, hide the peaks, smoke in stormy trails across the snows of the Higuerota. . . ."

How do humanity and environment come together in this novel? What is being said about the land and the human-nature interaction? The writer might explore the animal imagery throughout this novel. How does this relate to the human characters in the story?

Compare and Contrast Essays

A common way of writing a paper on a literary work is to compare or contrast elements of the work. This way, the writer can discover similarities and differences between certain aspects of the novel or story and then comment on the resonance of those comparative or contrasting elements and what it contributes to the work overall. This approach can help a reader focus on oppositions in the text and may bring into sharper detail the elements that need to be more closely observed.

It is important that the essay do more than merely list these similarities or contrasts. Thoughtful commentary helps to make your paragraph something more than just a list. Good writing is descriptive and thoughtful. Make sure to provide detail. Through critical thinking and analysis, a writer can look at differences between characters or patterns of imagery in the work. The writer might start by defining who each character is—as conveyed through his or her traits or behavior—or how each image is defined and presented. The differences or the ways Conrad alters or changes his representation can then be explored.

Sample Topics:

1. **Nature and political organization:** The writer may probe the contrast between nature and fragile political organization.

What structure does the San Tome mine, or the society of Costaguana, rest on? How are the forces of nature, and those of politics, involved in this place and how this story unfolds? Founders of national governments must be architects of enduring constitutions. Will anything endure in this tenuous political arrangement in Costaguana? What will happen if greed gets the better of a land's politicians and financiers? What if the natural resources of a nation are depleted? How is *Nostromo* a caution to the modern world?

2. **Benevolence and selfishness:** Which characters and which of their actions are greedy and selfish? Which characters are kind and benevolent?

The writer might consider how Nostromo's materialistic ends contrast with those of Charles and Emilia Gould. Emilia, in particular, is finally recognized by Nostromo as "Shining, Incorruptible" (420). Nostromo, in contrast, gives away or gambles away much of his money. His pride is injured and he feels exploited. Then he seeks the silver bars, as a form of recompense for the pride of name and position he does not have. How does his vanity play into this? In what respect does he feel betrayed? Has he betrayed the people of Costaguana? How does Nostromo gain moral sensitivity?

3. **Moral idealism and material interests:** How does *Nostromo* represent a conflict of values: one of moral idealism alongside the quest for material gain?

The theme of *Nostromo* is "the relation between moral idealism and material interests," suggests F. R. Leavis (191). Giorgio Viola, for example, is an idealist. He represents the age of heroic liberal faith, says Leavis (194). This idealist is in contrast to Costaguana politics. The writer might reflect on how the characters express this contrast. As Gould tells his wife:

> What is wanted here is law, good faith, order, security. Any one can declaim about these things, but I pin my faith to material

interests. Only let the material interests once get a firm footing, and they are bound to impose the conditions on which
alone they can continue to exist. That's how your money-
making is justified here in the face of lawlessness and disorder.
It is justified because the security which it demands must be
shared with an oppressed people. A better justice will come
afterwards. That's your ray of hope.

4. **"A better justice":** Will there be "a better justice" afterward?
   Is Gould's dream ever going to become a reality? Or is this an
   excuse for not practicing justice at the present time?

The writer may examine whether there will be more justice
in the future. The narrator describes Charles Gould as a "sentimental Englishman" who "cannot exist without idealizing
every simple desire or achievement. He could not believe his
own motives if he did not make them first a part of some fairy
tale." It may be that this is just a dream, a form of utopia used
as a rationalization for Gould's own private gain, rather than a
public purpose: "Charles Gould on going out passed his hand
over his forehead as if to disperse the mists of an oppressive
dream, whose grotesque extravagance leaves behind a subtle
sense of bodily danger and intellectual decay. . . ."

5. **Tradition, discipline, and moral ideals:** The writer may
   inquire into the moral ideals that Conrad brings to his story.

Conrad believes in "tradition, discipline, and moral ideals,"
observes F. R. Leavis. You might look at *The Great Tradition*
(173–226), in which Leavis considers Joseph Conrad's writing with special attention to *Nostromo.* Leavis recognizes that
Conrad reflects on human frailty. He considers absurdity.
He practices skepticism. Someone writing on Conrad might
examine the various ways in which Conrad does this in this
novel. Leavis notes the theme of isolation in Conrad's work
and says all readers will notice this (201). For the writer on
Conrad, this theme of isolation is very worth investigating.
Isolation and its contrast with solidarity or community can be

found throughout Conrad's works. By looking at Nostromo, Charles Gould, or other characters, you might examine how Conrad reflects on human frailty in this novel.

Bibliography and Online Resources for *Nostromo*

Berthoud, Jacques. *Joseph Conrad: The Major Phase.* Cambridge: Cambridge University Press, 1978.

Carabine, Keith. *Nostromo.* Introduction. Oxford: Oxford University Press, 1981.

Collits, Tony. *Postcolonial Conrad: Paradoxes of Empire.* London: Routledge, 2005.

Erdinast-Vulcan, Daphna. "*Nostromo* and the Writing of History," *Joseph Conrad: Voice, Sequence, History, Genre.* Ed. Jakob Lothe, Jeremy Hawthorn, and James Phelan. Columbus: Ohio State University Press, 2008, pp. 178–95.

Fitzgerald, F. Scott. Letter to Fanny Butcher. *Chicago Daily Tribune* (May 19, 1923): 9.

Fleishman, Avrom. *Conrad's Politics: Community and Anarchy in the Fiction of Joseph Conrad.* Baltimore, MD: Johns Hopkins University Press, 1967.

Hewitt, Douglas. *Conrad: A Reassessment.* Cambridge: Bowes and Bowes, 1952.

Jameson, Frederic. *The Political Unconscious: Narrative as a Socially Symbolic Act.* London: Methuen, 1981.

Jordan, Elaine. *Joseph Conrad.* Macmillan New Casebooks. New York: Macmillan, 1996.

Kettle, Arnold. *An Introduction to the English Novel, II, Henry James to the Present Day.* London: Hutchinson University Library, 1953.

Leavis, F. R. *The Great Tradition: George Eliot, Henry James, Joseph Conrad.* London: Chatto and Windus, 1948.

Miller, J. Hillis. "Material Interests: Conrad's *Nostromo* as a Critique of Global Capitalism." *Joseph Conrad: Voice, Sequence, History, Genre.* Ed. Jakob Lothe, Jeremy Hawthorn, and James Phelan. Columbus: Ohio State University Press, 2008.

Nostromo Online Page, www.nostromoonline.com/index/shtml, 2005.

Parry, Benita. *Conrad and Imperialism: Ideological Boundaries and Visionary Frontiers.* New York and London: Macmillan, 1983.

Russell, Bertrand. *Portraits from Memory and Other Essays.* London: G. Allen and Unwin, 1956, p. 82.

Said, Edward. *Beginnings: Intention and Method.* Baltimore, MD: Johns Hopkins University Press, 1975.

Sherry, Norman. *Conrad's Western World.* Cambridge: Cambridge University Press, 1971, pp. 137–204.

Warren, Robert Penn. "Nostromo," *Sewanee Review* 59 (1951): 363–91.

Watt, Ian. *Nostromo.* Cambridge: Cambridge University Press, 1988.

Williams, Raymond. "Joseph Conrad," *The English Novel from Dickens to Lawrence.* New York: Oxford University Press, 1978, pp. 140–54.

UNDER WESTERN EYES

READING TO WRITE

*U*NDER *WESTERN Eyes* is a psychological drama, dealing with the experience and choices of Kyrilo Sidorovitch Razumov. In this novel, the conflicts are moral and psychological. There are issues of human relationship and there is politics. In addition, there is a look at the East (Russia) from the West. There is also a concern with chance and fate, a topic that Conrad had been exploring since his writing of *Lord Jim. Under Western Eyes* was serialized in the *English Review,* edited by Conrad's friend Ford Maddox Ford. The story ran in 11 installments from December 1910 to October 1911. Although this story is now 100 years old, it has been called "an astonishingly contemporary novel" that is prophetic and pessimistic (Meyers xvi). Conrad's sensitivity about Russia and despotism lies behind his dramatic portrayal.

Fyodor Dostoevsky's *Crime and Punishment* is a clear model for this novel. Someone writing on Conrad's novel could effectively make this comparison. When Razumov meets Haldin, the assassin, it is almost as if Razumov has met Raskolnikov, who, in Dostoevsky's novel, is a murderer. Will he shelter him or give him up? Both Conrad's Razumov and Dostoevsky's Raskolnikov are characters who tend to consider themselves superior to others and to seek a calling. Both are existentially bereft of contact with others and subject to tensions in their environments. In this, each of them attempts to live apart from mankind.

Under Western Eyes is a frame narrative. A British teacher of foreign languages, who is never named, recalls the life experience of Kirylo Sidorovitch Razumov. The story starts with Razumov, who is a student at St. Petersburg University, writing an essay that he hopes will win a medal that will make set him on the path toward success in the future. Razumov has no family. He is the illegitimate son of Prince K—. He also has no connection with politics, but this soon changes. When he returns home one evening, he finds Victor Haldin, a fellow student, waiting for him. Haldin has just assassinated a political figure and has run away. He thinks that Razumov will be sympathetic toward him. Instead, Razumov finds what Haldin has done very disturbing. Razumov realizes that if Haldin were caught that he also might be considered a co-conspirator. He agrees to help him to escape—mostly to get rid of him. Razumov makes an arrangement with a sleigh driver, Ziemianitch, to hurry him away. However, Razumov finds the driver in a drunken state, falling asleep. Bothered and annoyed, he decides that he is going to give Haldin up.

This is a tragic event, an occurrence of chance encounter that launches Razumov into a new awareness of the complexity of the world. For him, security and the common world vanish. He is burdened. He has lost his life's direction. Razumov struggles with his betrayal of Haldin. At first he thinks that he has done the proper thing. Haldin has assassinated someone; he has killed people and he is a threat to Russia. However, in giving him up, Razumov experiences a sense of guilt. He can no longer concentrate on his studies, so he abandons them. He turns to revenge, targeting all of those people that he thinks have disrupted his life. He asserts, "perdition is my lot" (362). Curiously, the name Haldin is likely derived from the German word "*Held*," or "hero." The root of Razumov's name is "reason." The writer might inquire into how heroism and reason, or their opposites, cowardice and unreason or irrationality, are involved in this story.

TOPICS AND STRATEGIES

This section of the chapter will discuss possible topics for essays on *Under Western Eyes* and will offer some general approaches to these topics. This is a series of suggestions intended to inspire your own inquiry. You may find a topic that follows a useful place from which to start your essay. Use this material to prompt your thinking about the novel. After you jot down your ideas and analyze relevant passages in the novel, you should formulate your claim, the argument you want your essay to make. Then, you can go back to your notes and begin to provide the evidence for your claim, organizing and arranging your thoughts into a persuasive essay.

Themes

A novel's themes are those major ideas or issues that the story is considering. There are several key questions that Joseph Conrad reflects on in his works. Each work expresses a particular perspective on the themes with which it deals. Your job as a writer is to discover and articulate this perspective in your essay. Identify a central theme in the work and then think about how it is addressed in the narrative. In your view, what is being said about the theme? If you read closely and ask questions about what you have read, you will develop your own line of argument. Focus on close reading and what you think the work is saying about a particular issue. This will help you to develop a claim on which to build your essay. Always make sure to write to express the point that you have to make about the themes that you see in this novel. Clearly define the main points that you want to make. You do not need to write about the entire novel; stick to your main idea. Avoid straying into unrelated tangents of thought. Bring your essay back to focus on your main points. Whatever your interpretive approach, it should be supported with evidence from the text.

Sample Topics:

1. **Fate and chance:** How is Razumov representative of humanity, which is subject to fate?

   It appears as if Haldin has come into Razumov's rooms out of nowhere. Even though Razumov was simply minding his own business, Haldin draws Razumov into revolutionary conflict. What do you think of this? You might investigate how events may sometimes draw us into something we were not originally involved with.

   To begin work on his story about Razumov, Conrad set aside his work on a novel he called *Chance*. How is chance operative in this novel? The environment that surrounds this character seems to draw him inexorably into its conflicts. Is Conrad suggesting that Razumov has little control over his fate? Or is he suggesting that Razumov has not made the right choice?

2. **Betrayal:** In your view, has Razumov betrayed Haldin? How does Razumov's sense of guilt about this affect him and prompt his actions?

After Haldin, running from justice, winds up in his rooms, Razumov is trying to control his life and how he will be perceived. In attempting to regain some control, he betrays Haldin. However, this betrayal weighs on him. This experience pulls Razumov into the political world. What do you think about Razumov's feeling guilty about telling on Haldin and betraying his confidence?

Razumov will now work as a double agent who will infiltrate a revolutionary cell in Geneva. He holds the view that he is now guarding Russia against revolutionary activities. He wants to get back at Haldin and the revolutionaries that Haldin has associated with. Look carefully at how he begins to change as he meets Victor Haldin's sister, Nathalia Haldin, whom he finds honest and sincere. This moves him to confess what he has done to Victor. You might discuss how the relationship with Nathalia affects Razumov. Does this character grow, or learn anything, in the process?

Character

This story begins with an apparently chance occurrence, a dishonorable act and a moral failing, much like in *Lord Jim*. Razumov experiences hidden guilt for his betrayal of a young revolutionary. He becomes obsessed with the need to clear his conscience about what he has done. He falls in love with the sister of the man he has betrayed to the authorities. However, in your essay, you may take the position that Razumov is never quite worthy of her love. As you explore the characters, consider their motivations. Give some thought to how chance occurrences affect them. What choices are these characters making? How do they affect one another?

Sample Topics:

1. **Razumov:** How does Razumov define himself? Does he fit in anywhere? How does he change during the course of this story?

Razumov resembles Dostoevsky's Raskolnikov in *Crime and Punishment*. He is a loner haunted by guilt and troubled conscience who is affected by the love that he finds in a young woman. Through close reading, you can begin to discover Razumov's traits and his dilemma. What emotions does he experience? How does he react to the events in his life or to the sense of guilt he feels about betraying Victor Haldin? Follow Razumov as he becomes an agent, believing he is suppressing revolutionary activities. In what ways is he misguided? How is he humanized? What is the role of Nathalia Haldin in bringing about this change in Razumov? The writer might explore the ways in which Razumov is lost, or alienated. Can Razumov identify with anyone else? How does Nathalia bring a sense of humanness, care, and support into his life?

2. **Haldin:** What impact does Haldin have on the life of Razumov?

Haldin's sudden appearance in Razumov's rooms begins this novel. Haldin grows as a figure of stature in the book. He does not fade away. He is always on Razumov's mind. We see again here a kind of "double," for Haldin's isolation is similar to that of Razumov. The writer might explore how they might be doubles or reflections of each other. What happens when Razumov senses Haldin's sincerity and the way Haldin gave himself for a cause? How in his betrayal of Haldin does he destroy himself? In what respect does he have something like Haldin's idealism? How is Razumov a victim? Is Haldin one also?

3. **Nathalia:** What does Razumov learn from Nathalia? How does she play a significant role in the changes that we see in him? What are her qualities that affect him?

The writer can establish a thesis that, in his relationship with Nathalia, Razumov learns that revenge, patriotism, and other ideological notions do not mean as much as human connection and love. The writer can write on the importance of humanity in the relationship between Razumov and Nathalia. If this is your approach, you will need to probe the story for evidence that will demonstrate this. As you read, observe how Nathalia goes to meet Razumov, who she has heard has come to Geneva. Listen to Razumov, as he begins with "I believed that I had in my breast nothing but an inexhaustible fund of anger and hate for you both. . . . And do you know what I said to myself? I shall steal his sister's soul from her" (358–59). You may examine how, to the contrary, Razumov's heart and soul are challenged by Nathalia's presence. Investigate how Nathalia's genuine quality affects him. "I felt that I must tell you that I had ended by loving you," he says (361). He claims that she was a light that saved him from ignominy, "from ultimate undoing" (361). It would be valuable for a writer to explore this. How does Nathalia transform Razumov?

This is a world of human relationships. It is a story of Razumov and the people he interacts with. The writer might look carefully at his interaction with Haldin's sister and at the human sympathy that is summoned up inside him by this. Nathalia is a devoted person who cares little for politics. She cares deeply about her brother and how her mother is despairing over him. The writer can explore the contrast between this familial devotion and the harsh political world that appears in the novel. Nathalia represents humanity, emotion, and devotion in contrast with political and social ideas. How does she change Razumov? Patriotism is bound up with revenge in Razumov. How does his experience of Nathalia's loving nature affect him and his orientation?

4. **Tekla:** How is Tekla, while a loner, very much involved in the society of this story? What is her significance?

Tekla, like Razumov at the start of this story, is an isolated character. She is an outsider who gains identity by assisting others in their schemes. She recognizes her own anonymity. "No one talks to me, no one writes to me," she says. "I have no use for a name." What is the importance of Tekla in this story? It is Tekla who would help Razumov after his confession results in a beating and his crippling. What qualities do you see in her?

5. **Ziemianitch:** Describe the carriage driver. Why is love important to him?

One might also consider the divided character of Ziemianitch, the carriage driver. "Saint or devil, night or day is all one to Ziemianitch when his heart is free from sorrow" (29). We read that "Ziemianitch's passionate surrender to sorrow and consolation had baffled Razumov" (31). This character is not a romantic idealist or a revolutionary engaged in a political struggle. Instead, he is beset by love and the loss of it. In this, he might be contrasted with Haldin and the revolutionaries, who are passionate about their political agenda. You might describe Ziemianitch and set him alongside these other characters. How is the concern with love that is important to him different from their motivations?

6. **The revolutionaries:** How do people with misplaced ideals become fools in this story? How do they become ridiculous? How are such people to be humanized?

Razumov has played out a dangerous game with all seriousness. He has been like a marionette on strings. Mikulin, who represents Russian power, has a wisdom that is shortsighted. Haldin is a wild-eyed zealot full of energy. Kirylo will steal from his father and from the cause. The cab driver is too drunk to drive. Peter Ivanovitch, the revolutionary guide, is an ideologue who cannot guide anyone, except into misery. What is Conrad saying about these people?

History and Context

A writer's consideration of Conrad's own life story can add depth to any paper about *Under Western Eyes.* Conrad's Polish heritage lies behind this novel. Joseph Conrad's father, a Polish hero, was imprisoned by revolutionaries in 1861. Conrad was four years old at the time. His family was sent into exile in northern Russia. Conrad's experience told him that Russia had subjugated Poland. His father, Apollo Korzeniowski, wrote that "the form of government in Russia is despotism bounded by no other limit than assassination or palace revolution." Conrad fiercely deplored despotism but opposed revolutionary solutions.

Conrad had been thinking of the subject of this novel for a long time, Eloise Knapp Hay suggests, and he eventually "unburdened" himself of it (265). Conrad never mentions Poland in this novel. Yet, many commentators say that the Polish nationalist experience lies behind it. They also say that Conrad was critical of "messianic" Polish nationalism. Jocelyn Baines claimed that Conrad repudiated Polish politics. Hay says that Conrad still sought "sparks of truth" in this legacy and sought reason, not just "a gesture of blind defiance" (267). In V. S. Pritchett's view, "the corruption that has come from Moscow . . . has a generalized quality" and may reflect Conrad's childhood ("The Exile" in *The News Statesman,* August 24, 1957, p. 229). He sees the evil in Conrad's novels, including that of *Lord Jim,* emerging from this childhood experience. By reading a biography of Conrad's life alongside this story, you might reach similar, or different, conclusions.

Sample Topics:

1. **The story behind the story:** What were Conrad's sources for this story?

   In November 1869, a nihilist, Sergei Nechaev, murdered a student in Moscow who was a member of his secret organization of anarchists. He then fled to Geneva and was arrested in 1872 and extradited to Russia. This event was used by Dostoevsky for *The Possessed* (1872). It has been suggested that Conrad recalls and adapts this event for his own story. It has also been suggested that the anarchist Mikhail Bakunin was Conrad's model for Peter Ivanovich. You might explore the background for this story by reading of the history of the times or Conrad's letters and commentaries.

2. **Political issues:** What are the politics, or social issues, that this novel addresses? How are these characters motivated by politics? How does politics fill a void in Razumov's life?

It would be interesting for the writer to inquire into Conrad's politics in this novel. With the character Razumov, Conrad continues to explore ideas like self-imposed isolation. The writer might show how this is not independence and indeed no isolation is fully possible in this society. The individual must attempt to find some relationship with people and with values. What does Razumov join and why? How does Razumov, in his search, move from principles based on revenge or patriotism to ones based in love? What does he give up or renounce in this process?

3. **Noble humanism and a harsh political world:** How do noble humanism and political principles come into collision with a harsh world in this novel?

An act of terrorism is at the center of this novel. How is Conrad responding to this? In our time, how are noble humanism and political principles involved in responding to terrorism after 9/11? What are the citizen's loyalties and expectations of one's government? What are the expectations of justice? You might inquire into how this novel investigates these issues. Razumov assumes that he will become "a great reforming servant of the greatest of States . . . of the mightiest homogenous mass of mankind with a capability for logical guided development in a brotherly solidarity of force and aim such as the world has never dreamt of. . . ." How is there a warning against overzealousness in this novel? How might this guide our response to terrorism in the world?

Philosophy and Ideas

Under Western Eyes is filled with political issues. Conrad looks at the Russian government, at autocracy and revolution. The writer may explore how this government operates in this novel. How does this government's effort to preserve its power create an atmosphere of suspicion? How is this government repressive? Does Razumov turn in Haldin because he recognizes that this government and its secret police are repressive and he will be suspected? How are other characters, like Mikulin, affected by this government?

Sample Topics:

1. **Rejection of the revolutionaries:** Conrad sharply critiques this government but he does not favor the revolutionaries. Why does Conrad reject the revolutionaries' position?

The revolutionaries in this story are shown to be wrong and ineffective. The character of Peter Ivanovitch excels as a theoretical strategist. However, he treats Tekla poorly, even as he talks about improving humanity. Haldin is described as a wild idealist, as is Kostia. Nikita is a double agent who likes to kill. These revolutionaries are engaged in an attack in which innocent people also die. In writing on this novel, one might ask what Conrad is saying about such revolutionary conflicts. Conrad here faces an issue that would have much importance in the twentieth century.

The historical struggles between Poland and Russia may have occasioned this book. However, the writer could also engage in research to explore the history of the Russian revolution, the Mexican revolution, or other revolutionary situations and how the turmoil of these revolutions affected people. Following this line of questioning, the writer might trace through this novel to show that when the autocratic and repressive government and the revolutionaries get into altercations, innocent people get hurt. In this novel, both the government and the revolutionaries are cast in a negative light. People are dehumanized and discarded, whether they are friends or enemies. Humanity is devoured by revolution. What is Conrad's response to this?

2. **Survival of the fittest:** Is the world of this novel a world of the "survival of the fittest?"

In *Under Western Eyes* Conrad inherits the Darwinian vision, says George Levine (263). Conrad struggles with Darwinian thought in relation to concerns about value, continuity and disruption. Chance and necessity are central to Darwinian debates. Darwin believed that species evolved through a process of natural selection. To persist, species had to adapt to material conditions. Whatever you may think of this theory, it suggests an impersonal world, an environment that calls for a fight for survival.

In considering chance, this novel raises questions about science. Detached observation is important to Razumov in this novel. Conrad writes: "I had never been called before to a greater effort of detachment: detachment from all passions, prejudices and even from personal memories" (p. lx). How does reflection on science relate to this detachment? How is Razumov detached? Are the characters engaged in an aggressive battle, a fight for survival?

3. **Accidents and disruptions:** How does chance, or irrationality, enter into this story?

Haldin intrudes into Razumov's life, bursting in like sudden chance. Haldin is a disruption. He has broken into Razumov's space of privacy and challenged his detachment from the world. Razumov says, "Fatality enters your rooms while your landlady's back is turned; you come home and find it in possession bearing a man's name, clothed in flesh—wearing a brown cloth coat and long boots—lunging against the stove" (69–70).

The writer can explore how chance moves through this novel. If Ziemianich had not been drunk, perhaps he would have taken Haldin away. How is it that Razumov and Nathalia happen to be in the same part of the same city and meet each other? Why is Nikita present when Razumov offers his confession of what he has done to Haldin? Why was that streetcar there at the moment that Razumov stepped out? How is Conrad using these "coincidences?"

4. **Chance and choices:** Can people control their lives? What happens when events come along that affect them? How do political, economic, or social circumstances impact their lives?

What might Conrad be saying about chances and the choices that are made by characters in his novel? Is he suggesting that people do not have control of many events that may affect their lives? Or is he examining the choices of this one man, Razumov, and implying something about our own choices in life? Throughout Conrad's stories, we see this theme arise again and again. In "The Secret Sharer," the captain discovers a stranger on board who will have great impact on his life. In *Lord Jim,* the chance occurrence of the *Patna* hitting something that is adrift forces Jim to make a choice that has serious consequences. Here, the sudden arrival of Haldin, changes the course of Razumov's life. Why does he make the choices that he does? You might compare Razumov's situation and his choices with the situation and responses of characters in other Conrad stories.

There is a search for meaning in Razumov's narration: "What is this Haldin? And what am I? Only two grains of sand. But a great mountain is made up of just such insignificant grains. And the death of a man is an insignificant thing. Yet we combat a contagious pestilence . . ." (42–43). How does Razumov discover meaning?

Form and Genre

Focusing on these elements is actually an examination of how a literary work is put together and what kind of story it is. In Conrad's work, one frequent aspect of form is narrative point of view. In reading the novel, you will want to examine how the story is told, who tells it, and why. While initially these factors seem to be outside of the story proper, they are in fact an integral part of the narrative. Keep in mind that the author and the narrator are separate entities. You have Conrad, the author, who is writing the story, and you have the narrators, characters that Conrad creates to tell the story. If you remember to think of these narrators as storytellers created by the author, you will often gain interesting insights into the work's themes and meanings.

Sample Topics:

1. **The use of a diary:** How is Razumov's diary used as a literary device? What does this contribute to our knowledge about Razumov and other characters? How does the use of the diary advance this story?

The writer may focus on how this story is told. Along with the omniscient author, there is Razumov's diary and the narrative of the language teacher. The use of the diary is very important throughout. You can develop an essay that focuses on this diary and what it tells us. The diary sets up an interesting time sequence. The narrator gets his information from Razumov's diary. Why is this technique of storytelling important? How does it move the story along? What do we learn from this diary?

2. **Self-analysis:** How do narration and language contribute to our experience of this novel?

The writer ought to pay close attention to the way the narrator tells this story. Listen to how the characters speak and to the language that they use. The narrator of *Under Western Eyes* interprets experience to the reader. Sometimes the novel seems to reflect on itself. Razumov says, "I am not a young man in a novel" (100). How is there self-analysis in this novel, not only in Razumov but also in Conrad? In what ways is Conrad conscious of the mechanics of novel writing? Is this a novel reflecting on itself as a construction of words and language?

   In this story, the revolutionaries are not very efficient. Razumov's deception and his conflict about Haldin are played out amid their blindness. If Conrad identifies with the antirevolutionary attitudes, why is this? Are Conrad's conservative politics at odds with his innovative methods and techniques as a writer? That is, from a literary standpoint, Conrad's techniques are themselves revolutionary; they are disruptive of realist conventions. Yet, it appears that he writes to preserve traditional values. How has the world become a place of chance, a network of chance happenings?

Language, Symbols, and Imagery

One way to reflect on Conrad's use of symbols and imagery is to look at his details. How do they suggest something larger? Symbolism is of particular importance in much of Conrad's fiction. Your essay can probe the meaning of these symbols.

A significant or major symbol can serve as the anchor or the center of a novel. As you read, look for images, objects, or settings that seem to have particular resonance. Perhaps an image is repeated or it gradually becomes clear to you that it represents something more. An object, an action, or a word that calls forth associations may be a symbol.

Sample Topics:

1. **Language:** Does Razumov's writing of words, stating concepts, and applying reason in writing in his diary contrast with the strange, irrational event that happens: the breaking in of an assassin into his rooms?

"Words, as is well known, are the great foes of reality," says the Professor. Razumov has decided to enter an essay contest. It is then that Haldin enters his life. Why? Razumov will try to find some logic in a world that seems now illogical. Can he do this with words? The writer on Conrad ought to explore Conrad's reflections on language. How is language limited and how is communication challenged by these limitations?

Razumov seeks to be rational and to put reality into words. However, the way that things are often cannot be put into words. How does this novel express this idea? You will note that there is an old language teacher here. Does the presence of this character suggest a concern about language? How does this novel's language question language or distrust it?

2. **Imagery and perspective:** What are the most important images in this story? What do you see or hear as you read this story?

In this novel, Conrad insists on limited perspective, not omniscience. The narratives that make up this novel are not omniscient; they are partial views. What do you see and hear as you read through this story? Note the images that emerge and note the source of these images. Are they images from Razumov's diary? Or do they come from another narrative voice? What do these images tell us, or suggest, about the characters, the world they live in, and the way that they see that world? The writer can examine how Conrad is recognizing the limitations of any single individual perspective.

Compare and Contrast Essays

A common way of writing a paper on a literary work is to compare or contrast elements of the work. This way, the writer can discover similarities and differences between certain aspects of the novel or story and then comment on the resonance of those comparative or contrasting elements and what it contributes to the work overall. This approach can help a reader focus on oppositions in the text and may bring into sharper detail the elements that need to be more closely observed.

It is important that the essay do more than merely list these similarities or contrasts. Thoughtful commentary helps to make your paragraph something more than just a list. Good writing is descriptive and thoughtful. Make sure to provide detail. Through critical thinking and analysis, a writer can look at differences between characters or patterns of imagery in the work. The writer might start by defining who each character is—as conveyed through his or her traits or behavior—or how each image is defined and presented. The differences or the ways Conrad alters or changes his representation can then be explored.

Sample Topics:

1. **The ideal society:** How does this society fall short of an ideal society? What would an ideal society be?

   Nathalia Haldin had dreamt of an ideal society. She says, "Everything is inconceivable to the strict logic of ideas. And yet the world exists to our sense, and we exist in it" (89). However, this is hardly an ideal society that she and Razumov live in. You can compare the society in this novel with your own ideas of an ideal society. This story takes place in an artificially constructed setting. Here the vast Russian wilderness is a fundamental reality. In its brute force, it has a rough solitude that is beyond human comprehension. How is human reason to work within this irrational context?

   How is the human condition expressed by this setting? This story may be about finding humanity within conditions that include loneliness, darkness, and destruction. How do some of the characters find a sense of humanity in these conditions? You can inquire into how they act toward each other and how they respond to their situation. Often daily life preoccupies these characters, shielding some of them from the darkness that surrounds them. "The trivilialities of daily existence were an armour for the soul," writes Razumov (44). Irrationality and violence threaten this artificial order of daily life. They break into Razumov's detached little world. The writer can compare the characters with their environment and investigate how human interaction is affected by the environment or setting. Tekla says, "I have been starving for, I won't say kindness, but just for a little civility, for I don't know how long" (233). Where are civility and civilization here? Tekla is a revolutionary who has been mistreated by the other revolutionaries. For Tekla, revolution is connected with a fully human life. This contrasts with Peter Ivanovitch, for whom revolution is a matter of ideas and ideology. You could contrast the views of these characters.

2. **Conscience and political ideals:** Is there a conflict between matters of conscience and political ideals? You can contrast these.

Razumov struggles with a sense that he has betrayed Haldin to the authorities: "Betray. A great word. What is betrayal? They talk of a man betraying his country, his friends, his sweetheart. There must be a moral bond first. All a man can betray is his conscience. And how is my conscience engaged here; by what bond of common faith, of common conviction, am I obliged to let that fanatical idiot drag me down with him?" (44–45).

Razumov concludes, "In giving Victor Haldin up, it was myself, after all, whom I have betrayed most basely" (361). Does Razumov achieve a moral resolution with this? In what sense does he choose humanity in the end, rather than ideas and ideology? You might compare and contrast ideas of humanity and the political values that Razumov has held.

How does Razumov eventually experience a "break-through" and choose humanity over the political ideas that are swirling around him and through him? How is this character who becomes deaf and crippled actually more whole in the end than he was earlier in the novel? Razumov has previously withdrawn from this society. He wants to be left alone. However, he cannot remain neutral in this atmosphere because the revolution comes in his door, in the form of Haldin. Razumov is sucked into the conflict, as by a vacuum. He is bounced about between sides and ultimately flattened in an accident. What can be said about the impersonality of this situation in which an individual is caught between these dialectical forces?

Bibliography for *Under Western Eyes*

Billy, Ted. *Critical Essays on Joseph Conrad.* Boston: G.K. Hall, 1987.

Carrabine, Keith. *"Under Western Eyes." Cambridge Companion to Joseph Conrad.* Cambridge: Cambridge University Press, 1996.

Daleski, H. M. *Joseph Conrad: The Way of Dispossession.* London: Faber and Faber, 1977, pp. 184–209.

DiSanto, Michael John. *Under Conrad's Eyes: The Novel as Criticism.* Montreal: McGill-Queens University Press, 2009.

Erdnast-Vulcan, Daphne. *The Strange Short Fiction of Joseph Conrad: Writing, Culture, and Subjectivity.* Oxford and New York: Oxford University Press, 1999.

Fincham, Gail. "To Make You See: Narration and Focalization in *Under Western Eyes*," *Joseph Conrad: Voice, Sequence, History and Genre.* Ed. Jakob Lothe, Jeremy Hawthorn, and James Phelan. Columbus: Ohio State University Press, 2008, pp. 60–82.

Fincham, Gail and Myrtle Hooper, eds. *Under Postcolonial Eyes: Joseph Conrad after Empire.* Cape Town: University of Cape Town Press, 1996.

Johnson, Bruce. *Conrad's Models of Mind.* Minneapolis: University of Minnesota Press, 1971, pp. 140–58.

Karl, Frederick R. *Joseph Conrad: The Three Lives.* New York: Farrar, Straus and Giroux, 1979, pp. 668, 678–79, 680–83.

Levin, Yeal. *Tracing the Aesthetic Principle in Conrad's Novels.* New York and London: Palgrave Macmillan, 2008.

Moser, Thomas. "Conrad's Later Affirmation," *Joseph Conrad: Achievement and Decline.* Cambridge, MA: Harvard University Press, 1957, rpt. 1966, pp. 131–44.

Najder, Zdzislaw. "Conrad, Russia and Dostoevsky," *Conrad in Perspective: Essays on Art and Fidelity.* Cambridge: Cambridge University Press, 1997, pp. 117–38.

———. "Conrad and Rousseau: *Concepts of Man and Society*," *Conrad in Perspective: Essays on Art and Fidelity.* Cambridge: Cambridge University Press, 1997, pp. 139–52.

Rising, Catherine. "Raskolnikov and Razumov: From Passive to Active Subjectivity in *Under Western Eyes.*" *Conradian* March 28, 2001.

Smith, David. R. ed. *Joseph Conrad's Under Western Eyes: Beginnings, Revisions, Final Forms.* North Haven, CT: Archon Books, 1991.

Watt, Ian. *Joseph Conrad and the Nineteenth Century.* Cambridge: Cambridge University Press, 1981.

Wiley, Paul L. *Conrad's Measure of Man.* New York: Gordian Press, 1970, pp. 116–31.

Winner, Anthony. *Culture and Irony: Studies in Joseph Conrad's Major Novels.* Charlottesville: University of Virginia Press, 1988.

VICTORY

READING TO WRITE

*V*ICTORY FOCUSES on the story of the complex character Axel Heyst. In your essay, you might reflect on the ways that Heyst is detached and apart from others. He is "temperamentally . . . a spectator" (185), says the narrator. He is "temperamentally sympathetic" (70). Can Heyst be both detached and sympathetic? These appear to be opposing tendencies. You might consider the critic H. M. Daleski's idea that what we see in Heyst is a dualistic personality. How does he have both of these qualities?

In your essay you might investigate the interaction between Heyst and his society and world. Why does he stand so removed from it? How is he brought into involvement with the world? You may ask questions about his contact with other people and about his personal qualities. For example, does Heyst show sympathy or qualities of character when he rescues Captain Morrison from the Portuguese port authorities in Delli? You will see that Morrison then takes him along on his sea travels. Together they start the tropical belt Coal Company, with a central station on Round Island, or Samburan, in the Java Sea. You will notice that Heyst lives there alone and then goes to Sourabaya (today spelled Surabaya) in Captain Davidson's steamship. Is Heyst ready for attachment at this point? "There must be a lot of the old Adam in me, after all," he says. That is, to be like Adam is to seek to be a person in relationship. You may also note that Heyst is a solitary, yet he is "a ready letter-writer" who writes "pages and pages" to "his friends in Europe" (6).

Victory is among the novels produced during Conrad's final period. While Thomas Moser claimed was that there was a falling off in Conrad's skill, there is much about *Victory* that would disprove that claim. For F.

R. Leavis, *Victory* is one of those books "which deserves to be current as representing his claim to classical standing" (187). The novel raises questions about love and commitment, relationship and detachment. In this, it repeats some themes from earlier Conrad novels, such as issues about isolation and attachment, separateness and community. What do you think Conrad thinks about comrades? How do we live in a society with one another? When does Heyst, in his distance from people, show a need to be social?

Victory is also a study of the relationship between Lena, a musician, and Heyst. Contact between Lena and Heyst brings the element of romantic relationship into this story. However, there are several other relationships that are worth considering also. Business brings Heyst to Sourabaya. He is amiable, sociable there, inviting Mr. McNab to "come along and quench [his] thirst" with him (8). In relation to Morrison, he allows for feelings of connection. At first, he is a stranger to Morrison (15), and Morrison does not even see him when they meet. It is only when he is hailed from across the street that he looks up "with a wild worried expression" (12). He invites Morrison for a drink and offers him a loan to get his ship back. This reveals Heyst's quality of compassion. What do you think of this? The narrator later says that Heyst has "plunged after the submerged Morrison" (77). This is an active step toward someone else. It is a risk-taking action from a man who is supposed to be detached.

Heyst's interaction with Lena requires a break from his detachment. Lena provides Heyst with a heart-filled response. She speaks of her connection with him: "Do you know, it seems to me, somehow that if you were to stop thinking of me I shouldn't be in the world at all!" (187). When she speaks with him, she seems "to abandon to him something of herself" (188). She feels "in her innermost depths an irresistible desire to give herself up to him more completely, by some act of absolute sacrifice" (201). How can Heyst help but be affected by her? What do you think about Lena's impact on Heyst?

TOPICS AND STRATEGIES

This section of the chapter will discuss possible topics for essays on *Victory* and will offer some general approaches to these topics. This is a series of suggestions intended to inspire your own inquiry. You may find a topic that follows a useful place from which to start your essay.

Use this material to prompt your thinking about the novel. After you jot down your ideas and analyze relevant passages in the novel, you should formulate your claim, the argument you want your essay to make. Then, you can go back to your notes and begin to provide the evidence for your claim, organizing and arranging your thoughts into a persuasive essay.

Themes

A novel's themes are those major ideas or issues that the story is considering. There are several key questions that Joseph Conrad reflects on in his works. Each work expresses a distinctive perspective on the themes with which it deals. Your job as a writer is to discover and articulate this perspective in your essay. Identify a central theme in the work and then think about how it is addressed in the narrative. In your view, what is being said about the theme? If you read closely and ask questions about what you have read, you will develop your own line of argument. Focus on close reading and what you think the work is saying about a particular issue. This will help you to develop a claim on which to build your essay. Always make sure to write to express the point that you have to make about the themes that you see in this novel. Clearly define the main points that you want to make. You do not need to write about the entire novel; stick to your main idea. Avoid straying into unrelated tangents of thought. Bring your essay back to focus on your main points. Whatever your interpretive approach, it should be supported with evidence from the text.

Sample Topics:

1. **Inability to love, incapacity to act:** Is Heyst unable to love or to take action? If so, is this because he is so detached?

   Criticism has approached Heyst in many different ways. Conrad speaks of him as "a man of universal detachment" (1920, author's note, Dent Collected edition, p. x). This is a self-divided character. It has been said that this detachment is very much an aspect of Heyst's personality. According to Adam Gillon, he has "an inability to act or to love." This is echoed by Frederick R. Karl, who observes in Heyst an "incapacity to act" (*Reader's Guide*, 260). What kinds of human intimacy are sacrificed to Heyst's doubt and skepticism? Heyst cannot avoid this skepticism. "I have lost all belief in realities," says Heyst (350). Does Heyst ever regain his belief? How does Lena affect Heyst? You might write an essay in which you inquire into how the story shows her impact on him.

2. **Women and men:** What roles does Lena have? How is her relationship with Heyst significant?

In this novel appears Lena, one of Conrad's strongest female characters. Conrad began his writing career with *Almayer's Folly,* which included a well-rounded presentation of Nina Almayer. In his later novels he appears to give new attention to the subject of women. The writer can investigate what this novel has to say about women and men. Lena appears here as nurturance, as a woman who challenges Heyst by breaking down his stoic detachment. Is Conrad, who has often developed a masculine model of toughness and stoicism, interrogating gender roles here?

How do you view the women in this novel? What do you think that Conrad is suggesting about them? Schomberg's wife "twice interferes with his evil designs," Moser observes (114). Rita laughs at Ortega and rejects Blunt's marriage proposal. Mrs. Travers foils Jorgenson's plan by not delivering his message. The villains seem frustrated at every turn by the women, as Moser has pointed out (115). Do the women represent a force for good in this novel? Observe the actions of the female characters as you go back through this novel and see what you think.

3. **Chance:** How is chance, coincidence, or accident present in this story? How do the crises of the story come by chance?

You can trace through this story to locate many incidents in which chance happenings occur. Why do characters meet? Thomas Moser points out that this novel is filled with chance happenings: Heyst appears to just coincidentally go to the orchestra and is about to leave when he sees Lena. The villains appear suddenly at the hotel. Mr. Jones's fear of women,

Davidson's arrival, and Wang's interference are all apparently responsible for a chain of events (108). In the end, the relationship between Heyst and Lena encounters a scene of violence. How do you view this accidental convergence of people, and what occurs? In the end, has Lena contributed to Heyst's life or to his demise? Has he been brought down by chance, by other people, or by his own actions? Given the ending of this novel, is this story's title ironic?

Character

When you write about Conrad, consider character development and how he employs and pursues it in his work. As you read his novels and stories, observe how the characters act. Do his characters change? Do they reveal themselves as the story progresses? Your paper can focus on questions of character development or the author's method of characterization. It is helpful to investigate how we come to know the characters. In Conrad's work, this is particularly tricky at times because of the shifting of viewpoint narrators. So read closely. Characters in Conrad's work often use language and mannerisms of speech peculiar or specifically matched to them. The way in which a character speaks or inhabits a space can offer clues to his or her inner workings and motivations.

Sample Topics:

1. **Heyst:** What are Heyst's major characteristics? How does Heyst develop during the course of the novel?

   You can discuss Heyst's development in your essay. Follow Heyst, with special attention to what is said about him. He is a man of "tired eyes" in whom "the last vestiges of youth had gone out of his face and all the hair off the top of his head." How does Heyst become affected by the people around him? You might consider how Heyst's self-discovery is, in part, through other people. This occurs even as he insists on self-sufficiency:

   > Heyst was not conscious of either friends or of enemies. It was the essence of his life to be a solitary achievement, accomplished not by hermit-like withdrawal with its silence and immobility, but by a system of restless wandering, by the

detachment of an impermanent dweller amongst changing scenes. In this scheme he had perceived the means of passing through life without suffering and almost without a single care in the world—invulnerable because elusive!

Victory is a study of Heyst, who is uprooted, unattached, isolated, disillusioned. In his preface, Conrad called Heyst "the man of universal detachment." He suggests that Heyst has lost something in his character. What do you think he has lost? Does Heyst take responsibility for his life in the end? Heyst has been affected by his upbringing and his personal history. We hear that his father "in solitude and silence had been used to think clearly and sometimes even profoundly, seeing life outside the flattering delusion of everlasting hope, of conventional self-deception, of an ever-expected happiness." Of Heyst we learn: "The young man learned to reflect, which is a destructive process, a reckoning of the cost. It is not the clear-sighted who rule the world. Great achievements are accomplished in a blessed, warm mental fog, which the pitiless cold blast of the father's analysis had blown away from the sin."

Is it true that large decisions are determined "in a fog?" What does Conrad mean? How can one interpret the pose of skepticism that Axel Heyst takes? Is it tragic for Heyst to have a skeptical view toward life? Is this a character flaw? Does it serve him or fail him? How is Heyst's detachment a form of escapism or evasion? He sees himself as "the most detached of creatures in this earthly captivity, the veriest tramp on earth, an indifferent stroller going through the world's bustle" (198–99).

2. **Lena:** What qualities does Lena have and how does she affect Heyst's life? How is Lena symbolic? Is she transcendent? Can she go beyond suffering? Is she otherworldly?

Lena is a violinist in Zangiacomo's traveling orchestra. She has been pursued by Schomberg, a hotel keeper in Sourabaya.

When Heyst shows an interest in her, she flings herself into his arms (83). "You took me up from pity. I threw myself at you" (354). "She thought . . . that she would try to hold him as long as she could—till her fainting arms, her sinking soul, could cling to him no more" (246). In your view, is Lena a strong woman or not? Lena's way of life is different from Heyst's. Lena can take action. Is this because she is passionate? Or because she loves? How is Lena different from Heyst? Does she achieve any "victory"? Can life be sustained by intimacy and by love?

What kind of restorative energy does Lena have for Heyst? You might write about how she and Heyst are different from each other. In contrast with his mistrust of life, she is open. She is not detached. The expression on her face has about it "something indefinably audacious and infinitely miserable—because the temperament and the existence of the girl [are] reflected in it" (74). Lena has the courage to give herself, to place her trust in someone. She looks for a response from Heyst. "You do something. You are a gentleman. It wasn't I who spoke to you first, was it? I didn't begin it, did I? What did you want to speak to me for? I don't care what it is, but you must do something" (80). Later, Conrad writes, "He could not believe that the creature he had coveted with so much force and with so little effect, was in reality tender, docile to her impulses, and had almost offered herself without a sense of guilt, in a desire of safety, and from a profound need of placing her trust where her woman's instinct guided her ignorance" (95).

On meeting Lena, Heyst is transformed. You might observe in your essay how he forms an attachment with her and allows himself to love. His "skeptical mind" is now "dominated by the fullness of his heart" (83). You might also carefully observe how Lena is described in this novel. For example, when Heyst meets her outside the hotel, she is "white and spectral," "a white phantom-like apparition" (83). She is putting out her arms "like an appealing ghost" (86). You might look for ways in which Lena is portrayed as childlike, as someone with a spiritual nature.

3. **Morrison:** Describe Morrison and the impact that he and Heyst have on each other's lives.

Some critics have pointed out that Heyst lacks self-knowledge. He is a creature of habit, affected by influences from his past. He is moved by sympathy for Morrison and rescues this sensitive man. Morrison is a master of a trading brig. He is generous to a fault and later suffers economically for this. He meets Heyst on Timor in a town called Delli. He has trouble with the Portuguese around money issues. Morrison doesn't know what to do now that he has been rescued: "Poor Morrison actually laid his head down on the cabin table, and remained in that crushed attitude while Heyst talked to him soothingly with the utmost courtesy. The Swede was as much distressed as Morrison, for he understood the other's feelings perfectly. No decent feeling was ever scorned by Heyst. But he was incapable of outward cordiality of manner, and he felt acutely his defeat."

Why does Heyst help Morrison? He saves him and brings him into a business partnership. Does this suggest anything about Heyst? Did he only come to Morrison's aid for "amusement," as he tells Lena? In a sense, Heyst rescues Morrison, as Lena will later rescue Heyst. What do we know about Morrison? How do he and Heyst affect each other? You might contrast Morrison and Heyst. Heyst is detached from other people. Is this a defensive posture and an attempt to be invulnerable? He rejects contact and connection. Morrison is all about dialogue and interaction. The critic F. R. Leavis sees Morrison and Davidson as "complementary to Heyst" and as "upright, sensitive and humane individuals" (225). What "decency" do you see in these characters?

4. **Heyst's father:** What influence does Heyst's father have on his son's life?

You might write an essay about the influence that Heyst's father and his values and code have on Axel Heyst's life. Leaving school at the age of 18, Axel Heyst lives with his father. The father has a significant influence on him. His father is a man of "disillusion and regret." Heyst is subject to "the pitiless cold blasts of the father's analysis." We hear that "such companionship at that plastic and impressionable age" would "leave in the boy a profound mistrust of life" (91). You might show how it has done this.

The houses of London at night begin to look to Heyst "like the tombs of an unvisited, unhonoured cemetery of hopes" (174). The father encourages the son to "Look on—make no sound" and to "cultivate that form of contempt which is called pity" (174–75). H. M. Daleski points out that Heyst is thereby caught between contempt and compassion. The detached person drifts. He has no purposeful direction. Heyst is said to be "like a feather floating lightly in the work-a-day atmosphere" (60). (The word *feather* may reflect the word *father*.)

Heyst's father is like a ghost who draws his attention. The death of his father increases his influence on Heyst. If one were to speak in a Freudian sense, one might say that Heyst carries his father's ghost with him, as Daleski notes (116). "The father's influence on his son is thus clearly pernicious," says Daleski (111). Yet, the life Heyst lives is not only one imposed on him. There is something already deep in him that is "reinforced by his father's directives" (Daleski 111). It is already inherent within him. When Lena comes to the island, she finds the main room of Heyst's house "lined with the backs of books halfway up on its three sides" and notes "the gilt frame of the portrait of Heyst's father, signed by a famous painter, lonely in the middle of a wall" (168). "In the dusk and coolness," this appears as the only image that reflects light. His father is forever present. As he reads a book his father has written, we see him "shrinking into himself, composing his face as if under the author's eye, with a vivid consciousness of the portrait on his right hand . . ." (218–19).

5. **Schomberg:** In what ways is Schomberg an antagonist in this story? Can you compare him with Ricardo or Pedro and the evil that lurks in these characters?

Schomberg strikes some readers as a rather creepy character. The hotel proprietor stalks Lena. How does this hotel represent a place of meeting and passing through? Is it a good place or not? How is Schomberg like a melodramatic villain? You might discuss how Heyst expresses a kind of melodramatic chivalry in his unlikely rescue of Lena from Schomberg. Another narrator gives us a look into Schomberg's resentment, after Heyst saves Lena from his clutches. You might read again through these passages to determine more about Schomberg's character.

6. **Ricardo:** How is Ricardo a villain? What are the characteristics of this figure?

The vicious Martin Ricardo and the dehumanized or subhuman servant Pedro set up an illegal gambling operation in Schomberg's music room. Ricardo and Pedro are clearly portrayed as aggressive and seedy characters. What can be said of this angry character, Ricardo, and his involvements?

Ricardo sees the world as a jungle. He wants action. "Cross-legged, his head drooping a little and perfectly still, he might have been meditating in a bronze-like attitude on the sacred syllable Om. It was a striking illustration of the untruth of appearances, for his contempt for the world was of a severely practical kind" (267). In this passage we see that the appearance of Ricardo is not his reality. He appears as if meditating and attentive to transcendent visions. He is quite the opposite. He is a practical man with contempt for the world. Nor is Ricardo often still. Rather, he is disposed toward action. In Thomas Moser's view, Ricardo is "a voyeur," who is defeated by Lena (117–19). How does Lena defeat Ricardo? Is he a satanic figure?

History and Context

Another important approach to Conrad's novel is to research and write about the historical and social conditions surrounding the story. In one's effort to understand the motivation of the characters and the setting and action of this story, it is helpful to understand the novel's historical and social context. Conrad's *Victory* is set in a specific place and time. Heyst can be seen as a man without a home; a Swede by family origin who had lived in London before establishing a life in southeastern Asia, he is a mysterious figure who, on one hand, seems to have little or no personal history and yet who is, nonetheless, deeply intertwined with European colonialism and colonial practice. What are the European characters doing in the part of the world in which *Victory* is set? Such a question will lead to a more complex and sophisticated understanding of the historical implications of Conrad's work.

Sample Topics:

1. **Characters drawn from life:** What experiences in Conrad's life may have contributed to the making of this story? What has Conrad said about the building of his characters?

The character of Heyst was based on someone Conrad had met. In his Author's Note, Conrad writes that the person he met was "not the whole Heyst of course; he is only the physical and moral foundation of my Heyst laid on the ground of a short acquaintance. . . ." Is Heyst a part of Conrad's own personality? He writes in his preface, "I have lived longest with" Heyst. Is this because he is also filled with skeptical doubt? Certain themes seem to reappear in many of Conrad's stories. We see some of these in Heyst. He withdraws from the world, pursued by a double, Jones, who is a "secret sharer." Mr. Jones, likewise, is drawn from life and developed through imagination. Conrad says that he saw "Lena" in an orchestra in the south of France.

Conrad began writing *Victory* while he was still rewriting *Chance*. Conrad biographer Frederick Karl has suggested that the novel is interrelated with earlier novels, like *Nostromo* and *Chance* (715). "Berg" and "Dollars" were working titles for *Victory*. Writing it was at times a struggle (Karl 739). July 1, 1914, he gave the story its present title. You might read Conrad's author's note, then read from Frederick Karl's biography *Joseph Conrad: The Three Lives* (1979), and give some thought to how this novel emerged from Conrad's concerns.

Philosophy and Ideas

Conrad can be explored for his political and philosophical beliefs. We find in Joseph Conrad's work themes of isolation and community, meditations on death, concerns with guilt and shame, reflections on language, admonitions to see clearly and avoid illusions, understandings of human interaction with nature, and assertions of individuality, the power of love, and the value of hard work. As you read through his novels, you will see that Conrad offers his readers characters and situations that compel us to think about moral decision making, human sympathy and pity, the value of restraint and moderation, and the importance of honor. In Conrad's life and works, there is an emphasis on ethics, inquiries into colonialism, opposition to anarchism, and reflections on romance, marriage and family, science, and the emerging modern world.

In writing about a Conrad novel you might examine a few of the philosophical ideas that arise. With Conrad, you will have to spend some time reflecting on issues of identity, isolation, community, subjectivity and individuality, knowledge and skepticism. He was a writer who was concerned with ethics and responsibility and with knowledge and subjectivity. To inquire into ideas or problems such as these, you can look at the questions that the characters themselves ask. One might also work to identify themes that move through the novel.

Sample Topics:

1. **The divided self:** How is Heyst a divided man? How is he emotionally alienated? You might explore how his insistence on detachment affects him.

   Axel Heyst is a complex character. The writer may probe the ways in which he may be divided psychologically. Does self-deception appear as one of his qualities? Years ago, his father impressed on him a need for emotional detachment. Yet, when Lena enters his life, Heyst is challenged by emotion. You might examine how Heyst's external world is then in conflict with his interior life. Conrad called this "that part of our nature . . . kept out of sight." Heyst was taught by his father that a kind of detachment and pity for mankind were the only proper attitude. He was emotionally alienated, as Bruce Johnson points out (161). Heyst claims that his reasons for abandoning life are rational. Do you think so? Conrad notes "the use of reason is to justify the obscure desires that move our conduct, impulses, passions, prejudices and follies, and also our fears" (83, ctd. in Johnson 161). Is Heyst actually irrational in some ways?

2. **Facts and emotions:** How do emotions, chance, and irrational moments arise in Heyst's life?

Facts alone are not adequate to account for the world or for all of knowledge. Lena's affection goes beyond such facts. We see Heyst responding to this: "Oh, I am done with facts," says he, putting his hand to his helmet, sharply with one of his short bows" (25). What does Heyst learn about those things in life that go deeper than surface facts? As emotions are stirred by his experiences and his relationship with Lena, Heyst cannot maintain his detachment. He is also pulled into contact with people. After Jones, Ricardo, and Pedro arrive on the island, Jones says, "I am the world itself come to pay you a visit" (285). How is Heyst affected by the unexpected?

Heyst is drawn romantically to Lena. Yet, she seems "to infect his very heart" (II, 2). By her, he feels he is "enveloped in the atmosphere of femininity as in a cloud, suspecting pitfalls, afraid to move" (III, 5). What is the influence of Lena's presence on him? How is Heyst affected by the irrational?

Form and Genre

Focusing on these elements is actually an examination of how a literary work is put together and what kind of story it is. In Conrad's work, one frequent aspect of form is narrative point of view. In reading the novel, you will want to examine how the story is told, who tells it, and why. While initially these factors seem to be outside of the story proper, they are in fact an integral part of the narrative. Keep in mind that the author and the narrator are separate entities. You have Conrad, the author, who is writing the story, and you have the narrators, characters that Conrad creates to tell the story. If you remember to think of these narrators as storytellers created by the author, you will often gain interesting insights into the work's themes and meanings.

Sample Topics:

1. **Genre:** Is this a novel of romance or a critique of colonialism?

   Several critics have approached this novel's romantic aspects and have focused on the relationship between Heyst and Lena. Alternatively, the writer might look at this novel as a critique on European colonialism. The character of Wang is a colonial subject. The writer may examine how this character is presented.

   This may also be a novel in which romance is central. Heyst reflects that he has felt for Lena more than he has felt for anyone else in his life. What does love mean to him? What happens when his relationship with Lena seems imperfect? Does the denial of life he has learned from his father and has practiced stand in the way of an ability to love? Is this a romance or a tragedy?

2. **Interpretation:** How do you interpret the events in this story? How are characters in this story interpreting one another and their world?

   When you write about this story, you are engaged in interpretation. You are expressing your views about what occurs in this story. One approach may be to think about how the characters in this story are also interpreters of life. How do they view each other? What is their sense of the world around them?

   When Lena plans to trick Ricardo, misunderstandings occur between Heyst and Lena. Heyst becomes suspicious of her. Events seem to happen at the wrong moment: Heyst arrives with Mr. Jones when Lena is bending over Ricardo. How does Conrad make use of dramatic irony, human encounters, and misunderstandings? What is he saying about how people interpret things?

Language, Symbols, and Imagery

One way to reflect on Conrad's use of symbols and imagery is to look at his details. How do they suggest something larger? Symbolism is of particular importance in much of Conrad's fiction. Your essay can probe the meaning of these symbols.

A significant or major symbol can serve as the anchor or the center of a novel. As you read, look for images, objects, or settings that seem to have particular resonance. Perhaps an image is repeated or it gradually becomes clear to you that it represents something more. An object, an action, or a word that calls forth associations may be a symbol.

Sample Topic:

1. **Lena as a symbol:** Is Lena a symbolic presence in the novel and, if so, of what?

   If Lena is a symbol, what is she a symbol for? Love? Passion? Is she a ghostlike vision? When she arrives in the garden of the hotel, it is as a "white, phantom-like apparition" who clings to him (83). We see Lena: "white and spectral she is putting out her arms to him out of the black shadows like an appealing ghost" (86). She stands in opposition to the portrait of Heyst's father: her new life of spontaneity to his old life of heavy detachment. We follow the changes in this relationship. Heyst is unable to declare his love for Lena. Does Lena represent love or an appeal to involvement and commitment that he has never before known?

Compare and Contrast Essays

A common way of writing a paper on a literary work is to compare or contrast elements of the work. This way, the writer can discover similarities and differences between certain aspects of the novel or story and then comment on the resonance of those comparative or contrasting elements and what it contributes to the work overall. This approach can help a reader focus on oppositions in the text and may bring into sharper detail the elements that need to be more closely observed.

It is important that the essay do more than merely list these similarities or contrasts. Thoughtful commentary helps to make your paragraph something more than just a list. Good writing is descriptive and thoughtful. Make sure to provide detail. Through critical thinking and analysis, a writer can look at differences between characters or patterns of imagery in the work. The writer might start by defining who each character is—as conveyed through his or her traits or behavior—or how

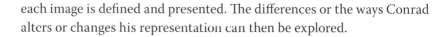

each image is defined and presented. The differences or the ways Conrad alters or changes his representation can then be explored.

Sample Topics:

1. **Heyst and Lena:** How might Heyst's qualities be characterized with those of Lena?

   Conrad writes that though he "lived the longest" with Heyst, it is his character Lena that most drew his "most sustained attention" (14–15). What about Lena draws your attention? Lena is a member of an orchestra who has been abandoned by her mother and left to a father who is an invalid. Schomberg, an unpleasant hotel keeper, is pursuing her and she has no friends that she can turn to. What is there about her being like an orphan that draws our sympathy? You might contrast Lena and Heyst. She has trust; he does not. She has faith in life; he doesn't. Lena has a voice "suggesting depths of wisdom and feeling," while Heyst is silent. How is Lena dreamlike? For her, God has "got to do with everything—every little thing." For Heyst, there is only absence. He is the opposite of such optimism. A writer might show this in an essay.

   You might also contrast the influence of Heyst's father with the influence of Lena on Heyst. Heyst explains to Lena that his father seems to have viewed life as a factory in which all men and women were workers. Their wages were paid in counterfeit money. What attitude does this suggest toward life? Heyst's last words to Davidson are: "woe to the man whose heart has not learned while young to hope, to love—and puts his trust in life" (part IV, chapter 14). Does this suggest that Heyst wishes that he had learned this? Has he been incapable of loving? Are hope, love, and trust spontaneous expressions of the heart or learned attitudes? How is Heyst disillusioned? Does he embrace or reject the world?

2. **Heyst and Mr. Jones:** How are Heyst and Mr. Jones doubles of each other?

   Mr. Jones is a curious character in this novel. Mr. Jones says to Heyst, "you and I have more in common than you think" (IV, 5).

How are they similar? How different? What is their alliance about? How are their goals different? How are they both wanderers who are "coming and going up and down the earth"? (IV, 5) Why do they both appear to dislike life? Jones says, "I am the world itself, come to pay you a visit" (IV, 11). In what respects does Mr. Jones present a challenge to Heyst's detachment from the world?

Bibliography for *Victory*

Anderson, John P. *Conrad's Victory: Resurrection Lost.* Boca Raton, FL: Universal, 2004.

Collits, Terry. *Postcolonial Conrad: Paradoxes of Empire.* London: Routledge, 2005, chapters 9–10.

Daleski, H. M. "Victory and Patterns of Self-Division." *Conrad Revisited: Essays for the Eighties.* Ed. Ross C. Murfin. Tuscaloosa: University of Alabama Press, 1985, pp. 107–23.

Geddes, Gary. *Conrad's Later Novels.* Montreal: McGill-Queens University, pp. 41–80.

Gillon, Adam. "Conrad's Victory and Nabokov's Lolita: Imitations of Imitations." *Conradiana* 12 (1980): 58.

———. *Joseph Conrad.* Boston: Twayne, 1982, pp. 140–52.

Hampson, Robert. "The Late Novels," *The Cambridge Companion to Joseph Conrad.* Ed. J. H. Stape. Cambridge: Cambridge University Press, 1996, pp. 144–46.

Johnson, Bruce. *Conrad's Models of Mind.* Minneapolis: University of Minnesota, 1971, pp. 159–76.

Jones, Susan. *Conrad and Women.* Oxford: Clarendon Press, 1999.

Karl, Frederick R. *Joseph Conrad: The Three Lives.* New York: Farrar, Straus and Giroux, 1979, pp. 144–45, 685–88, 714–24.

———. *A Reader's Guide to Joseph Conrad.* New York: Noonday Press, 1960, p. 260.

Moser, Thomas. *Joseph Conrad: Achievement and Decline.* Hamden, CT: Archon Books, 1957.

Najder, Zdzislaw. *Joseph Conrad: A Chronicle.* New Brunswick, NJ: Rutgers University Press, 1983.

Palmer, John. *Joseph Conrad's Fiction: A Study in Literary Growth.* Ithaca, NY: Cornell University Press, 1968, pp. 166–97.

Spittles, Brian. *How to Study a Joseph Conrad Novel.* New York and London: Macmillan, 1990.

Wiley, Paul L. *Conrad's Measure of Man.* New York: Gordian, 1970, pp. 150–58.

INDEX

Characters in literary works are listed followed by the title in parenthesis of the work in which they appear.

WLHS Library Media Center
58 South Elm Street
Windsor Locks, CT 06096
860-292-5736

DATE DUE
